FOR REAL
elementary

Martyn Hobbs and Julia Starr Keddle
with Tessa Hall and Rob Nicholas

Student's Book & Workbook

HELBLING
LANGUAGES

Contents

MODULE 4 ISSUES

UNIT	FUNCTIONS & REAL COMMUNICATION	GRAMMAR	VOCABULARY	SKILLS, STRATEGIES, PRONUNCIATION	INTERCULTURE, STORY, CLIL, SONG	TOWARDS EXAMS
7 **A busy life** p.68	• Talking about obligation • Talking about permission • **Having a discussion**	• *must / mustn't / (not) have to* • *So / Neither must I* • *(not) be allowed to*	• School • Computers	**Listening:** instructions on procedures to follow on a computer **Writing:** instructions on using a computer **Reading:** an article about safety when using chatrooms **Speaking:** discussing Internet safety **Strategies:** guessing the meaning **Pronunciation:** /uː/ /ʌ/	**Get into culture** Soft skills Shops in the UK **Interculture** Homes in the UK (LINKS pp.26-27) Schools and education in the UK (LINKS pp.28-29) **CLIL** Civic Studies: the UK political system (LINKS pp.52-53) **Song** Three Little Birds (LINKS p.63)	**PET Speaking Parts 3 and 4** (SB p.84) **Trinity ISE I Portfolio** (SB p.84) **PET Reading Part 2** (SB p.85) **PET Listening** (LINKS p.10)
8 **You shouldn't worry about it!** p.76	• Giving advice • Using articles • **Asking for and giving directions** • Having a debate	• *should / ought to / needn't* • Articles	• Relationships • Places in a town • Prepositions	**Listening:** teenagers researching age limits on the Internet **Reading:** a webpage on lowest age limits **Speaking:** group debate expressing opinions for or against age limits **Writing:** proposals on age limits for chatroom discussions **Strategies:** how to debate **Pronunciation:** /u/ /ɔː/		

MODULE 5 TRUE STORIES

UNIT	FUNCTIONS & REAL COMMUNICATION	GRAMMAR	VOCABULARY	SKILLS, STRATEGIES, PRONUNCIATION	INTERCULTURE, STORY, CLIL, SONG	TOWARDS EXAMS
9 **Life's like that** p.88	• Talking about the past • **Describing people** • Identifying people	• Past simple of *be* • Past simple regular • Past time expressions	• Physical appearance • Personality	**Reading:** an article on flash mobbing **Listening:** a news bulletin about flash mobbing incidents **Speaking:** reporting flash mobbing incidents **Writing:** inventing and describing a flash mobbing incident **Pronunciation:** /d/ /t/ /ɪd/	**Get into culture** Body decoration **Interculture** Multiculturalism in the UK (LINKS pp.30-31) Being British and sixteen (LINKS pp.32-33) **Story** The end of summer (LINKS pp.42-43) **CLIL** History: The Romans in Britain (LINKS pp.54-55)	**PET Writing Part 3** (SB p.104) **Trinity ISE I Portfolio** (SB p.104) **PET Listening Part 2** (SB p.105) **PET Listening** (LINKS p.12)
10 **Exploration** p.96	• Talking about the past • Talking about obligation • **Telling a story**	• Past simple irregular • Modal verb *could* • *was/were able to* • *had to, didn't have to / need to*	• Adventure	**Speaking:** discussing TV quiz programmes **Reading:** a general culture quiz **Listening:** a contestant answering quiz questions **Writing:** a set of questions for a TV quiz **Strategies:** agreeing and disagreeing **Pronunciation:** sentence stress		

MODULE 6 ONE WORLD

UNIT	FUNCTIONS & REAL COMMUNICATION	GRAMMAR	VOCABULARY	SKILLS, STRATEGIES, PRONUNCIATION	INTERCULTURE, STORY, CLIL, SONG	TOWARDS EXAMS
11 **Health** p.108	• Making comparisons • Qualifying what you say • **Talking about health**	• Comparative adjectives • *as… as…, more/less than* • Qualifiers: *a lot, a little, enough, really, fairly, too* • Comparative adverbs	• Parts of the body • Illnesses	**Reading:** an article on the founder of the UN Peace Day **Listening:** three students' contributions to Peace Day **Speaking:** discussing a project for Peace Day **Writing:** a personal opinion on the founder of Peace Day **Pronunciation:** /w/ /v/ /f/ /r/	**Get into culture** Health statistics The average British home **Interculture** Ireland (LINKS pp.34-35) **CLIL** Earth Sciences: Volcanoes (LINKS pp.56-57) **Song** Our House (LINKS p.63)	**PET Writing Part 3** (SB p.124) **Trinity ISE I Writing task** (SB p.124) **PET Reading Part 5** (SB p.125) **PET Listening** (LINKS p.14)
12 **Places** p.116	• Talking about the best • Asking for confirmation • **Homes**	• Superlatives • Question tags	• Houses • Landscape	**Reading:** a website article about World Heritage Sites **Speaking:** discussing a school trip to a World Heritage Site **Listening:** a girl talking about tourism in her own country **Writing:** a short article about a World Heritage Site **Pronunciation:** showing enthusiasm		

MODULE 7 EXPERIENCES

UNIT	FUNCTIONS & REAL COMMUNICATION	GRAMMAR	VOCABULARY	SKILLS, STRATEGIES, PRONUNCIATION	INTERCULTURE, STORY, CLIL, SONG	TOWARDS EXAMS
13 **Plans** p.128	• Talking about the future • **Making and accepting invitations**	• Present continuous for future • *be going to*	• Holidays	**Reading:** understanding holiday advertisements on the web **Listening:** four teenagers' predictions about their holidays **Speaking:** giving a talk about a holiday plan **Writing:** writing about a holiday plan **Strategies:** making notes as you listen **Pronunciation:** *going to*	**Get into culture** Barbecue Multicultural food **Interculture** British food (LINKS pp.36-37) **Story** Stars (LINKS pp.44-45) **CLIL** Biology: Nutrition (LINKS pp.58-59) **Song** Holiday (LINKS p.64)	**PET Speaking Part 4** (SB p. 144) **Trinity ISE The Interview** (SB p.144) **PET Listening Part 1** (SB p.145) **PET Listening** (LINKS p.16)
14 **Have you ever eaten a curry?** p.136	• Talking about experiences • **Ordering food**	• Present perfect • Present perfect with *for* and *since* • Prepositions of place and movement	• Food • Past participles	**Reading:** magazine interviews about favourite food **Speaking:** talking about food preferences **Listening:** a radio broadcast on healthy food **Writing:** a composition about the Mediterranean diet **Pronunciation:** consonants with 'r'		

Grammar present simple; *like, love, hate + -ing*; modal verbs *can, would*; question words; adverbs of frequency

Functions talking about the present, ability, routine, preferences; making arrangements; exchanging personal information

Vocabulary sports; hobbies; films; daily activities; jobs

Get started

1a CD1 40 **Listen and repeat the sports.**

1b Do the questionnaire and tick ☑ the things that describe you.

What sort of person are you?

1 Your favourite sports

 table tennis
 running
 riding
 diving

 volleyball
rugby
skiing
  athletics

 cycling
 karate
 sailing
 waterskiing

 gymnastics
 canoeing
 basketball
 hockey

2 Your hobbies and interests

acting in plays
playing an instrument
writing poetry, stories, blogs
drawing / painting pictures
collecting things
taking photos
playing computer games
reading books
other _____

3 Your favourite things

my mp3 player
my computer
my sports equipment
my diary
my dance shoes
my camera
other _____

4 My hero is...

a singer   a dancer
an artist   a politician
a writer   an inventor or business person
an actor   or someone you know: NAME _____

1c PAIRWORK Compare your answers with your partner.

2 Write sentences to describe your partner.
- He / She is good at art / computer games / sport, etc.
- His / Her favourite thing is his / her mp3 player, Harry Potter book, etc.
- He / She likes music / reading / writing / acting / dancing / taking photos, etc.
- He / She has / hasn't got a lot of hobbies.
- His / Her hero is the Italian writer Federico Moccia.

3 Tell the class about your partner.
Katrina likes singing. Her favourite thing is her mp3 player. Her hero is Rihanna.

Word expander   PLAY, GO, DO

play + ball sports	**play** table tennis
go + -ing	**go** running
do + others	**do** athletics

4a 41 **Decide if these sports and the sports above take the verb *play*, *go* or *do*. Then listen and check.**

football | swimming | golf | tennis | skydiving | judo | surfing | windsurfing

4b PAIRWORK Talk about the sports you do.
I play volleyball, I go skiing and I do athletics.

Unit 1
Free time

Unit objectives

Grammar present simple: all forms; *So do I, Neither do I*; object pronouns; *like, love, hate* + *-ing*; modal verb *can*

Functions talking about the present, ability, sport, likes and dislikes

Vocabulary musical instruments; films

Warm up

1 Look at the photos on page 9 and answer the questions.

1 Where are the friends?

2 What musical instrument do you think is in the case?

Comprehension

2 📀 **Listen and read** *Who's that girl?* **Circle T (True) or F (False).**

1 The new student's name is Rose. T / F

2 Jack and Charlie aren't interested in Rose. T / F

3 Rose studies the violin and the piano. T / F

4 Jack listens to rock bands. T / F

5 Rose doesn't like *Nirvana*. T / F

6 Rose can't sing. T / F

Talking about the present

3 Study the sentences and do the task.

Present simple

I study the piano.   *I don't like Coldplay.*

Mia plays the drums.   *Jack doesn't know her.*

Do you know her name? Yes, I do. / No, I don't.

Does she play the violin? Yes, she does. / No, she doesn't.

Complete the rules with *positive* and *negative*.

- The present simple _____ is the same as the base form of the verb. In the 3rd person singular (*he, she, it*) add *-s* to the base form.

- Form the present simple _____ with *don't / doesn't* + the base form.

- Form questions with *do / does* + the base form.

4 Complete the sentences with the correct form of the verbs in brackets.

1 Steve __plays__ the guitar. (play)

2 I _____ Chinese. (not speak)

3 _____ you _____ to rock music? (listen)

4 Claire _____ a blog. (write)

5 We _____ in a band. (not sing)

6 _____ he _____ the violin? (study)

7 He _____ the drums in the garage. (practise)

8 _____ she _____ with her parents? (live)

9 Gordon _____ in films. (not act)

5 PAIRWORK Ask and answer questions.

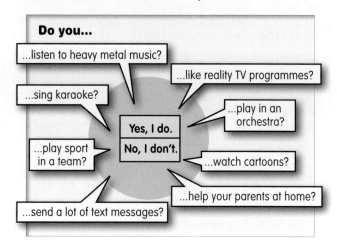

Do you...

...listen to heavy metal music?

...like reality TV programmes?

...sing karaoke?

...play in an orchestra?

Yes, I do.
No, I don't.

...play sport in a team?

...watch cartoons?

...send a lot of text messages?

...help your parents at home?

Talking about ability

6 Study the rules and the sentences.

Modal verb *can*

- Use *can* to talk about ability.

- *Can* or *can't* (*cannot*) is the same for all forms.

I/You/He/She/It/We/They can sing.

I/You/He/She/It/We/They can't sing.

Can I/you/he/she/it/we/they sing?

7 PAIRWORK Talk about you and your friends. Use these words and phrases.

play
the piano | the violin | the guitar | the drums | the clarinet | keyboards

speak
English | French | Spanish | Chinese

sing | dance | act | swim

A *I can play the guitar. Maria can play the drums.*

B *I can speak Chinese. Noah can speak French.*

Who's that girl?
EPISODE 1

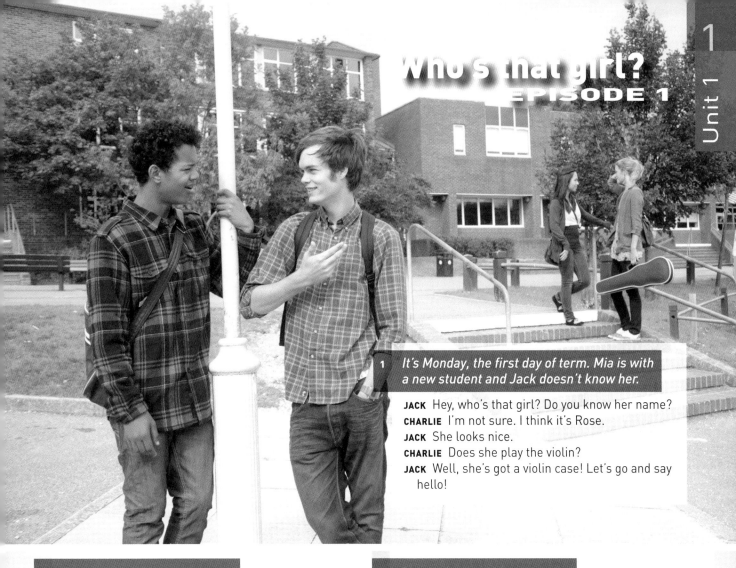

1 *It's Monday, the first day of term. Mia is with a new student and Jack doesn't know her.*

JACK Hey, who's that girl? Do you know her name?
CHARLIE I'm not sure. I think it's Rose.
JACK She looks nice.
CHARLIE Does she play the violin?
JACK Well, she's got a violin case! Let's go and say hello!

2 *Two minutes later...*

JACK And do you study the violin?
ROSE Yes, I do. I study the piano, too. Do you like classical music?
JACK No, I don't. Sorry! I listen to rock bands.
ROSE So do I. I love *Nirvana*.
JACK I like them, too. But I don't like *Coldplay*.
ROSE Neither do I!

3 *Charlie has an idea.*

CHARLIE You know, Jack and Mia have got a band. Jack plays the guitar and Mia plays the drums. But they haven't got a singer. Can you sing, Rose?
ROSE Yeah...
JACK Do you want to sing with us?
MIA Come to a rehearsal! We practise at my place.
ROSE OK. Cool.

REAL TALK   I'm not sure.   Sorry!   You know...   Cool.

SUPER HEROES

Young people going for  *gold*

Mo Farah – marathon runner
Born 28/03/1983

Mo comes from Somalia – his family are refugees. But he is British now. Mo, short for Mohammed, is an incredible runner – one of the best in Britain. He is an international gold medal winner. He trains every day. Mo loves playing football, but running is his life now. He doesn't like walking!

Tom Daley – diver   Born 21/05/1994

They call him 'Diver-boy'. He's young, but he's a brilliant diver. Tom doesn't really have free time because he trains every day. But he likes listening to hip hop and hanging out with his friends.

Johanna Jackson – race walker   Born 17/01/1985

Johanna is a race walker. She can walk 10 km in 45 minutes! All her family run in marathons. But Johanna is a top athlete. She's a student at university, too. She likes seeing her friends, going to the cinema and shopping!

Darius Knight – table tennis player
Born 22/02/1990

Darius comes from a poor part of London – an area with crime problems. But Darius has a talent for table tennis. He travels around the world and trains and plays in competitions. He likes earning money to help his family.

Talking about likes and dislikes

8a Read the article and write short answers.

1 Is Mo Somalian? **No, *he isn't.***
2 Does Mo train every day?
3 Do they call Tom 'Diver-boy'?
4 Can Johanna walk 20 km in 45 minutes?
5 Is Johanna a university student?
6 Does Darius come from a rich area of London?

8b Make notes about what each athlete likes / doesn't like or loves.

Mo Farah loves playing football.

9 PAIRWORK Discuss the questions.

• Which of the sports in the article do you know?
• Which are new to you?
• Which of the sports is easy / difficult / fun / cool?
• Which athlete do you admire?

10 Study the rule and the sentences.

> **like, love + -ing form**
>
> • Use *love, like, don't mind, don't like, hate / can't stand* + *-ing* form to talk about likes and dislikes.
> *I love playing football. I don't like studying.*

11 P T PAIRWORK Talk about these activities.

seeing friends | running | going to the cinema | walking | shopping | playing computer games | studying | cycling | skiing | cooking | playing tennis

A *I don't like playing tennis.*
B *I do. / Neither do I.*
A *I like walking.*
B *I don't. / So do I.*

Get the grammar

Present simple: all forms

1 Complete the tables with *do, don't, doesn't, play* or *plays*.

Positive

I/You	play	
He/She/It	_____	hockey.
We/You/They	_____	

Negative

I/You	_____		
He/She/It	does	not	do athletics.
We/You/They	_____		

Questions

_____	I/you		
Does	he/she/it	play	the guitar?
_____	we/you/they		

Short answers

POSITIVE	NEGATIVE
Yes, I/you do.	No, I/you _____.
Yes, he/she/it does.	No, he/she/it _____.
Yes, we/you/they _____.	No, we/you/they don't.

- Use the present simple to talk about:
  - actions in your daily routine.
    He trains every day.
  - what you like and don't like.
    He doesn't like walking.
  - things that are true.
    Mo comes from Somalia.
    Johanna is a race walker.

2 Complete the sentences with the correct form of the verbs in brackets.

1 My sister ___likes___ sport. (like)
2 You _____ volleyball. (not play)
3 Cathy and Rick _____ in the USA. (live)
4 I _____ to heavy metal music. (not listen)
5 We _____ a lot of photos. (take)
6 James _____ in their band. (not sing)

3 Write questions and short answers.

1 you / like / race walking? ☒
   Do you like race walking? No, I don't.
2 she / train every day? ☑
3 those students / come from Somalia? ☑
4 he / play in competitions? ☒
5 you / like *Sugababes*? ☑
6 they / go to the cinema with their friends? ☒
7 she / speak three languages? ☑
8 he / run in marathons? ☒

So do I. / Neither do I.

4 Look at the table and write answers below.

	Agree	Disagree
I like pizza.	So do I.	I don't.
I don't like cats.	Neither do I.	I do.

5 Write answers.

1 I love canoeing. DISAGREE _____*I don't.*_____
2 I don't like boxing. AGREE _____
3 I hate swimming. DISAGREE _____
4 I like jogging. AGREE _____
5 I don't like playing football. AGREE _____
6 I hate walking. AGREE _____

Modal verb *can*

6 Read the rules and complete the sentences.

Positive	Negative
I can swim.	You can't swim.
He can paint.	She can't paint.

Questions	Short answers
Can you swim?	Yes, I can. / No, I can't.
Can they paint?	Yes, they can. / No, they can't.

- *Can* is a modal verb – a verb that expresses the attitude of the speaker.
- Modal verbs do not take *-s* when the subject is *he, she* or *it*.
- Modal verbs are followed by the base form of the verb.
- Form the negative with the modal + *not* + the base form.
- In questions, put the modal verb before the subject.

1 ___Can___ you ___play___ the piano? (play)
2 We _____ this exercise today. (not finish)
3 They _____. (surf)
4 My grandfather _____ a computer. (not use)
5 _____ they _____? (drive)
6 I _____ pizzas. (cook)

7 Complete the sentences with the correct form of *can*.

1 A _____ you play the keyboards?
   B No, I _____, but I _____ play the drums.
2 My sister _____ act really well. She goes to drama school.
3 I _____ play tennis very well, but I am taking lessons.
4 A _____ you understand what she is saying?
   B No, I _____. It's so noisy.
5 A _____ you ski?
   B Yes, I _____, but not very well.

8 **Workbook pp 148-153; CD-ROM**

FILE

ASKING FOR IDEAS	SUGGESTIONS	OPINIONS	AGREEING
• What shall we do?	• What about...?	• I love / don't mind...	• Good idea. Great.
• Where shall we go?	• How about...?	• I don't like / can't stand / hate...	**DISAGREEING**
	• Shall we go and see...?		• Oh no! I can't stand...
	• I've got an idea...		• No, let's not.
	• What's on? [at the cinema]		

Vocabulary: films

1 **PAIRWORK** **Look at the film genres and add another film for each genre.**

Genre	Film title
horror films	*Halloween*
comedies	*Meet the Parents*
science fiction films	*Star Trek XI*
action films	*The Dark Knight*
teen movies	*High School Musical*
romantic films	*Pretty Woman*
thrillers	*The Silence of the Lambs*
fantasy films	*Lord of the Rings*
cartoons	*The Incredibles*
musicals	*Grease*

2 **P T** **PAIRWORK** **Ask and answer about the film genres in exercise 1. Use these verbs in your answers:**

 love like don't mind don't like  hate / can't stand

 Do you like horror films? *No, I can't stand them!*

Ⓐ *Do you like comedies?* Ⓑ *I don't mind them.*

3 **PAIRWORK** **Ask and answer about your favourite films.**

 What's your favourite action film? *Rambo.*

Going out

4 **43** **P** **Listen and write the times in the film listings on page 13.**

5 **44** **Listen and read the dialogue. Circle T (True) or F (False).**

1 Melissa doesn't like fantasy movies. T / F
2 Lauren likes comedies. T / F
3 Lauren and Henry love Jim Carrey. T / F
4 Henry wants to see *Hancock*. T / F
5 Lauren thinks romantic films are boring. T / F
6 The friends decide to see *What Happens in Vegas*. T / F

LAUREN What shall we do this evening, you guys?
MELISSA Let's go and see a film.
HENRY What's on?
LAUREN *The Golden Compass*.
MELISSA Oh, no! I hate fantasy movies. What else is there?
HENRY What about *Yes Man*?
LAUREN It's a comedy. I can't stand them.
MELISSA But Jim Carrey is in it. I love him. He's really funny.
LAUREN I don't like him.
HENRY Neither do I. Shall we go and see *Hancock*?
LAUREN No, let's not. Action films are boring.
MELISSA I've got an idea. How about *What Happens in Vegas* with Cameron Diaz?
LAUREN Yeah. Good idea. She's great.
HENRY Cool. What time is it on?

6 ROLE PLAY Work in groups of three.
- • You're going to a film.
- • Look at the film listings.
- • Have a conversation. Decide what film to see.
- • Use some of the words and expressions in the *File*.

○ ○ ○   @ http://www.brightoninfo/infothisweek   search:

Brighton INFO

CLUBS
SPORT
THEATRE
DANCE
FILM
CAFÉS
RESTAURANTS
BUSES
EXHIBITIONS
COLLEGES
MAPS

Now showing

The Golden Compass
Young Lyra travels to the far North to save her friend in this epic fantasy of good and evil.
Odeon: 1.30 pm, [1]_____ pm, 7.45 pm

Yes Man
A man decides to change his life by saying yes to everything.
Regent Cinema: [2]_____ pm, 5.00 pm, [3]_____ pm

Hancock
Funny, exciting and action-packed: it's Hancock against the bad guys of Los Angeles.
Ritzy: 2.30 pm, [4]_____ pm, 8.45 pm, Tuesday only [5]_____ pm

What Happens in Vegas
Cameron Diaz and Ashton Kutcher wake up married in Vegas!
Cineworld: [6]_____ pm, 6.05 pm, 8.50 pm

7 Read *Get into Culture* and do the task.

Get into *culture* GOING TO THE CINEMA

Cinema-going is popular in Europe. Italians go about twice a year, Britons about three times, but the Irish go four times a year! Teens go most often.

The most popular films are blockbusters: big, spectacular films such as *The Dark Knight*. Teen movies are also popular with teenagers. These are often set in American high schools. Two out of three films in the EU are American.

Many cinemas are multiplex cinemas with up to 20 screens and there are some megaplex cinemas with more than 20 screens!

How often do you go the cinema?
☐ once or twice a year
☐ three or four times a year
☐ more

What films do you like?
☐ American or British
☐ other

Is there a multiplex cinema where you live?

8 **LINKS Real communication pp 4-5**

POSSESSIONS

LifeStyle Teens, toys, and treasures. **Today's teens have more money to spend and more things to buy. Here's what one teen** can't live without....

AMY'S FAVOURITE THINGS.

1 ☐ I think these are really cool. I wear them all the time — in the winter, too.

2 ☐ I like reading on the train to school. The journey's so boring.

3 ☐ These trainers are very comfortable. I love wearing them. I walk a lot, so they're brilliant.

4 ☐ I've got posters all over my room. I guess Fernando Torres is my favourite. He's so good-looking.

5 ☐ This is really important. It carries all my favourite things. My boyfriend puts his horrible hat in it, too. I hate that hat!

6 ☐ I love listening to music. My favourite bands are *Kings of Leon* and *The White Stripes*. I like *Duffy*, too. She's got an amazing voice.

7 ☐ I love wearing jeans. These are my favourite pair. My mum thinks they are ugly. She prefers skirts.

8 ☐ This is my favourite thing. I send about 20 text messages a day. I sleep with it, and I take photos of all my friends!

a

b

c

d

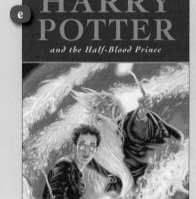

e

HARRY POTTER
and the Half-Blood Prince
J.K. ROWLING
BLOOMSBURY

f

g

h

Reading

1 Read the article. Match the pictures with the descriptions.

2 Circle the correct information.

1 Amy likes wearing *skirts / jeans / trainers / school uniform / trousers*.
2 Her favourite bands are *Kings of Leon / Coldplay / Killers / The White Stripes*.
3 She hates *her trainers / her boyfriend's hat / her mobile phone / her sunglasses*.
4 She likes *studying / reading / listening to music / sleeping / sending text messages*.

Pronunciation   LINKING

3   45 Listen and repeat.

1 She's got a computer.
2 I've got an iPod.
3 He's got a poster.
4 I've got a magazine.
5 You've got a pair of jeans.
6 We've got a blog.

Speaking and listening

Word **expander**   ADJECTIVES

Underline the adjectives in the text and write them in the correct list.

POSITIVE *cool* _____

_____

NEGATIVE *boring* _____

_____

4a What have you got in your bedroom? Write six things. Use adjectives to describe them.

posters	cool posters
an iPod	an amazing iPod

4b PAIRWORK Tell your partner about the things in your room. Try and add information.

 I've got an amazing mp3 player. It can hold 2,000 songs in its memory!

5a   46 P Listen and tick ☑. What have they got in their bags?

	Luke	Chiara	Max
a book	☐	☐	☐
a hairbrush	☐	☐	☐
keys	☐	☐	☐
a mobile phone	☐	☐	☐
money	☐	☐	☐
an mp3 player	☐	☐	☐

5b Listen again and answer the questions.

1 Who hasn't got a mobile?
2 Two people have got keys. Who are they?
3 Who has got a hairbrush?
4 What colour is Max's mobile?
5 Who has got an mp3 player?

Skills FOR life   LISTENING FOR KEY WORDS

• First identify the information that you need to find, eg. nouns such as *hairbrush* or *money*.
• While you are listening, watch out for the key words and whether the verb has a positive or negative meaning, e.g. *I haven't got a hairbrush. My favourite thing is this mp3 player. I hate wearing glasses.*

---

6 PAIRWORK What have you got in your bag? Tell your partner. Try and give more information.

I've got my mobile phone. I can take great photos with it. I love the colour. And it's really small!

Writing

7 P T Use the article about Amy as a model. Write short paragraphs about your three favourite things. Include:

• a short description using an adjective
• your opinion

RANDOM Fact Half of UK parents ask their teenagers for advice when buying a laptop or a mobile phone.

Unit 2
Daily life

Unit objectives

Grammar: present simple: question words; adverbs of frequency; *What's she like? / What does she like?*, modal verb *would / would like*
Function: talking about routine; preferences; exchanging personal information
Vocabulary: daily activities; jobs

Warm up

1 Look at the photos on page 17 and answer the questions.

1 Where are they in the pictures?
2 What musical instruments can you see?

Comprehension

2 🔊47 **Listen and read *Who's that girl*? Circle T (True) or F (False).**

1 Jack and Mia practise in a garage. T / F
2 Rose lives in London. T / F
3 Rose practises the violin and piano at the weekend. T / F
4 Mia goes running at the weekend. T / F
5 Rose isn't nervous. T / F
6 Jack doesn't like Mia's voice. T / F

Talking about routine

3 Study the rules and do the tasks.

Present simple: question words

• Use a question word for questions which ask for information.

When do you practise here?

Find questions in the dialogue with these words: *where, how often, how.*

Adverbs of frequency

• Use adverbs of frequency to say how often you do something.

We always practise at the weekend.

Complete the list with adverbs from the dialogue.

always _____ often _____ never

What's she like?

• Use *What's...like?* to ask for an opinion.

What's my voice like?

• Use *What does he/she like?* to ask about a person's preferences.

What does she like? She likes music and running.

4 Write the words in the correct order to make affirmative sentences.

1 usually / sister / my / cartoons / watches
2 are / you / at home / always
3 rock music / listen to / often / they
4 write / you / me / an email / never
5 I / go cycling / sometimes
6 practises / often / the violin / he

Vocabulary: daily activities

5a 🔊48 **Match the words and the pictures. Then listen and check.**

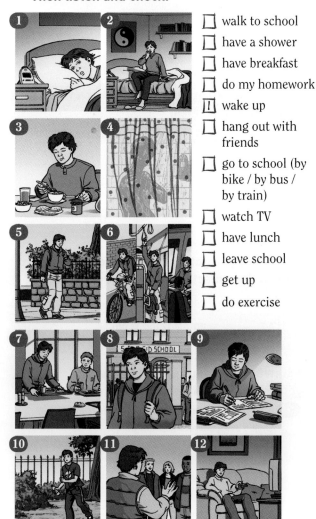

☐ walk to school
☐ have a shower
☐ have breakfast
☐ do my homework
☑ wake up
☐ hang out with friends
☐ go to school (by bike / by bus / by train)
☐ watch TV
☐ have lunch
☐ leave school
☐ get up
☐ do exercise

5b Put the activities in the order you do them.

💬 *I get up, then I have a shower...*

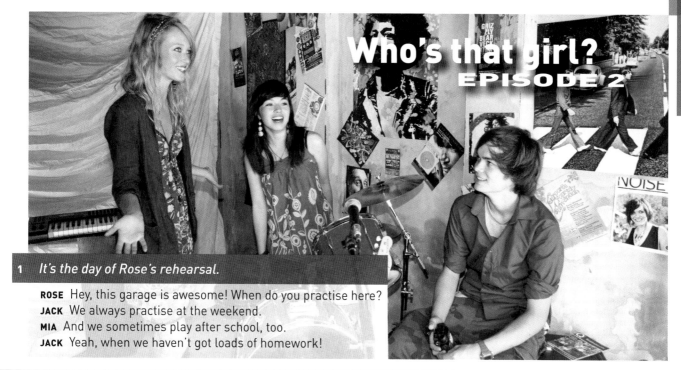

Who's that girl?
EPISODE 2

1 *It's the day of Rose's rehearsal.*

ROSE Hey, this garage is awesome! When do you practise here?
JACK We always practise at the weekend.
MIA And we sometimes play after school, too.
JACK Yeah, when we haven't got loads of homework!

2 *Jack wants to film Rose.*

JACK Can we film you, Rose? It's my mum's new DVcam.
ROSE Er... sure.
JACK OK, let me check this camera works...
MIA Where do you live, Rose?
ROSE In Kemptown.
MIA And what do you do at the weekend?
ROSE Well, I usually practise the violin and the piano. And I sometimes go shopping – for clothes. Oh, and I always go running!
MIA I never go running! How often do you run?
ROSE Every day. I really like it. It's important to me.
JACK OK, I'm ready. How do you feel?
ROSE A bit nervous.
JACK Don't worry. Just sing.

3 *Jack and Mia have an easy decision.*

ROSE What am I like on camera?
JACK You're great.
ROSE And what's my voice like?
MIA Fantastic!
JACK We've got a new singer!
MIA I really love her!

REAL TALK   awesome!   loads   sure   Don't worry.

Vocabulary: jobs

6 🔊49 **Match the pictures with the words. Then listen and check.**

12 a secretary	☐ a hairdresser
☐ a journalist	☐ a factory worker
☐ a police officer	☐ a shop assistant
☐ a housewife	☐ a computer programmer
☐ an electrician	☐ an office worker
☐ a nurse	☐ a sales representative

7 **Read the sentences. Which jobs do they describe?**

1 I work on a production line. *a factory worker*
2 I'm a manager in an insurance company.
3 I travel a lot for my job.
4 I develop software programs.
5 It's a manual job. I cut people's hair.
6 I serve customers in a department store.
7 I often work outside and I wear a uniform.

Talking about preferences

8 **Read the article and find:**
- unpopular jobs
- teen dream jobs
- popular jobs

@ http://www.jobscareersprofessions.com   search:

Number one teen dream

What would Italian teenagers like to be when they leave school? Well, they don't want to be politicians or judges, and they definitely don't want to be housewives. Only 0.2% of teenagers want that! The number one dream is to be famous. In fact 44% of teenagers would like to be a celebrity and 37% would like to be sporting personalities. An amazing 15% of boys want to be a footballer, and 11% of girls would like to be a dancer, a model, or a pop star.

Apart from these dreams, boys are interested in being engineers and sports stars. But girls would like to be hairdressers or beauticians. But both boys and girls would like to be doctors, teachers, vets or lawyers.

I just want to be famous!

---

9 **Study the rule and read the sentences.**

> **would like**
>
> - Use *would like* to talk about preferences.
>   *I'd like* to be a celebrity.
>   *Would you like* to work in an office? No, *I wouldn't*.

10 **P T GROUPWORK Discuss the question: What would you like to be in the future?**

a politician | a judge | a model | a footballer | a pop star | a dancer | a doctor | a teacher | a beautician | a lawyer | a celebrity

A *I'd like to be to be a judge.*
B *I want to be a teacher.*

Get the grammar

Present simple: question words

1 Complete the sentences with *do*, *does*, or *is*.

1 Who __is__ your best friend?
2 Where _____ you go to school?
3 What job _____ your father do?
4 What _____ your best friend like?
5 What time _____ you go to bed on Saturday night?
6 When _____ your teacher give you homework?
7 How often _____ you do sport?
8 How _____ you say 'celebrity' in your language?
9 Why _____ it good to learn English?
10 Which _____ your favourite day of the week?

2 Complete the dialogues.

1 A __What__ do you have for breakfast?
  B I have toast and coffee.
2 A _____ does he play the drums?
  B He usually plays in the garage.
3 A _____ do they live?
  B In London.
4 A _____ does Jenny cycle to school?
  B Once or twice a week.
5 A _____ does he practise?
  B He usually practises on the weekend.

3 PAIRWORK Ask and answer about your routines.
  A *What time do you get up?*
  B *At about half past six.*

4 PAIRWORK Ask and answer the questions in exercise 1.

Adverbs of frequency

5 Circle the correct phrase to complete the rules.

• Use adverbs of frequency *before* / *after* verbs in the present simple.
  We always visit my aunt on Sundays.
  Ben never phones me.
• Use adverbs of frequency *before* / *after* the verb *be*.
  I am often late for school.
  My dad is usually home by 7 o'clock.

6 Write the words in the correct order to make affirmative sentences.

1 sometimes / to school / walk / I
2 at seven / you / get up / always
3 often / they / lunch / at home / have
4 wears / never / jeans / my sister
5 secretaries / in an office / work / usually
6 travels / sometimes / my dad / for his job

7 Write eight sentences about you and your family. Use an adverb of frequency.
  My brother always gets up late on Sunday.

What's she like? v What does she like?

8a Match the questions and answers.

1 ☐ What's Paul like?
2 ☐ What does Paul like?
3 ☐ What are your new neighbours like?

a They're very nice. And they've got a dog.
b He's really funny.
c He likes sport, music and playing video games.

8b Complete the rules. Use *does* or *be*.

• Use *What* + the verb _____ + a pronoun / name + *like* to ask for an opinion about a person or thing.
• Use *What* + *do* / _____ + a pronoun / noun + *like* to ask if a person likes something.

9 PAIRWORK Ask and answer the questions.
What's your home like?   What's your town like?
What's your school like?   What's your friend like?

Modal verb *would / wouldn't like* for preferences

10 Look at the rule and circle the correct words.

• Use *would* / *wouldn't like* + *to* + the base form to talk about preferences.

1 My friend would *like* / *likes* to be a hairdresser.
2 Where would you like *to go* / *go* on your birthday?
3 *Would you like* / *Do you like* to live here all your life?
4 *Would* / *Does* your sister like to come to town with us?
5 What film *would you like* / *you like* to see tonight?
6 Would you like *to sing* / *sing* in our band? Yes, I would.

Object pronouns

11 Look at the sentences and complete the rules with *after* / *in front of*.

• Put the subject pronouns _____ a main verb.
  Do you want to try?
• Put the object pronouns _____ a verb.
  I like her. He likes her.
• Put the object pronouns _____ a preposition.
  I've got some music with me.

12 Complete the list with these object pronouns.
them | you | her | it | us | him | you

I __me__; you ____; he ____; she ____; it ____;
we ____; you ____; they ____

13 ⬅ **Workbook pp 154–159; CD-ROM**

FILE

PERSONAL DETAILS

What's your...
- first name / surname / full name?
- address / postcode?
- date of birth (day, month, year)?
- email address?
- home phone / mobile number?

ASKING FOR PERSONAL INFORMATION
- Are you... sporty / musical / interested in drama?
- Do you... like chatting online / belong to any clubs societies?
- What's your school / house like?
- What kind of music / TV programmes do you like?

Personal details

1 P 🎧 **Listen and circle the correct details.**

1 Name: *Tom Wilkins / Tom Wilkinson*

2 Date of birth: *14/07/94 / 04/06/94*

3 Address: *36 Meadow Lane, Norwich / 136 Meadow Lane, Northampton*

4 Postcode: *NO25 23H / NO25 2DH*

5 email address: *tom.boy@safemail.co.uk / tom. boy@safemail.com*

6 *home phone number / mobile number*: 06913 451211

Registering online

2 **Read the website on page 21 and answer the questions.**

1 Who can you chat with on LPO?

2 What languages do you chat in?

3 What age are the people you chat with?

4 How do you chat?

5 What does the school give you before you register?

6 What does LPO do when you register?

3 **Complete the form for you.**

4a **Number the questions and instructions in the same order as the information in the website.**

- ☐ What's your date of birth?
- ☐ What language do you speak?
- ☐ What are your hobbies and interests?
- ☐ Are you a boy or a girl?
- ☐ What's the name of your school?
- ☐ Write a short description of yourself.
- ☐ Do you belong to any clubs or societies?
- ☐ What language do you want to practise?
- ☐ What's your email address?
- ☐ Where do you live?
- ☐ What's your favourite type of music?
- ☐ What's your name?

4b **PAIRWORK Ask and answer the questions in exercise 4a. Make a note of your partner's answers.**

5 **Read *Get into Culture* and do the task.**

Get into *culture* **LANGUAGE TEACHING IN THE UK**

It is only compulsory for UK students to study a foreign language up to the age of 14. About 40% of UK students take a language exam at the age of 16. French and German are popular, but Spanish is very popular.

At the moment, about 60% of primary schools teach a foreign language. The government wants to increase this to 100% by 2010.

- **Is language teaching compulsory in your country?**
- **What languages are popular / unpopular?**
- **Do you think it is important to learn a foreign language? Why? / Why not?**

6 **LINKS Real communication pp 4-5**

@ http://www.languagepracticeonline.com   search:

LANGUAGE PRACTICE ONLINE

Click the ↻ button to play

Are you between 14 and 21 years old? Would you like to speak to students from other countries? **LPO** is an online language community with thousands of language students from schools in 46 different countries.

Register with us online and we match you with a student who speaks your target language as his/her first language. It's very easy. We put you in contact and you take it in turns to talk online in your language and your partner's language.

▸ **Register now...**
▸ **Make a new friend!**
▸ **Learn the real language of real people your own age!**
▸ **Talk about the things that really interest you!**

IMPORTANT: YOUR ONLINE SECURITY
Tell your school before you register with us.
The school gives you a password.
We check all registrations with the school.

1	School	
2	Name	
3	Gender	Male ☐ Female ☐
4	Date of birth:	Day ☐ Month ☐ Year ☐
5	Email	
6	Home country	
7	Your language	
8	Target language	
9	Description	
10	Hobbies / interests	
11	Clubs / societies	
12	Favourite type of music	

7 ROLE PLAY Work in pairs.
- Act out an online chat between language practice students.
- Write five more online questions.
- Ask and answer with your partner.
- Use expressions from the *File*.

Reading and speaking

1 Read the interview and complete the sentences.

1 Carrie likes…
2 In her free time she often… and she sometimes…
3 In her part-time job, the customers often…
4 At work, Carrie often…
5 She always…
6 She doesn't usually…

2 Write three things you have in common with Carrie.

Welcome to
THE FOR REAL INTERVIEW

This week we meet Carrie Tyson

Hi Carrie!
Hi Carrie!

Where do you live?
I live in Hereford in the UK.

Are you still at school?
Yes, I'm in my last year of secondary school.

What do you like doing in your free time?
I like going to movies, partying, and hanging out with friends.

What kind of music do you listen to?
Different kinds. I often listen to pop. But I also like R & B. And I sometimes listen to hip hop.

Do you have a part-time job?
I'm a shop assistant in a shoe shop. I work there on Saturday. I spend my money on going out in the evening and on clothes.

What do you do in your job?

Well, I do lots of different things in the shop. I help the customers choose their shoes. They often ask me for advice! I often serve customers with children: I always measure the children's feet and then help them choose their shoes. I don't usually work at the till because the full-time assistants do that.

Do you have a break in the day?
Yes, I have a ten-minute break in the morning and I usually have a coffee. Then I have an hour's break at one o'clock and I have lunch in town.

What's your ambition? Would you like to work in a shop when you leave school?
No, I wouldn't. It's OK for a part-time job, but I wouldn't like to do it full-time. I think I'd like to be a primary school teacher. I love children.

Word expander *HAVE*

Learn these expressions with *have*.

Use some of them to write six sentences about you.

have breakfast / lunch / dinner
have a drink / coffee / snack
have a bath / shower
have a lesson / a holiday
have a break / an accident

RANDOM Fact Top university subjects in the UK are law, design, psychology, management, business, computer science, English, medicine, social work and sports science.

3 PAIRWORK Look at the information about Georg. Role play the interview from exercise 1 with Georg.

Ⓐ *Where do you live?*
Ⓑ *I live in Innsbruck in Austria.*

Name: Georg Rolman

Home city:
Innsbruck, Austria
School:
Central Innsbruck Academy,
Year 12 (final year)
Hobbies:
skiing, athletics, playing
the drums, travel
Favourite music: heavy metal, rap
Part-time job: children's ski camp assistant
Duties: always checks the skis in the morning /
usually meets the children off the coach
/ often teaches the beginners / doesn't
work on his own – always works with a
full-time ski instructor
Ambition: to be a professional skiier

Writing

4a Write personal answers to the questions in the interview in exercise 1.

Where do you live?
I live in Milan, Italy.
What do you like doing in your free time?
I like swimming, hanging out with my friends and listening to music.

4b PAIRWORK Ask and answer the questions.

| Pronunciation /ɜ:/ /e/ |

5 🔊 51 **Listen and repeat the words.**

/ɜ:/	/e/
turn	get
work	ready
thirty	spell
birth	when
girl	ten

6 T Write about your normal day.

I always / usually… get up / have a shower at (half past seven).
I (usually) go to school by… I often… I sometimes… I get home at…

Listening and speaking

7 🔊 52 **Listen and write the jobs.**

Alex _____
Myra _____
Justin _____

8 PAIRWORK P T Talk about the routines of people you know.

💬 *My dad's a computer programmer. He works in London. He leaves home early in the morning and gets home late.*

Skills FOR life **USING A VOCABULARY NOTEBOOK**

You can organise your vocabulary notebook in alphabetical order. Write the word, a translation and an example sentence. Measure – misurare. I always measure the children's feet. Or you can organise it in groups, e.g. all words linked to *work in a shop*. Keep it up-to-date and read it regularly.

work at the till

part-time

shop assistant

WORK IN A SHOP

have a break

serve customers

FILE

SIGNS, LABELS, SHORT MESSAGES AND CARDS

We often have to read warnings, notices or labels in everyday life. So they are part of the Cambridge PET exam.

Towards PET Paper 1 Reading and writing, Part 1

Tips
- You don't need to understand all the words. Find the key words first. Where do you think the sign is?
- Next look at the grammar. Is the meaning positive or negative? What tense is it?
- Use any pictures or symbols to help you.
- Read the three explanations carefully.
- Choose the answer that is closest to the meaning.

---

1 **P Look at the text in each question. What does it say? Mark the correct letter A, B, or C.**

1 A Do not bring knives etc. onto the plane with you.
  B Put knives etc. in your hand luggage.
  C You must leave knives etc. at home.

2 A You can pay for certain tickets in euros if you travel from Oxford to London.
  B You can buy certain tickets in euros if you are in London.
  C In Oxford and London you can pay in euros.

3 In this restaurant
  A you can eat breakfast all day, but there is only cold food and you can't bring children.
  B you can eat breakfast until ten, there is hot and cold food and you can bring children.
  C you can eat breakfast all day, there is hot and cold food and you can bring children.

MOUNTAIN BIKE 4 SALE

PERFECT CONDITION, 21 GEARS
£80 ONO
PHONE: 0397737889

4 Someone wants to
  A sell a bicycle for £80.
  B buy a bicycle for £80.
  C borrow a bicycle for a mountain tour.

Julie,
Cindy wants to see you after school. Wants advice on some CDs to buy (Xmas presents!)
Mum

5 A Cindy wants to buy some CDs as Christmas presents for Julie's mum.
  B Cindy wants to talk to Julie after school about some CDs as Christmas presents.
  C Cindy wants some CDs from Julie.

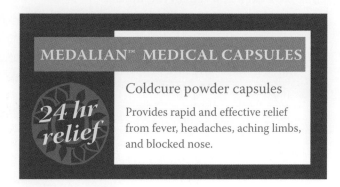

6 Take these pills if you
  A have a bad cold.
  B have earache.
  C have a problem with digestion.

FILE

HAVING A CONVERSATION

When we are talking to people, we chat about all sorts of things. In Cambridge PET you have an informal chat about your interests, routine, etc. And in Trinity you have a chat about a topic the examiner chooses. How can you prepare for informal chats? One way is to know lots of vocabulary on everyday topics.

Towards PET Paper 3 Speaking, Part 1
Trinity, ISE I

Tips

IMPROVING YOUR VOCABULARY
• Organise words into mind maps and vocabulary areas.
• Keep a vocabulary exercise book or notepad.
• Do a drawing or create a symbol for each word.
• Write the words in coloured pens.
• Say the words to yourself or even out loud.

ANSWERING *YES / NO* QUESTIONS
• Don't answer with one word, *Yes* or *No*. Use the correct short answer form: *Yes, I do. / No, I haven't*, etc.
• Try to add some extra information. This helps the conversation and shows your language skills!

1 PAIRWORK Here are the beginnings of some mind map word fields. Copy them and add words and expressions.

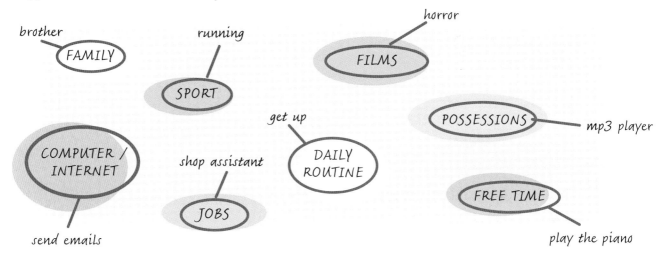

2 Circle the correct word to complete the short answers.

1 Do you like music? Yes, I *like / do*.
2 Have you got brothers and sisters? No, I *haven't / haven't got*.
3 Are you interested in football? Yes, I *am / do*.
4 Do your friends play computer games? No, they *doesn't / don't*.
5 Do you have a shower in the morning? Yes, I *do / have*.

3 Choose one of the subjects above. Try to maintain a conversation for two minutes!

Ⓐ *How many people are there in your family?*
Ⓑ *Oh I've got two brothers and a sister.*
Ⓐ *How old is your sister?*
Ⓑ *She's ten.*
Ⓐ *What music does she like?*
Ⓑ *Rap. And what about you?*

4 PAIRWORK P T Take it in turns to ask and answer with the correct short answers. Vary the order of the questions.

1 Are you sporty?
2 Do you often eat in restaurants?
3 Have you got a computer in your room?
4 Do you speak French?
5 Have you got a part-time job?
6 Do you and your friends like listening to music?
7 Does your mum use the Internet?
8 Is your house in a city?
9 Is your birthday in June?
10 Does your family eat a lot of pasta?

5 PAIRWORK P T Ask and answer the questions in exercise 4 again. This time, add a sentence with extra information.

Ⓐ *Are you sporty?*
Ⓑ *Yes, I am. I love playing basketball.*
Ⓐ *Do you often eat in restaurants?*
Ⓑ *No, I don't. I usually eat at home.*

6 **LINKS Exam listening p 5**

LANGUAGE CHECK

1 Choose the correct words.

1 Kelly often ____ computer games with her friends.
   a) play   b) does   c) plays   d) playing

2 My brothers ____ English.
   a) not study   c) don't study
   b) doesn't study   d) don't studying

3 ____ you like rap music?
   a) Are   b) Yes   c) Can   d) Do

4 'What's your town ____?' 'It's great.'
   a) like   b) likes   c) liking   d) is like

5 'I don't like jogging.' '____ do I.'
   a) So   b) Not   c) Neither   d) Never

2 Ask and answer questions about ability.

1 he / swim ? ☑
   Can he swim? Yes, he can.

2 they / paint pictures ? ☒
   _____

3 you / walk 20 kilometres ? ☑
   _____

4 she / play the guitar ? ☒
   _____

5 your friends / dance ? ☑
   _____

6 you / ride a horse ? ☒
   _____

TOTAL: ____/10

3 Complete the daily activities with these words.

to | leave | up | do | have

1 wake ____
2 _____ breakfast
3 go _____ school
4 _____ school
5 _____ exercise

4 Complete the words.

1 *Halloween* is a h _ _ _ _ r film.
2 In winter I aways go s _ _ _ _ g.
3 Children usually love c _ _ _ _ _ ns.
4 Mum's a d _ _ _ _r at the local hospital.
5 I love w_ _ _ _ _ g my blog.

TOTAL: ____/10

5 Circle the correct words.

A [1]*What's / Who's* on at the cinema?
B There's an action film at 3 o'clock. [2]*Do we / Shall we* go and see it?
A Oh no! I [3]*can't / don't* stand action films!
B How [4]*like / about* a comedy?
A Yes. Good [5]*mind / idea*.

6 Complete the factfile.

First name	Karen
1 _____	Phillips
2 _____	24 North Road, Culham, Oxfordshire, England
3 _____	OX23 lUR
4 _____ address	Karen.phillips@friendsmail.co.uk
5 _____ of birth	31 July 1995

TOTAL: ____/10

7 PAIRWORK Ask and answer the questions.

• What do you like doing?
• Do you like chatting to your friends online?
• Do you belong to any clubs?
• What's your school like?
• What kind of TV programmes do you like?

TOTAL: ____/10

TOTAL: ____/40

LINKS Interculture pp 18-21; CLIL (Sport) pp 46-47

A2
Key objectives

Grammar present continuous; *there is / there are*; countable and uncountable nouns; *how much / many*; *some / any*
Functions talking about present and temporary situations; buying clothes; talking about quantity; describing places; making arrangements
Vocabulary clothes; money; accessories; places

TEEN LIFE In the UK a typical teenager...

- ○ wears a school uniform.
- ○ sends a lot of text messages.
- ○ does a part-time job.
- ○ thinks school is boring.
- ○ watches TV in his or her bedroom.
- ○ gets weekly pocket money.
- ○ uses a computer at home.
- ○ spends a lot of money on going out.
- ○ doesn't speak a foreign language.
- ○ wants to be famous.

Get started

1 CD2 ② **Look at the survey above. Listen to Daniel Wood. Tick ☑ the things he does and put a cross ☒ by the things he doesn't do.**

2 PAIRWORK **Talk about Daniel's life. Is he a typical teenager?**

Ⓐ *Daniel wears a school uniform.*
Ⓑ *He doesn't send a lot of text messages.*

3 P T GROUPWORK **Compare your life with teenagers in the UK.**

Ⓐ *In my country we don't wear a school uniform.*
Ⓑ *We send a lot of text messages.*
Ⓒ *Most teenagers don't do a part-time job.*

4 ③ **Listen and circle the correct words.**

F MOBILE PHONE FACTS

⊠ An average of over *114 / 142* million texts are sent every day in Britain.

⊠ The first text message was sent on *3rd December / 25th December 1992.* The message was 'Happy Christmas'.

⊠ The most popular time of day for texting is from 10.30–11.00 *pm / am.*

⊠ About 5 million texts are sent every *day / hour* in Britain.

5 Find abbreviations in the text messages that mean the following.

are = R | for | to | at | you | see | wait | late | great | later | thanks | tomorrow | tonight | school | why | text back | come

SEE ALL MESSAGES FROM SENDER

1 ⊠↻ Lets go 2 the cinema 2nite
2 ⊠↻ Y dont U cum 2 my house?
3 ⊠↻ CU @scl 2moro
4 ⊠↻ C U L8R
5 ⊠↻ thx 4 the present :-)
6 ⊠↻ Sorry Im L8. Im leaving scl now
7 ⊠↻ RUOK? Tb
8 ⊠↻ Y R U sad? :-(
9 ⊠↻ w8 4 me!
10 ⊠↻ Gr8 2 c u!

menu   back

6 PAIRWORK **Write a message to your partner on a piece of paper. Then write an answer back. Use some of the abbreviations above.**

Unit 3
What are you doing?

Warm up

1 PAIRWORK Discuss these questions.

- Who is your favourite band / singer?
- Do you often go to concerts?

Comprehension

2 Read the ticket and text message. Answer the questions.

1 What has Jack got?

2 Where and when is the concert?

3 What time does Jack suggest?

3 **Listen and read *Who's that girl?* Answer the questions.**

DIALOGUE 1

1 Where are Jack and Charlie?

2 Where is Mia?

3 Who is Mia waiting for?

DIALOGUE 2

4 Where are Jack and Charlie?

5 Where are Rose and Mia?

6 What's the problem?

DIALOGUE 3

7 Are Rose and Mia on the bus?

8 Are they near the Zodiac?

9 Do you think the girls get to the concert?

Talking about present activities

4 Study the rule and read the sentences. Underline other examples in the dialogues.

Present continuous

- Use the present continuous to talk about things that are happening at this moment.

What are you doing?

We're sitting on a bus.

The bus isn't moving.

still

I'm still waiting for Rose.

- Use *still* with the present continuous to emphasise that a situation is continuing, and that it isn't finished.

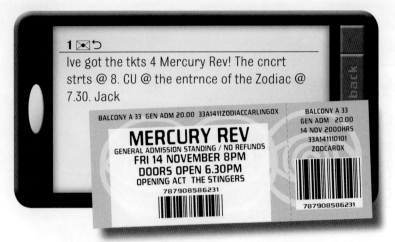

1 ✉↩
Ive got the tkts 4 Mercury Rev! The cncrt strts @ 8. CU @ the entrnce of the Zodiac @ 7.30. Jack

BALCONY A 33 GEN ADM 20.00 33A1411ZODIACCARLINGOX

MERCURY REV
GENERAL ADMISSION STANDING / NO REFUNDS
FRI 14 NOVEMBER 8PM
DOORS OPEN 6.30PM
OPENING ACT THE STINGERS
787908586231

BALCONY A 33
GEN ADM 20.00
14 NOV 2000HRS
33A141110101
ZODCAROX

787908586231

5 Write sentences in the present continuous.

1 Ryan / not watch TV / play computer games
Ryan isn't watching TV. He's playing computer games.

2 Tamsin / not do her homework / write email

3 we / not sit on bus / go by train

4 they / not study / listen to music

5 I / not read / study for my Maths test

6 you / not work / play

7 Rebecca / not shop / have a coffee

8 he / not cycle / walk

6 Write these text messages in full. Use correct spelling and punctuation.

Why are you texting me?

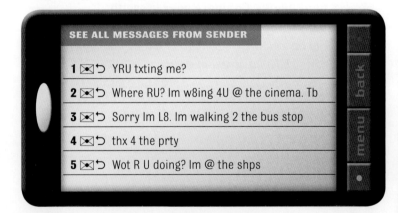

SEE ALL MESSAGES FROM SENDER

1 ✉↩ YRU txting me?

2 ✉↩ Where RU? Im w8ing 4U @ the cinema. Tb

3 ✉↩ Sorry Im L8. Im walking 2 the bus stop

4 ✉↩ thx 4 the prty

5 ✉↩ Wot R U doing? Im @ the shps

7 PAIRWORK Ask and answer questions about your family or friends.

Ⓐ *What's your mum doing at the moment?*

Ⓑ *I think she's driving home from work.*

Who's that girl?
Episode 3

1 *Jack and Charlie are waiting for the girls. But where are they?*

MIA Hi Jack. Where are you?

JACK I'm standing outside the Zodiac with Charlie. Where are you?

MIA I'm sitting in my room...

JACK What are you doing in your room?

MIA I'm still waiting for Rose. I think she's got a problem at home.

JACK Where is she?

MIA Don't panic. She's cycling here now. We can leave soon.

JACK Well, hurry up.

2 *Mia and Rose are sitting on the bus.*

ROSE Jack? It's me. I'm sorry we're late.

JACK That's OK. We're still outside.

ROSE I can't hear you properly. Are Mercury Rev playing?

JACK No, they aren't. It's the support band. What are you doing?

ROSE We're sitting on a bus. But it's a nightmare. There's a lot of traffic. The bus isn't moving.

JACK You've only got ten minutes!

ROSE Hang on, I've got an idea. Come on, Mia. See you soon, Jack!

3 *The concert starts in five minutes!*

JACK Are you OK? What's wrong?

MIA We're running... Oh dear! Rose is fast... We're nearly there! ... I can see you!

REAL TALK   Don't panic. It's a nightmare. Hang on. What's wrong?

Talking about temporary situations

8 Read the emails and write J (Jack) or M (Marco) next to the sentences.

At the moment…

- ☐ he's studying a lot.
- ☐ he isn't playing football.
- ☐ he isn't studying a lot.
- ☐ he's reading a lot.
- ☐ he's practising with his band.
- ☐ he's doing a school project.
- ☐ he isn't watching Chelsea.

Jack

Marco

Hi Jack

How are you? I'm studying a lot this term because we've got exams. I'm also doing a project on the history of science, so I'm reading a lot. ☹
But I'm not playing football this term. And I haven't got time to watch Chelsea on TV. Disaster!
What are you doing?
Write back soon.
Marco

Hi Marco

Thanks for your email. Poor you! I'm not studying at the moment. ☺ Our exams are next year. But I'm very busy. I'm practising with my band because we've got our first gig next month. We've got a new singer! Her name's Rose. She's got a great voice and she's good-looking, too!
Sorry you aren't playing football! There's a big Chelsea match on Saturday. Chill out and watch it!
Bye for now
Jack

Hi Jack

Good news about your new singer. Do you like her a lot?! Is Mia still playing the drums? She's cool. And are you practising in Mia's garage? I can't wait for the summer. I'm looking forward to seeing you all again.
Marco

Hi Marco
No comment! About Rose, I mean!
Jack

REAL TALK

Poor you!
Chill out!
I can't wait for...
No comment.

---

9 Study the rule and circle examples of the present continuous in the emails.

Present continuous

- Form the present continuous with the present of the verb *be* + the *-ing* form of the main verb.
- Use the present continuous to talk about temporary situations.

  I'm studying a lot this term.
  I'm practising with the band.

10 Write sentences that are true for you.

1 enjoy school this year
   I'm enjoying school this year. / I'm not enjoying school this year.
2 go to parties a lot this month
3 do a lot of sport these days
4 do lots of tests this week
5 listen to music a lot these days
6 my friends and I do a lot of things together at the moment

Present continuous all forms

1 Complete the table and read the rules.

are | are not/aren't | am/'m | is/'s | Is | is not/isn't

Positive		
I	am/'m	
He/She/It	_____	studying.
We/You/They	are/'re	

Negative			
I	_____		
He/She/It	_____	not	studying.
We/You/They	_____		

Questions		
Am	I	
_____	he/she/it	working?
Are	we/you/they	

Short answers: positive			Short answers: negative		
Yes,	I	am.	No,	I	'm not.
	he/she/it	is.		he/she/it	isn't.
	we/you/they	___.		we/you/they	aren't.

- Use the present continuous to talk about:
  - things happening at this moment.
    We're sitting on a bus.
    I'm not studying at the moment.
  - temporary situations.
    I'm studying a lot this term.
    I'm not playing football this term.

- We don't usually use the present continuous with:
  - verbs expressing likes and dislikes. We use the present simple.
    I like this film! **NOT** *I'm liking this film!*
    I hate wearing uniform. **NOT** *I'm hating wearing uniform.*
  - verbs of perception, such as *see, hear, feel, sound, smell, taste.* Use *can/can't* with *see, hear, feel, smell,* and the present simple with *sound, taste, look.*
    I can't see Sarah. **NOT** *I'm not seeing Sarah.*
    This tastes good. **NOT** *This is tasting good.*

2 Write questions and short answers.

1 Paul / watch a film ☑ watch / a comedy
   Is Paul watching a film? Yes, he is. He's watching a comedy.
2 your friends / cycle / to the cinema ☒ go / by bus
3 your mum / have lunch / in town ☒ have lunch / at home
4 you / do / lots of tests for school this week ☑ do / five tests
5 he / play / for Arsenal ☒ play / for Real Madrid
6 they / learn / a language ☑ learn / Chinese

3 Complete the sentences with the correct form of the verbs in brackets.

1 Look! The dog's *eating* the party food! (eat)
2 We _____ a lot of tennis this summer. (play)
3 I'm at my computer. I _____ my homework. (do)
4 Listen. I think a car _____. (come)
5 Kevin and Chloe aren't here this week. They _____ with their friends. (stay)
6 I'm busy. I _____ for the concert. (practise)

4 Write short answers and sentences about you.

1 Are you studying two languages?
   Yes, I am. I'm studying English and Italian.
2 Are you sitting in your classroom now?
3 Are you doing a lot of sport these days?
4 Are you seeing your friends a lot?
5 Are you reading an interesting book at the moment?

5 Correct these sentences.

1 I'm not hearing the phone from my bedroom.
   I can't hear the phone from my bedroom.
2 My mum's liking her new job.
3 You're seeing my friends in the photo.
4 They're loving this TV programme.
5 I'm smelling fish and chips.
6 Is he hating working in an office?

Prepositions

6 Match the pictures and the sentences.

1 ☐ He's outside the museum.
2 ☐ He's going past the museum.
3 ☐ He's going into the museum.
4 ☐ He's in the car.
5 ☐ He's getting into the car.
6 ☐ He's on the bus.

7 **Workbook pp 160-165; CD-ROM**

FILE

SHOP ASSISTANT
- Can I help you?
- What size are you?
- Would you like to try it / them on?
- Is it / Are they OK?
- Do you want anything else?
- Here you are.

CUSTOMER
- I'd like…, please.
- I'm a (size)…
- Can I have… / try on…?
- Have you got…
  any belts / umbrellas / jeans? a smaller / larger / cheaper one? it / them in blue?
- I'll take it / them.
- How much is it / are they?

Vocabulary: clothes, money

1a 🔊 **Match the words and pictures. Then listen and check.**

☐ dress	☐ T-shirt
☐ shirt	☐ trousers
☐ tracksuit	☐ trainers
☐ suit	☐ jeans
☐ jumper	☐ skirt
1 coat	☐ boots
☐ jacket	☐ shoes

1b PAIRWORK **Describe what you are wearing today.**

2 **Read *Get into Culture* and do the task.**

Get into *culture* SHOPPING IN THE UK

The UK is in the European Union but it is not part of the Eurozone. Its currency is Pounds Sterling. British people use credit cards a lot. Supermarkets can give customers 'cash back' on cards, like a cashpoint machine. Teenagers usually get monthly pocket money (or 'an allowance'). They can have bank accounts and debit cards to take money from cashpoint machines, but they don't usually have credit cards.

- **What is the currency in your country?**
- **Do you get pocket money? If so, how much?**
- **How do people usually pay for things in your country?**

3 🔊 **Listen and repeat.**

UK CURRENCY

1p one 'p'
2p two 'p'
£5 five pounds

5p five 'p'
10p ten 'p'
£10 ten pounds

20p twenty 'p'
50p fifty 'p'
£20 twenty pounds

£1 one pound
£2 two pounds

£1.50 one pound fifty / one fifty
£13.35 thirteen pounds thirty-five / thirteen thirty-five
Informally, English people call the pound 'a quid'
  e.g. ten quid = £10.

Shopping

4 🔊 **P Listen and write the prices of the items.**

1 the blue tracksuit
2 the long skirt
3 the black jacket
4 the red party dress

5 🔊 **Look at the photos, then listen and complete the dialogues with these words.**

sale | much | sorry |
have | want | size | small |
try | looking

SHOP ASSISTANT Hello, Can I help you?
JOSH Yes, I'm ¹_____ for a T-shirt.
SHOP ASSISTANT What ²_____ are you?
JOSH Medium.
SHOP ASSISTANT Well, we've got these ones here.
JOSH Cool. I really like this one. How ³_____ is it?
SHOP ASSISTANT £45.
JOSH Phew! ⁴_____ you got a cheaper one?

SHOP ASSISTANT Well, these ones are in the ⁵_____ at £20.
JOSH Oh, they're really nice. I'll have this one, please.
SHOP ASSISTANT Sure. Do you ⁶_____ anything else?
JOSH No, thanks.
SHOP ASSISTANT That's £20.
JOSH Here you are.

NADIA Hello. I'd like to ⁷_____ on these boots.
SHOP ASSISTANT Of course. What size are you?
NADIA Size 38.
SHOP ASSISTANT One moment, please… Here you are.
NADIA Thanks.
SHOP ASSISTANT How do they feel?
NADIA They're a bit ⁸_____ Have you got a bigger pair?
SHOP ASSISTANT No, I'm ⁹_____, we haven't.
NADIA OK. Thanks.

6 Study the rules and the sentences.

one / ones

• Use the pronouns *one* and *ones* to avoid repeating a noun.
I'd like a small yellow T-shirt. Have you got one?
Which shoes do you prefer? The red ones.
Have you got these trainers in blue? Sorry, we've only got these ones.

would like

• Use *Would you like to…?* to invite people to do things.
Would you like to try it/them on?
• Use *I'd like to* + verb *to say* what you want to do politely.
I'd like to try them on, please.

7 PAIRWORK Practise the dialogues.

8a P ROLE PLAY Work in pairs.

• **Act out dialogues in shops.**
• **Use expressions from the dialogues and the *File*.**

8b Write out your dialogues.

9 ⇄ **LINKS Real communication pp 6-7**

Vocabulary: accessories

1a 🔊 **Look at the photos and study the words. Answer the questions. Then listen and check.**

What can you…

☐ wear on your fingers?   ☐ wear over your eyes?
☐ wear round your neck?   ☐ wear round your waist?
☐ wear in your nose or ears?   ☐ carry?
☐ wear on your wrist?

1b **PAIRWORK** Which of the things are you wearing or have you got with you today?

2 Look at Nicole on page 35. What is she wearing?

1 earrings
2 sunglasses
3 scarf
4 ring
5 stud
6 belt
7 necklace
8 handbag
9 bracelet
10 chain

Rate my look

Nicole Brand is nineteen and comes from Glasgow. She is a Media student at University College Falmouth.

What are you wearing at the moment?

I'm wearing boots, a grey skirt, a T-shirt and this designer coat. It isn't new. It's second-hand. Oh, and my hat and favourite red belt, of course. And I've got a red scarf round my neck, too.

What do you never wear?

Jeans! I look terrible in them. And I really hate suits. They're so old-fashioned. And I hate really high heels.

What are your favourite shops?

I love charity shops. I buy all my clothes from them. I like retro clothes — you know, from the 70s and 80s. I also love designer shops but the clothes are too expensive.

How often do you go shopping for clothes?

Maybe once or twice a month. But I go window shopping a lot, and I make my own clothes!

Which accessories do you always wear?

I wear rings, chains and earrings. I like really long ones. And big sunglasses. I've got lots of pairs. Oh, and I love scarves.

What's your favourite item of clothing or accessory?

This belt. It's retro and I love it.

Are you a fashion junkie?

No, I'm not, but my look is very important to me.

VOTE!

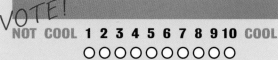

NOT COOL   1 2 3 4 5 6 7 8 9 10   COOL

Reading

3a Read the interview and answer the questions.

1 How old is Nicole?
2 What clothes does she hate?
3 Where does she buy her clothes?
4 Why doesn't she buy designer clothes?
5 Does she wear a lot of accessories?
6 Don't forget to rate Nicole's style!

3b Read the interview and find the words to match the meanings:

1 not new when you buy it
2 not fashionable
3 looking at things in shops but not buying them
4 a person who is obsessed with fashion

Listening and speaking

4   10 Listen to Martin. Which clothes and accessories does he wear/not wear? Put a tick ☑ or a cross ☒ beside the items.

☐ designer T-shirts   ☐ jeans
☐ boots   ☐ trainers
☐ tracksuit   ☐ jacket
☐ coat   ☐ sunglasses
☐ earrings and studs   ☐ belt

Pronunciation   /m/ /n/ /ŋ/

5a   11 Listen and repeat the words.

/m/ money | museum | message | jumper
/n/ nose | new | fashion | designer
/ŋ/ wearing | clothing | ring | shopping

5b Underline the sounds. Say the words again.

6 PAIRWORK Interview your partner. Use the questions from the article.

Writing

7 T Describe what someone in the class is wearing. Swap texts with a partner. Guess who the person is.

🗨 *X is wearing… X isn't wearing…*

8   **12 Go to LINKS p 62 and listen to *What a wonderful world.***

Unit 4
Is there any good music?

Unit objectives

Grammar *there is / are*; countable and uncountable nouns; *a / an*, *some / any*, *How much? / How many?*

Functions describing places; talking about quantity; planning a day out; making arrangements

Vocabulary everyday technology; places; *lend* and *borrow*

Warm up

1 Do you agree or disagree with these statements? Why?

- My city / town / area is a good place for teenagers.
- There are a lot of activities for teenagers in my area.
- There are places where teenagers can go.

Comprehension

2 🔊 Listen and read the interviews on page 37.
Match the places with the descriptions.

1 d OX4
2 ☐ the university parks
3 ☐ the university sports centre
4 ☐ cafés in Oxford
5 ☐ the multiplex cinema
6 ☐ Oxford clubs and dance venues
7 ☐ the town of Reading

a They are big green spaces in Oxford.
b It's outside the city.
c It's a cool place to shop.
d You can hear new bands there.
e They're too expensive for teenagers.
f Hannah plays volleyball there.
g People under 18 can't go to them.

3 Read the interviews again and answer the questions.

Who...

1 goes to fast food restaurants?
2 goes to Reading for shopping?
3 goes to a nightclub once a month?
4 plays football?
5 plays volleyball?
6 likes the music scene?

Describing places

4 Study the rules and do the tasks.

Countable and uncountable nouns

- Countable nouns can be singular or plural.
  a park – two parks   a band – two bands
- Uncountable nouns only have a singular form.
  water   music   NOT *~~waters~~   ~~musics~~*
- Use singular verbs with singular countable nouns and uncountable nouns.
  There's a night club.
  The music is great.
- Use plural verbs with plural countable nouns.
  There are cafés and restaurants.

Find two more uncountable nouns in the interviews.

a / an, some / any

- Use *a* or *an* with singular countable nouns.
  a multiplex, an ice rink
- Positive sentences: use *some* with both plural countable nouns and uncountable nouns.
  It's got some really good bands.
  I've got some information.
- Negatives and questions: use *any* with both plural countable nouns and uncountable nouns.
  Are there any good shops?
  There isn't any information.

Underline sentences in the interviews with *some* or *any*.

5 PAIRWORK Ask and answer five questions about these places in your city / town / area.

multiplex cinema | sports centre | stadium | parks | cafés | clubs | chain stores | music venues | ice rink

 Is there a multiplex cinema in your town?
Yes, there is. / No, there isn't.

6 P T Write a paragraph about what there is to do in your town. Give it a score at the end of your paragraph.

My town
I live in ... There are lots of parks in my town. There is a sports centre near my house.

This week we are asking teens in Oxford about their town.

OUT & ABOUT
TEEN LIFESTYLE

Is there a good cinema near you?

Yes, there is. It's a big multiplex. It's near the stadium, outside the city. You can see all the new films there.

Brandon **Rate my city** fun ☺☺☺☺☺

Are there any green spaces?

Yes, there are. There are brilliant university parks. They are really big. We often hang out in the parks during the summer. We play football and have a laugh.

Silas **Rate my city** cool ☺☺☺☺☺

Are there any places to do sport?

Yes, there are. There are two new sports centres near me, but I prefer the university sports centre. It's cheap. I play volleyball there once a week.

Hannah **Rate my city** sporty

Are there any good dance venues?

No, there aren't. It's a real problem. There aren't any clubs or dance venues for teenagers. They're all for over-18-year-olds. There's a nightclub that does an under-18s evening once a month and we all go to it!

Zac **Rate my city** no good ☹

Are there any places to hang out?

No, there aren't. There aren't many things for 14–16 year olds to do. We hang out in the city centre when it isn't raining! Or we go to fast food restaurants. There are some good cafés, but they're expensive... and we haven't got any money.

Jasmine **Rate my city** no fun ☹

Are there any good shops in Oxford?

There are some big chain stores in Oxford. So you can buy fashionable clothes. But it's a bit boring sometimes. There aren't any small shops for teens. So we go to Reading – the shopping is really cool.

Liz **Rate my city** a bit boring ☹☹☹

Is there any good music?

It's not bad. There's a new venue called OX4. There are some new bands on tonight – I've got some information about them. They sound great.

Joe **Rate my city** musical ☺☺☺

REAL TALK   hang out   have a laugh   a bit boring

Teenagers in the UK

A How many friends have UK teens got?
33 friends (7 close friends and 26 acquaintances)
86 buddies on their instant messaging list

B How much time per week do they spend on different activities?

surfing the web and chatting online	20 hours
listening to music	14 hours
watching TV	12 hours
playing video games	12 hours
doing homework	6 hours
looking after younger children / relatives	4.5 hours
playing a musical instrument	2 hours
doing other hobbies	3.5 hours

D How much pocket money do they get a month?

13 year olds	£45
16 year olds	£80

C How many 16 year olds play team games?
Boys 75%
play a team game
Girls 42%
play a team game

E How much technology do they use?

own a mobile phone	96%
own music CDs	95%
own an mp3 player	92%
do instant messaging	90%
use the Internet	90%
use email	89%
have a computer at home	87%
use social networking sites	73%
have a TV in their bedroom	73%
watch film clips on their mobile phone	30%
own a webcam	15%

Talking about quantity CLIL

7 Read the statistics about teenagers in the UK and match the numbers with the descriptions.

1 ☐ six		5 ☐ ninety-six
2 ☐ fourteen		6 ☐ fifteen
3 ☐ twenty		7 ☐ seventy-five
4 ☐ seven		8 ☐ eighty

a number of close friends
b percentage of mobile phone owners
c percentage of webcam owners
d hours per week surfing the web and chatting online
e hours per week doing homework
f hours per week listening to music
g percentage of boys playing team games
h monthly pocket money for 16 year olds

8 Study the sentences and do the task.

How much? / How many?

How much information technology do you use?
How many friends do teenagers in the UK have?

Complete the rules with *countable* or *uncountable*.
- Use *How many...?* to ask questions with _____ nouns.
- Use *How much...?* to ask questions with _____ nouns.

9 P T PAIRWORK Compare your life with UK teenagers. Read the statistics again and ask and answer questions.

Ⓐ *How much time do you spend surfing the web?*
Ⓑ *About two hours a week.*

Word **expander** FREQUENCY

Use *per hour / per day / per week* and *an hour / a day / a week*
to talk about how often you do things.

I usually go swimming once / twice / three times a week.
The average British teenager eats five pieces of fruit per week.

there is / there are

1 Complete the table with *are*, *aren't*, *is* or *isn't*.

Positive	Negative
There's a cinema.	There ¹_____ a cinema.
There are some cinemas.	There aren't any cinemas.

Questions	Short answers
Is there a cinema?	Yes, there ²_____. No, there isn't.
³_____ there any cinemas?	Yes, there are. No, there ⁴_____.

2 Complete the sentences with *There is/isn't/are/aren't* to make true sentences about you.

1 _____ a computer in my bedroom.
2 _____ two Spanish people in my class.
3 _____ an ice rink in my town.
4 _____ four people in my family.
5 _____ a pencil case in my bag.
6 _____ a poster on my wall.

3 Complete the questions with *Is* or *Are* and write true short answers.

1 __Is__ there a multiplex cinema in your town?
   Yes, there is. / No, there isn't.
2 _____ there boys and girls in your English class?
3 _____ there a webcam in the room?
4 _____ there clothes in your bedroom cupboard?
5 _____ there a sports centre near your house?
6 _____ there a TV in your bedroom?

Countable and uncountable nouns

4 Complete the table with these nouns and study the rules.

information | student | homework | venue | mistake | computer | help | pocket money | cat | friend | box | car | shirt | food | fun | alcohol | love | school | music | poster | bread | water | bottle | oil | email | work | time | knowledge | text message | laptop

Countable	Uncountable

- Some nouns may be countable in your language and uncountable in English, e.g. *hair, information, money.*
- Some nouns can be countable and uncountable, e.g. *cake, coffee, cheese.*
- When making generalisations, use the plural of the countable noun, e.g. *I like cats.* NOT ~~I like the cats~~.
- *work* is an uncountable noun, *job* is countable.

a / an, some and any

5 Study the rules and circle the correct words.

a / an
- Use *a/an* before singular, countable nouns in positive and negative sentences
  There's an orange in the fridge. I haven't got a book.

some
- Use *some* before singular, uncountable nouns and plural countable nouns.
  There's some water in the cup.
  There are some new students this year.

any
- Use *any* before singular, uncountable nouns and plural countable nouns in negative sentences and questions.
  There isn't any information. Are there any questions?

1 There's *a* /*some* text message on my mobile.
2 There are *some* / *any* parks in the town.
3 I've got *a* / *some* pen in my bag.
4 There isn't *some* / *any* sugar in this coffee.
5 Has Tom got *an* / *some* idea about the project?
6 She hasn't got *a* / *any* job at the moment.
7 This website has got *some* / *any* photos of the band.
8 Have you got *an* / *any* oil for this salad?

6 Complete the text with these words.

~~there~~ | isn't | some | a | any | are | is | aren't

My name's Tania and I'm sixteen. I live in a small village outside Manchester. ¹_There_ isn't a cinema here and there ²_____ any music venues. There's a primary school in the village but there ³_____ a secondary school. I go to school in Manchester. There ⁴_____ a sports centre in the village, and it's got ⁵_____ football pitches. We play football there. There's ⁶_____ good bus service into Manchester. There ⁷_____ some activities for teenagers in the village. The big problem is that there aren't ⁸_____ shops at all!

How much? / How many?

7 Complete the questions with *How much* or *How many*. Then write true answers.

1 _How much_ traffic is there in your city centre?
2 _____ friends have you got?
3 _____ money do you spend per week?
4 _____ people are in your family?
5 _____ films do you see a month?
6 _____ chocolate do you eat a week?
7 _____ CDs / magazines / ice creams do you buy a month?

8 ➡ Workbook pp 166–171; CD-ROM

Places to go

1 Read the brochure and answer the questions.

1 Which place is a modern art gallery?
2 Where can you see models of famous people?
3 Which place is fun for shopping and eating out?
4 Where can you admire the views of London?
5 How many visitors go to Madame Tussaud's each year?
6 Where can you buy old clothes?

2a 🔊 **P Listen and complete the brochure with the opening times and admission prices.**

2b P Decide on the best place for each person.

1 Andy hasn't got much money. _____
2 Jordan likes modern art. _____
3 Lawrence wants to eat Thai food. _____

What to see in London

Portobello Road market

This world-famous street market is popular with Londoners and tourists. Portobello Road is 2 miles long and there are over 200 stalls and lots of shops, too. You can buy designer and second-hand clothes, jewellery, books, antiques and lots of interesting things. There are stalls selling hot food, and a wide choice of cafés, restaurants and pubs.

NEAREST TUBE STATIONS: NOTTING HILL GATE AND LADBROKE GROVE
OPEN MONDAY TO WEDNESDAY:
9.00AM UNTIL [1]_____
THURSDAY: 9.00AM TO 1.00PM
FRIDAY AND SATURDAY: [2]_____ UNTIL
7.00PM
ANTIQUES ONLY ON FRIDAY AND
SATURDAY

Madame Tussaud's

Where can you meet David and Victoria Beckham, the Queen, Nelson Mandela and Albert Einstein? At Madam Tussaud's waxworks, of course! Over 2 million visitors go there every year to see the models of hundreds of historical figures, cultural icons and royalty.

OPEN MON TO FRI:
FROM [3]_____ UNTIL 5.30 PM
[4]_____
SUN: FROM 9.00 AM UNTIL
[5]_____

ADMISSION: ADULT [6]_____
CHILDREN UNDER 16: £21

Tate Modern

This is London's most spectacular modern art gallery. Originally a power station, its huge spaces make it the ideal showcase for international modern art from 1900 to the present day, including work by Dali, Picasso and Warhol. There are magnificent views, especially from the café on Level 7, and the gallery is very popular with students.

[7]_____ ADMISSION
OPEN MON TO THURS & SUN:
FROM [8]_____ UNTIL 6.00
PM, [9]_____ AND SAT: FROM
10.00 AM UNTIL [10]_____ PM

Making arrangements

REAL TALK I mean...   Come on
How boring is that?

ANDY Why don't we go to London on Saturday, Lawrence?

LAWRENCE Good idea.

JORDAN Cool. I'd like to go to Madame Tussaud's.

LAWRENCE I'd rather go to Portobello Road market. There's lots to do – you can spend the day there. And I like looking at the old records and the retro clothes. And there's really good Thai food stalls! Yum.

ANDY I don't want to spend much money.

JORDAN Andy, I can lend you some money. Chill out!

ANDY Thanks, Jordan, but I don't really want to borrow any money.

LAWRENCE Well, there's no admission fee to a market! Come on, you guys!

ANDY Yeah, Lawrence. But there are things to buy. It's no

fun going to a market with no money!

JORDAN Hey, Tate Modern's free. We could go there.

LAWRENCE But it's a *museum*! How boring is that?

JORDAN It isn't a typical museum. It's all modern art, it's really cool. And we could hang out in the café.

LAWRENCE I guess that sounds OK. So let's go to Tate Modern, then.

3 15 **P Cover the dialogue and listen. Circle T (True) or F (False).**

1 They agree to go to Madame Tussaud's. T / F
2 Lawrence wants to go to Portobello Road. T / F
3 Andy's got lots of money. T / F
4 Jordan wants to help Andy. T / F
5 Andy accepts money from Jordan. T / F
6 Jordan suggests going to Tate Modern. T / F
7 Lawrence decides not to go. T / F

4 **P ROLE PLAY Work in groups of three.**
• **Imagine you are going to the nearest town for the day with your friends.**
• **Invent new dialogues.**
• **Use expressions from the *File* and the *File* from Unit 1, p12.**

5 Read *Get into Culture* and do the task.

Get into *culture* GOING OUT IN THE UK

Teens in the UK and the US often hang out in shopping malls because there are lots of cafés and it doesn't rain. They also meet up in parks, skate parks or leisure centres. In big cities they get together in fast food restaurants or in cafés in fashion shops. There are special teen areas in some libraries – with headphones so they can listen to music and large computer screens for films.

Wherever teens hang out, they like to meet up with their friends. And if that's not possible they can always hang out online!

• **Where do teens get together in your country?**
• **Are there any special facilities for them?**

Word **expander**   *LEND* AND *BORROW*

lend you give a thing to a person and expect to get it back later.
I can lend you some money.

borrow you take a thing from a person and give it back later.
Can I borrow your dictionary?

6 **LINKS
Real communication
pp 6-7**

CITY GUIDES

London *must-see* places!

You've got two days —→ *in London* *Where do you go?*

1

Over seven million people live in London, and around 25 million people visit it a year.

2

From the London Eye, in the heart of London, you can see a lot! A trip on the wheel takes thirty minutes. On a clear day, you can see up to 40 kilometres.

3

See the Crown Jewels in the 900-year-old Tower of London and the famous Beefeaters, too. Buckingham Palace is the official residence of the Queen. You can't visit the 600 rooms, but you can see the Changing of the Guard. The Houses of Parliament opposite Parliament Square are the home of the British Government.

4

The Globe Theatre is a modern reconstruction of Shakespeare's original theatre. The actors perform the plays in the open air!

5

The River Thames runs through the city. Tower Bridge has two levels, one for traffic and one for pedestrians. The Millennium Bridge is London's newest bridge and is only for people.

6

The British Museum contains a world famous collection of 7.5 million objects. You can only see a small part in one day. St Paul's Cathedral is a huge church that dominates London's skyline. Its 350 steps take you to the top of a dome with wonderful views.

7

London is the capital of shopping! Harrods is a world famous department store with 330 different departments. Don't forget Oxford Street for shopping. It's over two kilometres long and has 300 shops. Or visit Camden Market for its cool fashion and second-hand clothes.

8

Where can you relax in beautiful green spaces? In London's parks, of course. In Hyde Park you can go horse riding or rowing. In Regents Park you can visit London Zoo.

RANDOM Fact Big Ben is actually the name of the bell, not the famous clock tower.

Vocabulary: places

1 Scan the article and find these words. Guess their meaning from the context.

palace | park | market | bridge | river | theatre | city | museum | cathedral | church | department store | zoo

Reading CLIL

2 Skim the article and write the headings with the paragraphs.

Eating out | The people of London | Power and ceremony | A breath of fresh air | A new building | The big picture | Culture | The river | Night Life | Shopping

3 Read the article and answer the questions.

How many…
1 people visit London each year?
2 rooms are there in Buckingham Palace?
3 departments are there in Harrods?
4 steps take you to the top of St Paul's?
5 objects are there in the British Museum?

Listening

4 🔊 A tourist guide is taking tourists to places in the article. Where do they visit?

1 _____
2 _____
3 _____
4 _____

Pronunciation   PLACE NAMES

5 🔊 Some place names in London are difficult to pronounce. Listen and repeat.

Leicester Square | Piccadilly Circus | Wimbledon | Trafalgar Square | Wembley | Greenwich | Buckingham Palace | Notting Hill

Speaking

6 PAIRWORK Talk about a famous city – but don't name it! Your partner says what it is.

Ⓐ *It's a small city. There are lots of old buildings and churches. There's a very famous square. And there are lots of bridges!*
Ⓑ *It's Venice.*

Writing

7 T Write a brochure about three important sights in a famous city. Use the article as a guide.

9

You can eat food from all over the world. But at Planet Hollywood you can have a great meal and watch famous film clips on a big screen at the same time.

10

And at the end of the day, why not go to one of London's many theatres? Most are located in the West End. *The Phantom of the Opera,* with its costumes and special effects, is really spectacular!

FILE

POSTCARDS

In daily life, we often write postcards to friends and family when we are on holiday. So they are part of the Cambridge PET exam. There are tips that will help you write them.

Towards PET Paper 1 Reading and Writing, Writing Part 2

Tips

Postcards often use certain verb tenses:
• present simple of verb *be* + adjective to describe weather, etc.
• present continuous to describe what the writer is doing.
• present simple of *like* / *don't like* / *love* / *hate*, etc.
• past simple to describe a memorable activity.

Useful language

Hi / Hi there / Dear (name)
We're having a great / terrible time.
It's really hot / cold / sunny / wet.
The hotel / B& B / campsite is fantastic / awful.
I love / hate the food / shops / architecture.
We're visiting museums and galleries / swimming in the sea / going for walks / relaxing.
At the moment I'm sitting in a café / waiting for a train / eating an ice cream.
I'm (not) looking forward to getting home.
Lots of love / Love / All the best / Take care

Postcards

1 Complete the postcard with the verbs in the correct tenses.

Hi!
We ¹*'re having* (have) a brilliant holiday in the Alps. The weather ² _____ (be) perfect – very cold and sunny. I ³ _____ (love) the mountains, they ⁴ _____ (be) beautiful. Kate and I ⁵ _____ (ski) every day and Mum and Dad ⁶ _____ (walk) in the mountains. At the moment I ⁷ _____ (watch) TV in my hotel room before dinner. Austrian TV ⁸ _____ (not be) very good!
I'm not looking forward to getting back to school next week!
Love
Adrian

Greetings from the Alps

2 Complete the instructions for the e-postcard with these phrases.

the recipient's email address | your text message | Click on | your email address

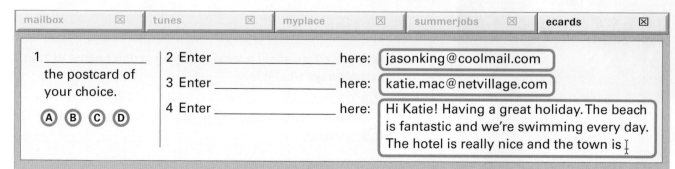

| mailbox ☒ | tunes ☒ | myplace ☒ | summerjobs ☒ | ecards ☒ |

1 _____ the postcard of your choice.
Ⓐ Ⓑ Ⓒ Ⓓ

2 Enter _____ here: jasonking@coolmail.com

3 Enter _____ here: katie.mac@netvillage.com

4 Enter _____ here: Hi Katie! Having a great holiday. The beach is fantastic and we're swimming every day. The hotel is really nice and the town is

3 P Write a postcard to a friend from your summer holiday. Use phrases from the *File*.

FILE

GREETINGS CARDS

People in the UK send a lot of greetings cards. But e-cards are also becoming popular, too. Greetings cards usually have a greeting on the front and a short printed message on the inside. The sender adds a personal message. These greetings and messages can be useful in the PET exam, and if you have English-speaking friends!

Towards PET Paper 1 Reading and Writing, Reading Part 1

Useful language

CARDS
Happy / Merry Christmas   Happy New Year
Happy Birthday   Congratulations
Get well soon   Good luck
Happy Anniversary

SENDER'S MESSAGES
To (name)
I hope you have a great day...
Have a lovely day...
Best wishes / Love / Lots of love (from)

1 **Do a quick survey round the class. Ask the question and compile the results in percentages.**

Which do you send on a friend's birthday?

a an e-card?   b a traditional card?   c a text message?   d nothing?

2 **Match the situations and the cards.**

a Carla's getting married.
b It's Oliver's birthday.
c Robert and Marian got married 25 years ago today.
d Kelly's taking her driving test.
e Ian is ill.

3 **Complete the messages inside the cards with the words.**

Have | wishes | from | New | To | Lots | hope

To Simon
HAPPY BIRTHDAY!
I ____ you have a fantastic day.
Love ____
Marisa

____ Rebecca
Congratulations on your exam results.
____ a wonderful holiday after all your hard work.
Best ____ from Aunt Sue

To Paul and Anna
Happy ____ Year!
Hope you have a great year in 2012.
____ of love,
Bethan and Henry

4 **P Write a card for each person/situation.**

• Jack/New Year's Day
• Ella/passed her driving test
• Laura/18 today

5 **LINKS Exam Listening p 7**

LANGUAGE CHECK

LANGUAGE **I CAN NOW TALK ABOUT PRESENT AND TEMPORARY SITUATIONS / AMOUNTS / DESCRIBE PLACES**

1 Write complete sentences.

1 you / study / English / now ?

_____

2 I / do / a part-time job / this year

_____

3 He / not play / football a lot / these days

_____

4 they / still / live / in Cardiff ?

_____

5 She / use / the computer / at the moment

_____

2 Choose the correct words.

1 I ____ the river from my house.
   a) see   b) am seeing   c) can see   d) is seeing

2 'Are they waiting for their exam results?' 'Yes, ____.'
   a) they are   b) they wait   c) they do   d) they waiting

3 He ____ his new boots.
   a) love   b) is loving   c) are loving   d) loves

4 Is there ____ good music venue in this town?
   a) any   b) a   c) an   d) some

5 How ____ people are there in the classroom?
   a) any   b) much   c) some   d) many

TOTAL: ____/10

VOCABULARY **I CAN NOW TALK ABOUT CLOTHES / MONEY / ACCESSORIES / PLACES**

3 Complete the words for clothes.

1 Angelina is wearing a beautiful blue d _ _ _ s.
2 I usually wear a t _ _ _ _ _ _ _ t and trainers for football practice.
3 Mr Green wears a j _ _ _ _ t and trousers to school.
4 On Saturdays Alexandra wears a T-shirt and j _ _ _ s.
5 My dad wears a s _ _ t to work.

4 Find the words for places in London.

1 BUCKINGHAM A C E L A P _____
2 THE BRITISH S M M E U U _____
3 THE GLOBE H R A T E E T _____
4 TOWER G B E R I D_____
5 HARRODS P R A M T E N E D T R O T S E

_____

TOTAL: ____/10

COMMUNICATION **I CAN NOW BUY CLOTHES / MAKE ARRANGEMENTS**

5 Complete the dialogue with these words.

rather | could | like | would | don't

MICHAEL ¹_____ you like to go to London tomorrow, Amy?

AMY Good idea! Why ²_____ we go to Madame Tussaud's?

MICHAEL It's very expensive. I'd ³_____ go to Tate Modern. That's free.

AMY OK. We ⁴_____ have lunch in the café. It's got a fantastic view.

MICHAEL Yeah, and I'd ⁵_____ to see the new Picasso exhibition.

TOTAL: ____/10

6 PAIRWORK Ask and answer questions.

1 you / wear / now ?
   What are you wearing now? _____

2 you / wear / a lot of accessories?
   _____

3 you / send / a lot of text messages ?
   _____

4 how much time / you / spend / watching TV ?
   _____

5 there / be / interesting places / in your town ?
   _____

6 which / shops / you / like ?
   _____

TOTAL: ____/10

TOTAL: ____/40

LINKS Interculture pp 22-23; Story pp 38-39; CLIL (Technology) pp 48-49; DVD My Look, London

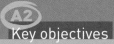

A2
Key objectives

Grammar modal verbs: *can, could, may*; present simple v present continuous; *much / many / a little*, etc.

Functions talking about permission and possibility, the present, quantity

Vocabulary transport; shapes and materials; food; souvenirs

Get started

1 **Look at the photos. What are the activities?**

2 🔊 **Listen and tick ☑ the activities the people say in the first column.**

3 **Read the text. Tick ☑ the six things which best describe your idea of happiness.**

4a **Write four sentences about you. Use these verbs.**
Happiness is… reading… playing… going to… being with… talking to… meeting… having… eating…

4b **PAIRWORK Tell your partner your sentences. Ask and answer questions about the activities.**

What is happiness to you? Well, it means different things to different people.

Happiness is...

☐☐ dancing all night
☐☐ going to a party
☐☐ scoring a goal
☐☐ sunbathing
☐☐ jogging

☐☐ learning a new song or guitar chord
☐☐ playing the latest computer game
☐☐ listening to my favourite music

☐☐ painting a picture
☐☐ buying new clothes
☐☐ getting text messages
☐☐ playing with my pet
☐☐ seeing a good film
☐☐ reading a great book
☐☐ writing my diary or blog
☐☐ going to a cool museum

☐☐ being with my family
☐☐ hanging out with friends
☐☐ watching my team win
☐☐ eating a huge ice cream
☐☐ walking in the countryside
☐☐ chilling out in my bedroom
☐☐ getting good exam results

Can you do it?

Unit objectives

Grammar modal verbs: *can, could, may* for ability, permission and possibility; *So can I. / Neither can I.*; present simple v present continuous

Functions talking about ability, permission and possibility; the present; travelling by Underground; understanding announcements

Vocabulary transport; shapes and materials

Warm up

1 Look at the photos on page 49 and answer the questions.

1 Where are Jack, Mia and Rose?
2 Who is talking on her mobile?
3 What is the man's job?
4 Does he like the band's music?

Comprehension

2 🔊19 Listen and read *Who's that girl?* Circle T (True) or F (False).

1 Jack wants Rose to hurry up with her phone call. T / F
2 There is a special night at the Zodiac every week for local bands. T / F
3 Harry doesn't watch demo tapes. T / F
4 The band have got their instruments with them. T / F
5 They perform for Harry in his office. T / F
6 Harry asks them to play at the Zodiac next Wednesday. T / F

Talking about permission and possibility

3 Study the rules and do the task.

> Modal verbs: *can, could, may*
>
> - [1]Use *can* to talk about ability.
>   *You can sing quite well.*
>
> - [2]Use *can*, *could* or *may* to ask for permission or help. Only use *may* with the first person, *I* or *we*.
>   *Can I see you tomorrow?*
>   *Could we play next week?*
>   *May we leave early?*
>
> - [3]Use *can / can't* or *could / couldn't* to talk about possibilities.
>   *I can't leave now.*
>   *We could see you later.*
>   *I can't come to the party.*
>   *Can you be there by 10 am?*
>
> - Use *can*, *may* or *could* in short answers.
>   *Yes, you can. No, you couldn't. Yes, you may.*

Underline the examples of ***can, could*** and ***may*** in the dialogue and decide if they are using rule 1, 2 or 3.

4a Write PE (permission), A (ability) or PO (possibility) next to each sentence.

1 Can I borrow your mobile phone?
2 Sean can swim twenty lengths of the swimming pool.
3 Can we watch TV now, please?
4 You can buy food and drink on this train.
5 Can you take photos with this mobile phone?
6 I can speak French quite well.
7 Can you tell me the time, please?
8 I'm sorry, I can't come to the party.

4b Write the words in the correct order.

1 can / we / Sara's / go / party / to
We can go to Sara's party.
2 come / in / I / may / ?
3 can't / sing / they
4 can't / room / dad's / we / work / in / my
5 help / you / me / work / my / could / with / ?
6 get / fish / you / in / restaurant / good / this / can

5a PAIRWORK Ask for and give permission or help for these things.

Ⓐ *Can I use your dictionary?*
Ⓑ *Yes, of course.*
Ⓐ *Can you help me carry this bag?*
Ⓑ *Sure!*

> use your dictionary

> help me carry this bag

> use your mobile phone

> help me with my project

> work on this table

> help me install this game on my computer

5b Invent other situations.

Who's that girl?
Episode 4

1 *It's an important day. Jack, Mia and Rose have got a meeting with the manager of the Zodiac!*

ROSE Hi guys.

MIA Hi Rose. How's things?

ROSE OK... Oh, I'm sorry. Can I take this call?

JACK Yeah, OK. But hurry up. Our meeting is in five minutes.

2 *Harry is a busy man. And Jack is nervous.*

HARRY Harry Lime speaking... What?... No, I can't change the date. We've got a contract. Yeah, bye. ...
Sorry about that. How can I help you?

JACK Well, you know you have a special night every month for local bands? Could we be one of the bands?

HARRY You're joking! You're very young. Can you perform in front of an audience?

JACK I think so. And we've got film of the band on this tape.

HARRY I don't watch demo tapes.

ROSE We could play a song for you now. We're very good.

MIA Rose, we haven't got our instruments with us.

ROSE Have you got a guitar and drums here, Mr Lime?

HARRY Yeah, they're in the studio.

ROSE May we use them?

HARRY Go ahead.

3 *The band perform a song.*

HARRY I'm impressed! You can play very well. Listen, one of my bands can't play next Wednesday. Can you do it?

JACK Yes, I can.

MIA So can I.

ROSE Me too!

HARRY Great. You've got your first gig.

REAL TALK How's things? guys hurry up You're joking! Go ahead. I'm impressed.

Talking about the present

6a **Read the messages. Then complete the information for Jack and Rose about a) their routine and b) their temporary situations.**

Jack

Routine

does his homework,

Temporary situation

practising every day after school,

Rose

Routine

Temporary situation

6b **PAIRWORK Talk about Jack and Rose.**

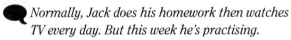
Normally, Jack does his homework then watches TV every day. But this week he's practising.

7a **Read the sentences and do the task.**

Present simple v present continuous

I do my homework.

I'm writing new songs.

Complete the rules with *simple, continuous, routines, happening.*

- Use the present _____ to talk about actions _____ at this moment and for temporary situations.
- Use the present _____ to talk about daily _____, what you like and don't like, and things that are always true.

7b **Read the messages again. Underline examples of the present simple and the present continuous.**

8 **ROLE PLAY Work in groups of four.**
- Go to LINKS page 61 for your role cards.
- Before you start choose A, B C or D.
- Read your role card and memorise your new identity.

Go to LINKS page 61 for your role cards.

CHAT-TIME **Jack is ONLINE**

Hi Marco – Life is very exciting at the moment. You know my normal week – I do my homework, I watch TV and listen to music in the evening, I often hang out with Charlie. And Mia and I practise our music at the weekend. Well, this week is different. I'm not watching TV and I'm not hanging out with Charlie. Why? Because I haven't got time! We're practising every day after school. And I'm writing new songs, too! Guess what? We've got a gig next week. That's right. Yellow Fish have got a real gig at a real club!!! I can't sleep at night. I'm really nervous!

Hey, Jack. That's fantastic! How's Rose? Is she happy in the band?

Yes, I think so. But she's always very busy. She does a lot of other things. She goes running every day (I don't understand it!). She always studies a lot. And she has two or three music lessons every week. And this week she's learning all our songs and going to all the rehearsals as well!

Wow! Is Rose cool? Do you fancy her?

Sorry, Marco. I can't write now. I've got a rehearsal with the band! PS You're so nosey!

REAL TALK Guess what?   That's right.
fancy   You're so nosey!

Get the grammar

Modal verbs: *can, could, may*

1 Complete the table with *can, can't,* or *I*.

Positive	I _____ speak French.
Negative	I _____ speak French.
Questions	_____ you speak French?
Short answers	Yes, _____ _____. No, _____ _____.

2 Write PE (permission or help), A (ability) or PO (possibility). Then translate the sentences.

1 Could you show me how to play this song on the guitar? PE
2 I can't swim very well.
3 May I open the window?
4 Jeremy's ill. He can't come to the concert.
5 I can read this in English.
6 May we come with you?
7 Could you pass me the milk, please?
8 You can get nice candles in that new shop.

3 Circle the correct word.

1 My baby sister is crying because she *can't / couldn't* have a chocolate.
2 *May / Could* you help me with this bag?
3 He *can / may* play tennis brilliantly. He's a champion.
4 A Can they perform next week?
 B Yes, they *do / can*.
5 I've got my guitar. I *may / could* play some music now.
6 A May I read your magazine?
 B Yes, you *may / can*.

Can: agreeing and disagreeing

4 Study the table. Then write answers to agree or disagree with the sentences below.

	Agree	Disagree
I can ride a horse.	So can I.	I can't.
I can't play tennis.	Neither can I.	I can.

1 I can balance a chair on my head.
 So can I! / I can't!
2 I can't go to parties during the week.
3 I can ski very well.
4 I can't play the clarinet.
5 I can write five text messages in one minute.
6 I can't always remember people's names.

Present simple v present continuous

5 Study the sentences. Match them with the correct use.

1 ☐ I usually get up at seven.
2 ☐ She's studying hard for the test next week.
3 ☐ They're building a new multiplex.
4 ☐ She doesn't like coffee.
5 ☐ The earth revolves around the sun.

a Use the present continuous to talk about things happening at this moment and for temporary situations.
b Use the present simple to talk about daily routine, what you like or don't like, and things that are true.

6 Complete the dialogue with the correct form of the verbs in brackets.

A They _____ (build) a new shopping centre near the airport.
B Near the airport? I _____ (not like) that idea.
A No? Why's that?
B Well there's a lot of traffic already. A lot of people _____ (drive) to the airport every day.
A I _____ (not agree). People _____ (go) by train to the airport, too.
B Hang on a minute. My mobile _____ (ring). It's my boss.
A Right.
B Guess what? He _____ (wait) for me at the airport. Sorry, I have to go!

7 Complete the sentences with the correct form of the verbs in brackets so that they are true for you.

1 I _____ jeans at the moment. (wear / not wear)
2 I _____ to school every day. (walk / not walk)
3 At my school, we _____ a lot of homework. (get / not get)
4 The sun _____ today. (shine / not shine)
5 I _____ my homework at the moment. (do / not do)
6 I _____ watching reality shows on TV. (like / not like)

8 Look at the table and write sentences about the people.

	job	this summer
Susie	work in shop	travel in Australia
Pete	look after mum	have holiday with friends
Ken	clean offices	do volunteer work
Abby	teach guitar	play in orchestra
Lily	fly planes	walk in Himalayas

1 Susie usually works in a shop, but this summer she's travelling in Australia.

9 **Workbook pp 172-177; CD-ROM**

FILE

BUYING A TICKET
- Can I have a ticket to...?
- Two singles to the centre, please.
- Can I have a single / day return to...?
- Can I have a Travelcard / an Oystercard, etc?
- Here you are.
- Cheers. / Thanks.

ASKING FOR INFORMATION / HELP
- Does this bus go to...?
- Can you tell me when to get off?
- Excuse me, where do I get off for...?
- Which line do I need to get to...?
- What time is the next train?
- Does this train go to...?
- Which platform does the train leave from?
- Is this train going to...?
- I'm sorry, I can't get through the barrier.

Travelling by London Underground

1a Read the information leaflet and match the headings with the paragraphs.

Leaving the station | On the platform | On the train | Getting to the platform | Finding your way around | Buying tickets

 The Tube: useful information

1_____

The Underground has ticket zones with different fares. You can buy different sorts of tickets, e.g. a single, a return, a One Day or Weekend Travelcard. The best value card is an Oystercard. In the ticket hall there is a ticket office but most people use the ticket machines. You can pay with coins, notes or a credit card.

2_____

Signs tell you the direction of the trains. Before you start, look at the map and check if your train is Northbound, Southbound, Eastbound or Westbound. The last station on your line is its destination.

3_____

On the escalator people stand on the right. They walk on the left side. Smoking isn't allowed in the stations.

4_____

On the platform stand behind the yellow lines. Look at the displays for the next train and its destination. Don't go onto the railway line because the rail is electrified. The announcement 'Mind the gap' warns people when they get on and get off the train. There is often a big gap between the train and platform.

5_____

The announcement 'Stand clear of the doors' means the doors are about to close. Londoners usually read on the Underground or talk quietly. They don't make much eye contact or start conversations.

6_____

There are no litter bins on the stations so take your litter away with you. You need your ticket or Oystercard to get through the barriers so have it ready.

RANDOM Fact *The most popular Tube trip for tourists is from Leicester Square to Covent Garden. But it's quicker to walk than go by Tube!*

1b Use the highlighted words to make an Underground travel mini-dictionary for a trip to London. Write a translation for each word.

Understanding announcements

2 🔊 **Listen to the announcements and match them with the pictures.**

Vocabulary: transport

3a 🔊 **P Jordan, Andy and Lawrence are travelling to Tate Modern. Listen and write two types of transport, A–H, for each dialogue. Which two types of transport aren't mentioned?**

A bike	E train
B on foot	F car
C boat	G plane
D motorbike	H coach

DIALOGUE 1 It's 9 am. Jordan is at her sister Amy's house in Oxford. ☐ ☐

DIALOGUE 2 It's 11 am. Andy is at home in South London. ☐ ☐

DIALOGUE 3 It 's 12.25 pm. Jordan is calling Lawrence on his mobile. ☐ ☐

3b Listen to the dialogues again. Who says these things? Write J (Jordan), A (Andy), L (Lawrence), Am (Amy) or D (Andy's dad).

1 ☐ How much is it by coach?
2 ☐ I'm on foot…
3 ☐ Could you give me a lift…?
4 ☐ It's ten pounds single and thirteen pounds return…
5 ☐ It's a regular ferry service…
6 ☐ There's a good cycle path…

Word **expander** TWO - WHEELED VEHICLES

- *Bike* can be an abbreviation of *motorbike* or *bicycle*.
- *Mopeds* and *scooters* are motorbikes with small engines.
- Special types of bicycles include *mountain bike*, *racing bike* and *BMX bike*.

On the bus

4a 🔊 **Listen and repeat the dialogues.**

1 A Excuse me, does this bus go to Wimbledon?
   B Yes, it does.
   A Thanks.
2 A Can I have a ticket to Wimbledon, please?
   B Single or return?
   A Return, please.
   B That'll be £2.60.
   A Here you are.
   B Thanks.
3 A Can you tell me when to get off, please?
   B Yes, of course.

4b ROLE PLAY Work in pairs.
  • Act out the dialogues.
  • Change the destinations and prices.

5 Read *Get into Culture* and do the task.

Get into *culture* BUS TRAVEL IN THE UK

In most cities in the UK you buy your ticket from the bus driver, or you show the driver your weekly or season ticket. Sometimes there is a machine for you to insert your travel card.

Do the British still love queuing? Yes, and no. The traditional image of a long orderly line at a bus stop is not so common now. People often stand at bus stops in groups, and only queue to get on the bus. Observe the local customs – if there is a queue, then go to the end. If you don't, people can get upset!

• Do you queue for buses in your country?
• Do you buy your tickets on the bus?

6 **LINKS Real communication pp 8-9**

WEIRD THINGS PEOPLE LOSE

What happens
if you lose something in a bus, black cab or on a train in London?
It goes to the London Transport Lost Property Office, an office under Baker Street, near Madame Tussaud's.

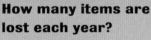

How many items are lost each year?
About 133,000.

How many of the owners come to get their things?
About 60%.

How does the office get rid of the things?
There's an auction twice a month.

What are the most commonly lost items?
In order of frequency: cases and bags, books, clothes, handbags, purses and wallets, mobile phones, umbrellas, keys, glasses, jewellery, gloves.

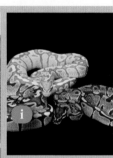

What are the **weirdest** things found in the London Transport system?

- three dead snakes
- two human skulls
- £150,000 in two white supermarket bags
- a well-cared-for kitten in a cat box
- a baby in its baby buggy
- a 4-metre-long boat

Reading

1 Match the words with the photos in the text.

- ☐ skulls
- ☐ a handbag
- ☐ jewellery
- ☐ keys
- ☐ boat
- ☐ snakes
- ☐ baby
- ☐ a kitten
- ☐ money

2 Read the text. What do the numbers refer to?

1 four   *a 4-metre long boat*
2 three
3 one hundred and fifty thousand
4 sixty
5 two
6 one hundred and thirty-three thousand

3 What fact do you think is incredible? funny? boring? surprising? disgusting?

Vocabulary: shapes and materials

4 (23) **Match the adjectives with the pictures. Then listen and check.**

a woolly   f wooden
b cotton   g cardboard
c paper   h leather
d glass   i metal
e plastic

| 1 | 2 | 3 | 4 | 5 | 6 | 7 | 8 | 9 |

Word **expander** ADJECTIVES

- Follow this order when there is more than one adjective. We don't usually use lots of adjectives at once!

QUANTITY	OPINION	SIZE	AGE	SHAPE	COLOUR	ORIGIN	MATERIAL	NOUN
a	lovely	large	new	round	blue	Chinese	glass	vase
some	horrible	big	old	square	pink	Spanish	plastic	sunglasses

Listening

Skills FOR life LISTENING WHILE LOOKING

Always read the task carefully! It helps you predict the language. In this exercise there are people at a lost property office. So you can expect a description. Before you listen look at the pictures. What is the difference between them? In this case, focus on size, age, materials, shape and colour. Notice any special features such as stickers before you listen.

5 (24) **P Listen to the people at the Lost Property Office. Tick ☑ the things they describe.**

1   a   b   c

2   a   b   c

3   a   b   c

Speaking and writing

6 **Describe these things with three different types of adjectives in the correct order.**

your pencil case | your shoes | your mobile phone

I've got a nice new red pencil case.

Pronunciation /e/ /æ/

7 (25) **Listen and repeat the words.**

/e/   leather | red | pen | said | beg | well
/æ/   Spanish | bag | plastic | man | hand | bad

8 **GAME Choose an object that you can see in the room. Then ask and answer questions.**

Ⓐ *Are you wearing it?*
Ⓑ *No, I'm not.*
Ⓐ *Is it square?*
Ⓑ *Yes, it is.*
Ⓐ *Is it on the desk?*

9 **Write a description of some of the objects in your bag. Write sentences with three or more adjectives.**

Unit 6
Too much chocolate!

Unit objectives

Grammar: *much / many / a lot of / a little / a few*; *(not) enough / too much / too many*; uses of the *-ing* form; *such / so*

Function: talking about quantity; emphasising opinions; asking for information

Vocabulary: food; souvenirs

Warm up

1 🔊 **Listen and complete the recipe opposite for a Fruit Smoothie.**

Comprehension

2 🔊 **Listen and read *Who's that girl?* Circle T (True) or F (False).**

1 Mia is making a milk drink. T / F
2 She has got a pot of yoghurt. T / F
3 She needs apples for the drink. T / F
4 They've got a lot of milk. T / F
5 Charlie decides he wants a smoothie. T / F
6 Charlie puts a lot of chocolate on top. T / F

Talking about quantity

3 **Study the sentences and do the tasks.**

---

much / many / a lot of / a little / a few

You need a lot of fruit.

There are a lot of apples and a few bananas.

I don't need many bananas.

There isn't much yoghurt.

Put a little chocolate on top.

Complete the rule with *large* or *small*.

• Use *much*, *many* and *a lot of* for run on _____ quantity; use *a little* and *a few* for a _____ quantity.

Look at the sentences and complete the rules with *countable* and *uncountable*.

• Use *a lot of* in positive and negative sentences with countable and uncountable nouns.

• Use *much* in negative sentences and questions with _____ nouns.

• Use *many* in negative sentences and questions with _____ nouns.

(not) enough / too much / too many

One carton is enough yoghurt.

That's too much chocolate.

We've got too many peaches.

Look at the examples and complete the rules with *enough*, *much* and *many*.

• Use *enough* and *not* _____ with countable and uncountable nouns.

• Use *too* _____ with uncountable nouns and *too* _____ with countable nouns.

Fruit Smoothie

Fruit Smoothie (for 2 people)

What you need:
• 2 small glasses _____
• 3 ripe apricots or peaches
• 1 ripe _____
• 1 125g carton of yoghurt
• some grated _____
• 1 teaspoon honey
• a blender and _____

What to do:
• _____ all the ingredients in a blender.
• Mix until smooth.
• Pour into the _____ .
• Sprinkle with the _____. (optional).

4 **Circle the correct words.**

1 There aren't *much / many* boys in Jo's class.
2 I can do it with *a little / a few* help from my friends.
3 I always eat *too many / too much* ice cream.
4 I need more milk. That's *not enough / enough*.
5 I haven't got *much / many* time for you at the moment.
6 Sue only runs *a little / a few* kilometres every day.

Vocabulary: food

5a **PAIRWORK Copy and complete the table with these words. Check in your dictionary if necessary.**

cheese | orange | potato | apple | yoghurt | lettuce | cod | onion | sardine | pear | banana | carrot | courgette | peach | beef | mushroom | egg | cabbage | lamb | milk | apricot | prawn | butter | chicken | bacon | strawberry | tomato | salmon | aubergine | sausage | red pepper | pork

Fruit	Vegetables	Meat	Fish	Dairy products

5b 🔊 **Listen and check your answers.**

Who's that girl?
Episode 5

Charlie wants a cola, but Mia has other ideas.

CHARLIE Hey, Mia, what are you up to? Have you got a cola?

MIA Wait a minute. I'm a bit busy. I'm making a smoothie.

CHARLIE Cool. How do you do it?

MIA Well, you need a lot of fruit. Can you have a look in the fruit bowl?

CHARLIE Sure. There are a lot of apples and peaches, and a few bananas. Here you are.

MIA Stop, Charlie! Don't put all that fruit on the table! I don't want any apples and we've got too many peaches and bananas. Look at the recipe! I only need three peaches, and I don't need many bananas. One banana is enough.

CHARLIE What else?

MIA I need some yoghurt and some milk. Can you look in the fridge?

CHARLIE Erm... There isn't much yoghurt. There's only a small carton.

MIA That's OK. One carton is enough yoghurt. I don't need a lot. What about milk?

CHARLIE No problem. There are two litres.

MIA Great. So now I mix it all together... pour it out... and put a little chocolate on top.

CHARLIE Here, let me do it!

MIA No, that's too much chocolate!

CHARLIE You can't have too much chocolate. Can we drink them now?

MIA We? This isn't for you. You want a cola.

CHARLIE No way! I want a smoothie!

REAL TALK What are you up to? Wait a minute. No problem. No way!

Emphasising opinions

6a Read the questionnaire and tick ☑ your answers.

6b Compare your results with a partner.

'Such a perfect day,
Feed animals in the zoo
Then later, a movie, too,
And then home.'

Well, Lou Reed sings that in his famous song. But what's your idea of a perfect day? Do our questionnaire and find out.

A perfect day

1 It's the morning of your perfect day. When do you get up?
  a Very early – there are such a lot of things to do.
  b At your normal time – that's OK!
  c At 10 o'clock – it's so lovely in bed!

2 It's the morning. Which of the following activities do you prefer?
  a Going shopping – there are such great shops!
  b Going to a big museum – it's so interesting!
  c Going for a walk in the countryside – it's so green and beautiful.

3 It's time for lunch. Where do you want to eat?
  a At a pizzeria with friends – it's such a noisy place!
  b At an expensive restaurant with a good friend – the food is so delicious!
  c At home with my family – it's so nice!

4 In the afternoon you go to the cinema. What type of film do you watch?
  a An action film – it's so exciting!
  b A love story – it's so romantic!
  c A comedy – it's so funny!

5 It's the evening of your perfect day. Which of the following do you prefer?
  a Having a party – you have such a lot of friends. It's great to get together.
  b Playing video games with a good friend – you always have such a good time together.
  c Sitting in a beautiful place with someone you love, watching the sun go down – it's so romantic!

Score

MAINLY A – You're so busy. A perfect day for you has an early start and includes lots of fun activities with your friends.

MAINLY B – You have got a balanced life. A perfect day for you includes time with your family and friends, but also some time on your own.

MAINLY C – You like an easy life. A perfect day for you includes a lazy start and time spent with the people you love.

7 Study the sentences and the rule. Find more examples in the questionnaire.

such / so

It's *so* lovely in bed!
You always have *such* a good time together.

• Use *such* or *so* in exclamations to strengthen what you want to say.

8 Complete the sentences with *so* or *such*.

1 The Greek islands are _____ beautiful.
2 James is _____ a good student.
3 You look _____ fantastic in that jacket.
4 There are _____ interesting programmes on TV tonight.
5 Learning a new language is _____ difficult.
6 Emily Watson is _____ a good actress.

much / many / a lot of / a little / a few

1 Study the sentences. Circle countable nouns. Underline uncountable nouns. Then complete the rules.

> There are only a few (sandwiches) left.
> I don't drink much <u>coffee</u>.
> There is a lot of salt in this meal.
> Just a little sugar, please!
> There aren't many biscuits in the cupboard.
> What a lot of people!

- Use *many* and *a few* only in front of countable nouns.
- Use *much* and *a little* only in front of _____ nouns.
- Use _____ in front of countable and uncountable nouns.

2 Circle the correct quantity word or phrase.

1 Can I have *a little / a few* ice cream, please?
2 I haven't got *much / many* text messages today.
3 Do you drink *many / a lot of* coffee, Zoe?
4 I've got *much / a few* good songs on my mp3 player.
5 The museum closes at 5 pm. There isn't *much / many* time to look around.
6 Is £20 *a few / a lot of* money in euros?
7 Could you give me *a little / a few* information about the tour, please?
8 There aren't *much / many* people at this party.

(not) enough / too much / too many

3 Study the examples and complete the rules with *uncountable* or *countable*.

> There are too many things in the fridge. I can't close it!
> There's too much milk. We can't drink it all!
> I haven't got enough information or enough notes to do this homework.

- Use *too many* with _____ nouns.
- Use *too much* with _____ nouns.
- Use *(not) enough* with _____ and _____ nouns.

4 Complete the sentences with *too much, too many* or *enough*.

1 **A** Is there _____ salt in the soup?
  B Yes, it's perfect.
2 He can't hear the teacher because there's _____ _____ noise in the classroom.
3 She can't decide what to wear because she's got _____ _____ clothes.
4 I can't give you the job. You haven't got _____ _____ experience.
5 I'm feeling sick. I had _____ hot dogs.
6 My mother thinks I spend _____ money on sweets.

such / so

5 Study the sentences and complete the rule with *such* or *so*.

> This is such a nice pair of boots!
> And that black jacket is so cool!
> These peaches are so good.
> They're such fantastic musicians!

- Use _____ in front of adjectives that are not followed by a noun.
- Use _____ in front of an adjective + a singular or plural noun.

6 Complete the sentences with *such* or *so*.

1 I'm _____ cold. Can I borrow your jacket?
2 This is _____ a good smoothie. Yum!
3 They're _____ sorry they can't come.
4 I'm _____ angry about my sister.
5 You make _____ delicious drinks!
6 This book is _____ funny.
7 He buys _____ expensive clothes.
8 I love this café. It's _____ nice.

Uses of the *-ing* form

7 Match the rules 1–4 with the sentences a–d.

- Use the *-ing* form of the verb as a noun form in the following sentence types.

  1 As the subject, at the beginning of a sentence.
  2 After verbs of preference (*like, love, hate*, etc.) and other verbs including *stop, start, finish* and *mind*.
  3 After the expressions *How about...?* and *What about...?*
  4 After phrases ending in prepositions including *good at..., interested in..., keen on....*

  a ☐ *How about going horse-riding this weekend?*
  b ☐ *Stop eating sweets in the car, please!*
  c ☐ *Corinne is very interested in learning the guitar.*
  d ☐ *Watching reality TV is my favourite entertainment.*

8 Complete each sentence with a verb in the *-ing* form so that it is true for you.

1 I'm good at _____.
2 I want to start _____.
3 (Make a suggestion to a friend) How about _____ _____ this weekend?
4 I'm not very keen on _____.
5 _____ is my favourite sport.
6 My parents love _____.
7 (Make a suggestion about holidays) What about _____ _____ this summer?
8 I can't stand _____.

9 **Workbook pp 178-183; CD-ROM**

FILE

ASKING FOR INFORMATION

- Excuse me, Where...
  ...are the toilets? / ...is the cloakroom? / ...is the café? / ...is the shop?
- Is there...
  ...a multimedia room /...a café /...an audio tour /...a wheelchair?
- May / Can I...
  ...take a photo / ...use my mobile phone?
- How do I get to the...?
- Can you tell where the ... is?

DIRECTIONS INSIDE A BUILDING

- on the left / right
- go left / right
- it's the first / second door on the left / right
- basement / ground / first / second / third floor, etc.
- take the lift
- go up / down the stairs
- go along that corridor

BUYING IN A GIFT SHOP

Customer
- I'd like... Can I have...?
- How much is...?
- Do you have a / any...?
- I'll have these.
- Can I pay for this / these?

Shop assistant
- I'll have a look.
- That'll be £...
- I'm sorry, but we haven't got any ... at the moment.

Getting around a museum

1 🔊 **29 P Listen and complete the dialogues with these words.**

right | draw | left | ground | shop | photo | toilets | second | through

1 **LAWRENCE** Excuse me. Where's the
  ¹_____?

  WOMAN It's on the ²_____ of the main hall. Take the lift to the ³_____ floor.

  LAWRENCE Thank you very much.

2 **ANDY** Excuse me. May I take a ⁴_____ of this?

  MUSEUM ATTENDANT No, you can't. But you can ⁵_____ it.

  ANDY Ah, right. OK.

3 **LAWRENCE** Excuse me. Can you tell me where the ⁶_____ are, please?

  MUSEUM ATTENDANT Sure. They're the ⁷_____ door on the ⁸_____ over there.

  LAWRENCE Cheers, mate.

4 **JORDAN** Hey, there's Andy over there.

  LAWRENCE But look at all the people!

  JORDAN Excuse me. Can we get ⁹_____, please? Thank you.

2 ROLE PLAY Work in pairs.

- **Look at the map and make new dialogues.**
- **Use expressions from the *File*.**

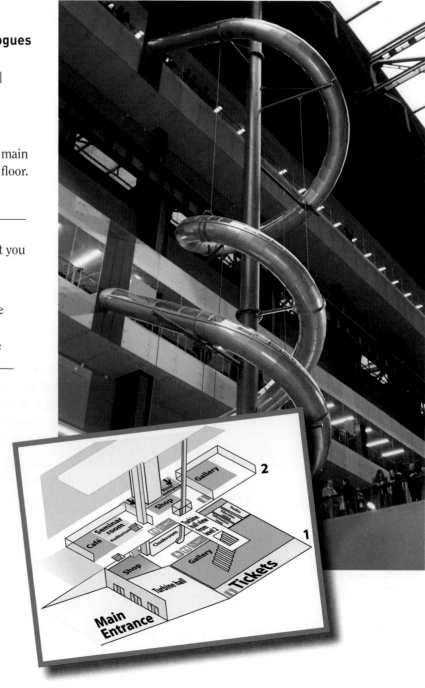

Vocabulary: souvenirs

3 🔟 **Match the words and the pictures. Then listen and check.**

a key ring   d pencil   g fridge magnets

b postcards   e eraser   h pencil sharpener

c mug   f T-shirt

4 **PAIRWORK Do you like the souvenirs in the photos? Do you buy souvenirs?**

 I like the pencil. It's a nice colour.

🅑 *I often buy souvenirs when I visit a museum.*

Shopping for small things

5 🔟 **Listen and put the dialogue in order.**

☐ SHOP ASSISTANT Is this mug yours as well?

☐ SHOP ASSISTANT Five postcards, the fridge magnets and two mugs. That'll be £23.50.

☐ SHOP ASSISTANT It's £6.50.

☐ SHOP ASSISTANT I can check... I'm sorry, but we haven't got any at the moment.

☐1 JORDAN Excuse me. Have you got any more of these bags?

☐ JORDAN Yes, but can you tell me how much the mug is?

☐ JORDAN Oh, well. Never mind. Can I pay for these things, then?

☐ JORDAN That's a good price. Hold on. I'll get another one.

6 **P PAIRWORK Act out the dialogues. Use the *File* and the photos of souvenirs.**

7 **Read *Get into Culture* and do the task.**

Get into *culture* MODERN ART

Modern art is very popular in the UK. The Turner Prize is a famous British art competition. One artist wins from a shortlist of artists. There are often some very controversial artists on the list, such as installation artists. The British press reports the competition. People may like the art or not, but they always have an opinion!

- **Do you like art?**
- **What sort of art do you like?**

8   **LINKS Real communication pp 8-9**

FESTIVALS

The Notting Hill Carnival

...where you can see amazing dancers, eat delicious food, listen to reggae and steel bands, and have a great time

This summer festival is a major tourist attraction. Notting Hill is only a small area in West London but two million people come from all over the world to have fun. The carnival's at the end of August each year, and the main days are Sunday and Bank Holiday Monday.

The festival started as a local West Indian event, but from a small procession through the streets of Notting Hill, it is now a huge multi-cultural arts festival. In fact, it is the largest street carnival in Europe. Only the Rio Carnival in Brazil is bigger. The carnival isn't only a Caribbean event, groups from many parts of the world take part including Bangladesh, Bulgaria and Afghanistan.

At the heart of the festival is a spectacular parade. The Carnival route is three miles long and hundreds of groups move along it. There's music, decorated floats, elaborate costumes and dancing. It's a very loud festival because there are 45 static sound systems in the street playing reggae, soul, hip hop, funk, house and garage. In addition, there are three live stages where live artists from all over the world perform, but there's a lot more to the festival than just music. There are 300 food stalls selling exotic international food so you can't get hungry. There's theatre and arts and crafts, too.

You can sing and dance or you can just watch. But there's no need to be quiet. You can buy whistles and blow them to make lots of noise! The Notting Hill Carnival welcomes visitors and tourists. Its motto is 'Every spectator is a participant'.

Reading

1 **PAIRWORK** What festivals are there in the UK and in your country?

2 Look at the photographs and the heading on page 62. What do you think the article is about?

3 **P** Read the article and answer the questions. Choose the correct answer (a, b, c or d).

1 How often does the carnival take place?
   a Every August   c Every two years
   b Every month   d Every three years

2 When is Notting Hill Carnival?
   a on Monday   c on Saturday and Sunday
   b on Sunday   d on Sunday and Monday

3 What is the origin of the carnival?
   a It was a small music festival.
   b It was a small Brazilian festival.
   c It was a small Bulgarian event.
   d It was a small West Indian event.

4 How big is the carnival?
   a bigger than the carnival in Rio
   b the biggest in Europe
   c the biggest in the world
   d bigger than the carnival in Bangladesh

5 What can you see in the parade?
   a a small procession
   b 300 food stalls
   c decorated floats, music and dancing
   d 45 static sound systems

6 Where can you listen to music at the carnival?
   a in the houses and garages
   b on three live stages
   c at 45 discos
   d at 300 stalls

Word expander LINKING WORDS

Use words like *and, but, because, so, or* to link ideas.
*We give presents and cards, **and** even send emails.*
Find linking words in the article on page 62.

4 Read the article again and find words that are associated with the following.
Music and gigs: sound system
Carnivals and festivals: procession, costumes

Skills FOR life KEY WORDS

Use your vocabulary notebook. When you read an article make a list of the words linked to the topic (see exercise 4).

Listening

5 **32 P** Listen to a radio phone-in about popular festivals. Circle the correct information in the table.

F A C T F I L E Diwali, the Festival of Lights

Type of festival? religious music

When? September October November

How many days? five six seven

Special food? sweets and cakes curry and rice

Best bit? dancing lights food

F A C T F I L E Glastonbury Festival

Type of festival? religious music

When? June July August

How many days? two three four

Special food? yes no

Best bit? camping music dancing

6 Report to the class about the festivals.

Pronunciation /ə/

7 **33** Listen and repeat the words. The underlined syllables are a very common short sound in English. Many words contain this sound.

1 Septemb<u>er</u>   3 Saturd<u>a</u>y   5 numb<u>er</u>
2 lett<u>er</u>   4 danc<u>er</u>   6 list<u>en</u>

Speaking and writing

8a Make some notes about your favourite festival or public holiday. Think about these things.

type of festival | when and how long | what happens | historical associations | food | decorations | costumes | music / dancing | fireworks | procession / parade | favourite thing

8b **T GROUPWORK** Talk about festivals and holidays in your country.

 My favourite time is Christmas because we have a big tree and lots of presents.

9 **T** Use your notes from exercise 8a to write a website article. Try to use linking words.

10 **34** Go to LINKS page 62 and listen to *Happy Xmas.*

FILE

LISTENING FOR INFORMATION

We often need to identify specific pieces of information when we are listening, so this is part of the Cambridge PET exam. It may be in a conversation, a radio programme, a public announcement or a message on an answering machine.

Towards PET Paper 2 Listening, Part 3

FIND KEY INFORMATION
- You don't need to understand every word. You are listening for specific information.
- Look at the questions first to find out what information you need. Often it relates to factual information such as places, events, activities, days of the week, opening hours, prices, etc.
- Try to predict key words, such as days of the week or times, and listen for them.

MAKE NOTES
- Take notes to help you understand and remember. Only write down the main points.

1 ㉟ **Answer the Beatles miniquiz. Then listen and check.**

1 Where did the Beatles come from?

2 What decade are they most associated with?

3 Rearrange the names to make the four Beatles.

   George Lennon   John McCartney
   Ringo Harrison   Paul Starr

4 Name the Beatles that are still alive.

5 Which Beatles member is also a painter?

6 Which Beatles member married Yoko Ono?

2 ㊱ P **You will hear a teacher telling a class about their day trip to Liverpool. For each question, fill in the missing information in the numbered space.**

The Beatles tour: School trip to Liverpool
Departure
    Meet at Euston station at ¹ _____. Train leaves at 7.00 am.
Arrival ² _____.
Magical Mystery Tour starts at ³ _____.
Lunch at ⁴ _____ at Albert Dock. Remember to bring ⁵ _____.
Going to the museum
    Assemble at ⁶ _____. Meet up at museum ⁷ _____ at 4.00 pm.
Shopping
⁸ _____ hour to explore and go shopping.
Going home
    Minibus to station at ⁹ _____. Train leaves at ¹⁰ _____. Train arrives in London at ¹¹ _____.
    All students must have a parent to meet them, or arrange to travel home with another student.
Rules
    NO personal stereos or ¹² _____ in the museum.

FILE

DISCUSSION OF A TOPIC

Giving a talk is a good way to improve your English. It is also a useful preparation for daily life when we often explain, teach or describe something to our friends and family. So it is part of the Trinity exam.
In a talk you need to organise ideas, facts and opinions and explain them. You also need to be able to have a discussion about your ideas and answer questions.

Trinity ISE I topic phase

Tips

• Choose a topic that really interests you –a sport you like, your town or city, a hobby, or an aspect of your culture.
• Plan your talk in sections, each with a main point.
• Write the four main points on a Topic form.
• Plan a very short introduction and a conclusion.
• Support your talk with photos, pictures, diagrams and objects.
• Prepare your talk carefully. Write notes with key words for each part of the talk.
• Practise it a lot.
• Learn to use only notes. You sound more natural and more interesting.

1   **Look at the pictures and guess Chiara's topic.**

2   **Read Chiara's presentation. Match the pictures of the things with the right place in the presentation.**

3   **Read the presentation again and write the topics in the Topic form.**

food | nativity scene | the atmosphere | Jesi

TOPIC FORM

Candidate name *Chiara Lombardi*
Centre *Ancona*
Date of examination *June 20---*
Title of topic *Christmas in my town*

Main points for discussion

1 ....
2 ....
3 ....
4 ....

Present this form to the examiner during the examination

4   🔊37 **Listen and make a note of Chiara's answers to the examiner's questions.**
   • What sort of presents do you buy at Christmas?
   • What can you see and do in Jesi?
   • Are any famous people from Jesi?
   • What is the typical food and drink from Jesi?
   • And what does your family do at Christmas?

5   T **Now plan and prepare a talk about a festival in your country.**

6   **Give your talk to the class. Bring photos and objects to show people. Think about the questions people could ask you.**

7   ↗ **LINKS** Exam listening p 9

My topic is about Christmas in my town in Italy.

Jesi is a small medieval town near the east coast. Christmas is very important for us and we all look forward to it. There are lots of special events in December. Sometimes it snows. Then it is really beautiful and I feel very excited. Here is a picture of Jesi. ☐

There is a great atmosphere at Christmas. There are Christmas things in the shops – decorations, models of Father Christmas and so on. In the evening, people look in the windows and buy Christmas presents. The streets look really pretty because they have Christmas lights. And there's a big Christmas tree in the main square. Sometimes there is Christmas music playing. Here is a photo. ☐

We eat a lot of special food at Christmas. I look forward to traditional Christmas dinner with the family. In Jesi the food shops sell traditional Italian Christmas food including special cakes. Panettone is a sort of bread with dried fruit in it. I have one here to show you. ☐

The 'Presepio' is a traditional Italian scene. You say 'nativity scene' in English. It is a model, sometimes life-size, with Mary, Joseph and the baby Jesus in a stable. There is a church in Jesi with an incredible 'presepio' with scenes from daily life in the old days. It takes people all year to make it! I have a small nativity scene to show you. ☐

I hope you can come to Jesi one day and experience our Christmas!

LANGUAGE CHECK

1 Choose the correct words.

1 I've only got ____ lessons today.
   a) much   b) many   c) a little   d) a few

2 There aren't ____ trains to Leeds.
   a) such   b) so   c) much   d) many

3 Kurt doesn't like ____ sugar in his coffee.
   a) too much   b) enough   c) too many   d) some

4 She's interested in ____ Japanese.
   a) learn   b) learning c) to learn   d) learns

5 ____ you help me with my homework, please?
   a) May   b) Do   c) Are   d) Could

6 You're only six but you ____ ride a bike!
   a) can   b) may   c) could   d) are

7 They ____ a new sports centre in the town.
   a) build   b) builds   c) are building d) building

8 My dad usually ____ to work.
   a) drive   b) drives   c) is driving   d) can drive

9 'I love fruit smoothies.' '____.'
   a) I do.   b) I don't. c) Neither can I. d) So does I.

10 Katie makes notes in lessons and ____ does Nathan.
   a) neither   b) so   c) such   d) too

TOTAL: ____/10

2 Find the words to complete the table.

Transport		Materials		Souvenirs	
gnduoerdnou	underground	toctno	c_____	erdifg natgem	f_____ m_____
hacoh	_____	robcradad	c_____	mgu	_____
bomktrioe	m_____	helarte	l_____	yke nrgi	_____ _____
elpan	p_____	clstpai	_____		

TOTAL: ____/10

3 Complete the dialogues with the phrases.

can I take
where are
go down
how do I get
can you tell me
excuse me
how much is
in the basement
on the left
does this bus go

1 A ¹_____ to Liverpool, please?
   B Yes, it does.
   A ²_____ a return ticket, please?
   B It's £6.70.
   A Here you are. ³_____ when we're in the city centre, please?
   B Yes, of course.

2 A ⁴_____, I'm a bit lost. ⁵_____ to the Picasso exhibition?
   B Take the lift to the second floor and it's ⁶_____.
   A Thank you. ⁷_____ photos in here?
   B No, you can't.
   A Oh, OK. And ⁸_____ the toilets, please?
   B They're ⁹_____. ¹⁰_____ those stairs on the right.
   A Thank you.

TOTAL: ____/10

4 Write a paragraph about the types of transport you/your family use to go:
   • to school   • to work   • to the cinema   • to your friend's house   • on holiday

TOTAL: ____/10

TOTAL: ____/40

 LINKS Interculture pp 24-25; Story pp 40-41; CLIL (Geography) pp 50-51

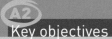
A2 Key objectives

Grammar *must / mustn't / (not) have to; be allowed to; should / ought to / needn't*; articles
Functions talking about obligation; having a discussion; giving advice; asking for and giving directions
Vocabulary school; computers; relationships; places in a town; prepositions

Get started

1a Do the questionnaire. Make a note of your answers.

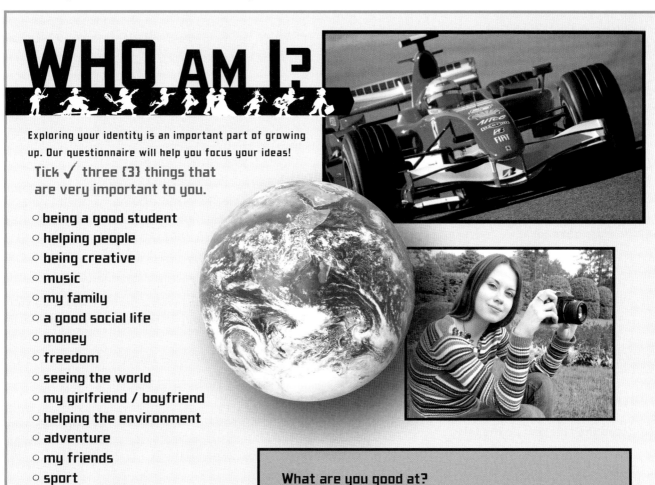

WHO AM I?

Exploring your identity is an important part of growing up. Our questionnaire will help you focus your ideas!

Tick ✓ three (3) things that are very important to you.

- being a good student
- helping people
- being creative
- music
- my family
- a good social life
- money
- freedom
- seeing the world
- my girlfriend / boyfriend
- helping the environment
- adventure
- my friends
- sport
- making things

NOW....answer these questions.

What are you good at?
What would you like to be good at?
What do you worry about?
What scares you?
What bores you?
What world problem would you like to solve?
Which person, living or dead, do you admire?
What's your dream for the future?
What object, animal or thing represents you? Why?

Look at your answers to the questions.

Now think of one thing you can do to get new skills, help the world, achieve your ambitions. Make it a simple thing, e.g. start guitar lessons, talk to your family, join an environmental group.

1b **PAIRWORK** Compare your answers to part 1. Ask and answer the questions.

Unit objectives
Grammar *must / mustn't / (not) have to;*
So / Neither must I; (not) be allowed to
Functions talking about obligation, permission,
having a discussion
Vocabulary school; computers

Warm up

1 **Look at the photos on page 69 and answer the questions.**

1 Where are Charlie and Mia?

2 What do you think Charlie's problem is?

3 What do you think Jack is asking Rose?

Comprehension

2 **38 Listen and read *Who's that girl?* Complete each sentence with one word.**

1 Charlie and Mia have got a lot of <u>Maths</u> homework.

2 Charlie's parents are getting heavy about his _____.

3 Mia needs to talk to Jack and Rose about their _____.

4 Rose says she's got a _____ memory.

5 Jack invites Rose to go for a _____.

6 Rose has to go for a _____.

3 **What do you think?**

- Does Jack like Rose?
- Does Rose like Jack?
- Does Charlie like Mia?

Talking about obligation

4a **Read the rule and do the task.**

> *must / mustn't / (not) have to*
>
> - The use of *have to* and *must* both express obligation and are often interchangeable. But *have to* is more frequent than *must* in spoken English.
>
>   *I have to go for a run now.* = *I must go for a run now.*
>
> - Use both [1] _____ and [2] _____ to say that it is important or urgent to do something.
>
> **Complete the rules with *have to, don't have to, must* or *mustn't.***
>
> - Use [3] _____ to express prohibition.
> - Use [4] _____ in questions to ask about obligation.
> - Use [5] _____ to express negative obligation / to say that it is not necessary to do something.

4b **Look for sentences expressing obligation in the dialogue and underline them.**

5 **Complete the sentences with the correct form of *have to* or *not have to.***

1 You <u>have to</u> believe me. It's really true.

2 He _____ give me any money. I've got enough.

3 You _____ ring John. He's waiting for your call.

4 I know the answer. You _____ tell me.

5 She _____ join us. We can go without her.

6 The students _____ learn this. There's a test tomorrow.

6 **Complete the sentences with *must* or *mustn't.***

1 Sorry, I <u>must</u> go now. I'm tired.

2 What's Joe's girlfriend's name again? I _____ forget it.

3 We _____ ask Kevin. He can help us.

4 They _____ find this letter. Can you hide it?

5 He's going out with Vicky, but you _____ tell Sue.

6 I'm hungry. I _____ remember to buy some food.

7 **PAIRWORK Discuss with a partner. What do you have to do this week? What don't you have to do this week?**

A *I have to go to the dentist.*

B *I don't have to do any English homework.*

1 *School's finished for the day, but Charlie isn't happy.*

CHARLIE What do we have to do for our Maths homework?
MIA All the exercises on page 80.
CHARLIE I don't believe it. We have to do lots of extra work this year!
MIA So what? You never study!
CHARLIE I know, but I must do well in my exams. My parents are getting really heavy.
MIA Listen, Charlie. I have to talk to Jack and Rose about our gig now.
CHARLIE And I have to go home and do my Maths! What a pain!
MIA You don't have to do it on your own. Call me later and I can help.
CHARLIE Thanks, Mia. That's really sweet of you.

2 *Later, over coffee...*

JACK Listen guys, we're really lucky to get this gig. We must do a good job.
ROSE Right! And I must learn all the songs. But I've got a terrible memory!
JACK You mustn't be negative, Rose.
MIA Don't worry, Rose. You're great.

3 *Jack walks home with Rose.*

JACK Hey, Rose. Do you fancy a coffee or something?
ROSE I'd love to, but...
JACK But what?
ROSE I have to go for a run now. Maybe another time?
JACK Yeah, maybe. See you tomorrow.
ROSE OK. See you, Jack.

REAL TALK   I don't believe it.   So what!   heavy   What a pain!   That's really sweet of you.

Vocabulary: school

8a Make a list of words connected with school.

pupil | geography | assistant | gym

8b **PAIRWORK** Compare your list and add more words.

Speak Up!

Tell us what YOU think by email or text message.

This week:

SCHOOL RULES

SUZY posted UK time 22 May 9.02PM   Comments (2)

We aren't allowed to wear jewellery or short skirts. And we aren't allowed to wear trainers – we have to wear black shoes. I think that's silly. Trainers are so practical.

WEIRD RULE We have to go outside during the breaks. Even in the rain!

BAZ Posted UK time 22 May 9.02PM   Comments (1)

We have to stand up when a teacher comes into the classroom. We aren't allowed to use our mobile phones during lessons. But we often text each other in class! The teachers don't see us.

WEIRD RULE You aren't allowed to yawn in class.

AISHA Posted UK time 22 May 9.02PM   Comments (0)

We have to wear a school uniform – a blue blazer, a white shirt and tie, grey trousers or a skirt. It's really formal! Boys aren't allowed to wear hair gel and girls can't have dyed hair. You're allowed to wear a scarf for religious reasons.

WEIRD RULE At registration we have to wear our blazer.

STEPHEN Posted UK time 22 May 9.02PM   Comments (3)

We aren't allowed to bring knives into the school. There is a security control at the entrance. We can't eat junk food. We have to choose at least one healthy option from the menu.

WEIRD RULE We all have to walk on the left side of the corridor.

Talking about permission

9 Read the messages in *Speak Up!* and write the name of the student next to each rule.
1 No junk food *Stephen*
2 No jewellery
3 Wear your blazer during registration
4 No knives in school
5 No yawning in class
6 No short skirts
7 No hair gel
8 No mobile phone use in class

10 Study the rules and find examples in Speak up!

(not) be allowed to

- Use (*not*) *be allowed to* to talk about permission.
  We aren't allowed to wear jewellery.
  You're allowed to wear a scarf.

Impersonal *you*

- Use *you* to talk about permission in an impersonal, general way.
  You aren't allowed to yawn in class.

can / can't

- You can also use modal verb *can / can't* to talk about permission.
  Girls can't have dyed hair.

11 **P T PAIRWORK Does your school have the same rules as the students above?**

 We mustn't use our mobile phones in school.

 We can wear short skirts.

A *You are allowed to wear a head scarf.*

12 🔊39 Listen to some students talking about school rules. Number the topics in the order you hear them.

☐ eating in the street   ☐ uniforms
☐ mobile phones   ☐ computers
☐ homework

13 What are your school rules? Make a list.

We mustn't chew gum in class.

Modal verb *must* and modal form *have to*

1 **Read the rules and complete the examples with the correct form of the verbs.**

must
- *Must* is a modal verb. It doesn't take *-s* when the subject is *he, she* or *it*.
  Rose _____ learn the songs.
- Modal verbs are followed by the base form.
  We must wait here.
- Form the negative with the modal + *not* + the base form.
  Students _____ run in the corridor.
- The question form of *must* is rare.

have to
- *Have to* uses the auxiliary *do* or *does* in questions and the negative.
- *Have to* is the usual question form for *must*.
  Do we have to do this exercise?
- *Have to* has the same form as present simple verb *have*.
  He _____ to go. I have to study.

needn't
- It is often possible to use *needn't* instead of *don't have to* for lack of obligation.
  You don't have to come. = You needn't come.

2 **Study the sentences and complete the rules with *must, have to, mustn't* or *not have to*.**

- *Have to* and _____ often mean the same thing in positive sentences.
  I have to go home. = I must go home.
- We usually use _____ to talk about personal obligation.
  I must do well in my exams.
- We usually use _____ for an external obligation.
  You have to show your passport at customs.
- _____ is often used in public announcements, signs and notices.
  You must turn off your mobile phones.
- Use _____ to express a habitual obligation.
  I have to tidy my room on Saturdays.
- Use _____ to say that something is forbidden.
  You mustn't park here.
- Use _____ to say it is not obligatory to do something.
  You don't have to write this down.

3 **Complete the sentences with the verb in brackets and the correct form of *must* or *have to*. Sometimes both are possible.**

1 We _____ our mobiles in class. (turn off)
2 We're late. We _____ her. (call)
3 _____ you _____ a uniform at your school? (wear)
4 He is usually late, but this time he _____ late! (be)
5 A _____ we _____ these words? (study)
  B Yes, you do.
6 She _____ us money. We have enough. (lend)
7 All visitors _____ at hospital reception. (sign in)
8 Tom _____ the dog for a walk every morning. (take)

4 **Write sentences that are true for you.**
1 At the weekend I don't have to…
2 When you do an exam you mustn't…
3 My parents don't have to tell me to…
4 I always have to…
5 I must remember to…

Must: agreeing and disagreeing

5 **Study the dialogues. Then write answers to agree or disagree with sentences 1-8.**
1 **A** I must read this book.
  B So must I. / I don't have to.
2 **A** I don't have to be home before eleven tonight.
  B Neither do I. / I do.
3 **A** I have to do my homework now.
  B So do I. / I don't.
4 **A** I don't have to hurry.
  B I do. / Neither do I.
5 **A** I mustn't eat sweets.
  B Neither must I. / I can.

1 I must get up before six tomorrow.
2 I don't have to study a lot.
3 I have to take a bus to get to school.
4 I have to help a lot at home.
5 I must tidy my room.
6 I have to do a lot of music practice.
7 I mustn't watch TV tonight.
8 I don't have to make my bed.

(not) be allowed to

6 **Complete the rules with *be allowed to* and *not be allowed to*.**

- Use *can* and _____ to express permission, and use *can't* and _____ to express prohibition.
  We can use dictionaries in our lessons. / We are allowed to use dictionaries in our lessons.
  I can't go out tonight. / I'm not allowed to go out tonight.

7 **Write sentences which are true for you using *be allowed to* or *not be allowed to*.**
1 I / sleep over at a friend's house on a school night
  I'm not allowed to / I'm allowed to sleep over at a friend's house on a school night.
2 we / wear jeans to school
3 my friends / go out late on Saturday night
4 I / drive at my age
5 I / take money from my mother's bag
6 my friends / travel by train on their own
7 I / have a computer in my bedroom
8 I / have a part-time job

8 **Workbook pp 184-189; CD-ROM**

FILE

GETTING STARTED
• Are you ready? / Ready?
• Let's start.

LISTENING
• Yes. / Yeah.
• OK.
• Right.

FILLERS
• Um / Er.
• I mean...
•...you know...

ELICITING
• What do you think?
• What about you?

SUGGESTING AND RESPONDING
• Why don't we...? / Shall we...?
• Good idea! / Let's do that.

EXPRESSING PREFERENCE
• I think...
• I prefer...

AGREEING AND DISAGREEING
• I agree. / I don't agree.
• You're right / Yes, definitely.
• Me too. / Me neither.
• I'm not sure. / I don't know.

Multiple intelligences CLIL

1a Read the article and match each intelligence with the correct definition.

Do you like moving and doing sport? And hate sitting still at your desk? Or maybe you are good with numbers, but not so good with words? Perhaps you learn best when you're listening to music on your mp3 player? Or are you the artistic genius of the class?

Well, there is a theory that says we all have different intelligences. And we learn best when we are using our special intelligences. In this theory the brain has nine different intelligence centres.

How smart are you?

1 **Body smart**   a you have a strong spiritual sense

2 **Number smart**   b you love words and learning languages

3 **Myself smart**   c you like listening to and playing music

4 **Visual smart**   d you enjoy being outside in the natural world

5 **Word smart**   e you are analytical and you like logical answers

6 **People smart**   f you use your body a lot, you do sport or dance

7 **Music smart**   g you are self-aware, you like working on your own

8 **Nature smart**   h you are artistic and can visualise things

9 **Spirit smart**   i you enjoy being with people, you understand how they feel

1b Choose three intelligences that are strong for you.

2 PAIRWORK Try these multiple intelligence activities.

 Mime verbs to each other.

 Give each other sums to do.

 Discuss these questions. *Do you like working on your own / playing team games / doing pairwork activities / doing puzzles on your own?*

 Think of a noun and draw it for your partner. They have to guess it.

 Play the adjective game.
Ⓐ *The teacher's cat is an angry cat.*
Ⓑ *The teacher's cat is a bad cat.*
Ⓐ *The teacher's cat is a clever cat, etc.*

 Tell a sentence each of a continuing story.
Ⓐ *Marco woke up at three o'clock in the morning.*
Ⓑ *He was scared because...*

 Play *Name that tune*. Sing the first five notes of a song. Your partner has to guess the song.

 Make word maps for these words: *the country, the seaside.*

 Discuss these questions: *Do you believe in ghosts / extra-terrestrials / magic?*

3 Write sentences about yourself for each type of intelligence.

Body smart: I like dancing and sport. I don't enjoy sitting still for a long time. I prefer learning by doing something physical.

4 Read *Get into Culture* and do the task.

Get into *culture* SOFT SKILLS

Young people work hard to get their qualifications. But many workplaces are looking for extra skills – soft skills. So what are soft skills? Well, they include things like managing your time, communicating with other people and working in a team. People with these skills do a good job. Many of these skills are useful in your education as well. You can develop them by learning about the way you think and the way you communicate.

Tick two things you do well. Circle one thing you need to improve.

work in a team | plan your work | be adaptable | manage your time | be reliable | give talks | communicate with other people | be creative | listen well | solve problems | work on your own | accept criticism | start a job

Improve your teamwork!

5 **P** **GROUPWORK** Work in groups of four or five.
- Read the situation below and do the preparatory task.
- You have ten minutes to agree together on your solution.
- Use the expressions in the *File*.

You are on a desert island for three months. You are allowed only five foods on your island! Your group must decide unanimously on your answer.

Desert island food!

Preparatory task

Here is a list of food to help you. Can you divide them into the different groups? Can you add any other food?

potato | oil | pasta | peas | butter | pork | apple | beans | cabbage | lamb | orange | beef | tomato | fish | cheese | sugar | banana | bread | carrots | onions | nuts | green beans | chicken | rice | yoghurt | grapes | pear | spinach

meat and fish	fats
carbohydrate	vegetables
fruit	dairy

6 Present your group solutions to the class. Explain your reasons.

7 **LINKS** Real communication pp 10-11

Vocabulary: computers

1 🔟 **Match the pictures with the words. Then listen and repeat.**

- ☐ printer
- ☐ speakers
- ☐ keyboard
- ☐ mouse mat
- ☐ monitor
- ☐ hard disk
- ☐ mouse
- ☐ cable
- ☐ processor
- ☐ USB ports
- 9️⃣ buttons
- ☐ plug

2 🔟 **Listen and repeat the words.**

plug in / unplug the computer / printer
turn on / turn off the computer / printer
start up / close down the computer
key in words / letters / numbers
delete / print / send / receive documents
click on the mouse

Listening and writing CLIL

3a 🔟 **P Listen to the instructions and number the pictures in the order you hear them.**

3b Listen again and make a note of the words that helped you decide.

4 Now write instructions for the pictures. Use the words in your notes and/or words from exercises 1 and 2.

Word **expander** MULTI-WORD VERBS

Some verbs have a verb and a preposition, e.g *stand up, get up, sit down*. They have a different meaning from the base verb. These verbs have special grammatical rules, but you can learn them individually first.

Find the multi-word verbs in exercise 2 with: *plug, turn, start, close and key.* **Keep a special page in your Vocabulary notebook for multi-word verbs.**

Reading and speaking CLIL

5 Read about safety on the Internet and match the headings with the paragraphs.

Bullying | Personal details | Stranger danger | Passwords | Chatrooms

Skills FOR life **GUESSING THE MEANING**

When you don't understand a new word, look at its position in the sentence. Which words are near it? What type of word is it? An adjective, a verb, a noun? Is it like a word in your language? Try to guess these words from the article: *identity theft, well-monitored, moderator.*

Internet safety

The Internet is fun. And it's fine to chat. But you must be careful. Read our advice so you can be safe on the net!

1 ....

Use a nickname in chatrooms. Don't give your name, home address, email address or phone number in online social areas. Don't give personal information about where you live, where you go to school, etc., as someone can use this to identify you. And don't give your phone number.

2 ....

Use different passwords. And keep your passwords secret: this protects you from identity theft. Don't tell your friends your passwords.

3 ....

Good chatrooms are well-monitored and have safety features, including a moderator. Most chatrooms have some public areas for group conversations and private areas for one-to-one chat. Chat in the public areas, not the private areas.

4 ....

Online bullying is a big problem. When a person bullies you, don't respond – that is what they want you to do. Always tell a parent, trusted adult or a teacher. They can report the bully or bullies to the Internet Service Provider or the chatroom moderator. Make notes of names, times and contact details.

5 ....

Many teenagers want to meet new online friends. This can be very dangerous. It is very easy to create false identities online. NEVER arrange a meeting on your own. Don't agree to meet someone secretly. Always tell your parents. Always take a friend or your mum or dad. Arrange the meeting in a safe public place during the day.

6 PAIRWORK Complete the table with information from the article.

You mustn't ...	You must ...
It's a good idea to ...	**It isn't a good idea to ...**

Pronunciation /uː/ /ʌ/

7a 🔊43 **Listen and repeat.**

/ʌ/ must, sun, just

/uː/ computer, music, use

7b 🔊44 **Listen and write the words in the table.**

/ʌ/	/uː/

7c Now listen and check.

8 P T PAIRWORK Ask and answer about the Internet.

How often do you use the Internet?
What do you do on the Internet?
Do you use chatrooms? Which ones?
Do you use a nickname in chatrooms?

You shouldn't worry about it!

Unit objectives

Grammar: *should / ought to / needn't*; articles
Function: giving advice, using articles, asking for and giving directions, having a debate
Vocabulary: relationships; places in a town; prepositions

Warm up

1 PAIRWORK What can you do to get help when you've got a problem? Write a list.

talk to your parents, talk to a teacher

Vocabulary: relationships

2 ⁴⁵ Complete the text with these phrases. Then listen and check.

break up | get back together | asks her out | go out together

True Love

Jack really likes Lucy so he ¹ _____. He sends her a text message – 'Would you like to see a film with me tonight?' They like each other. And they ² _____ for six months. But then they have problems, so they ³ _____. But they miss each other. So they ⁴ _____ again!

Comprehension

3a Read the letters to the agony column on page 77. Write the names Lucy, Daniel or Alice at the top of the replies.

3b P Circle T (True) or F (False).

1 Lucy has lots of problems at school. T / F
2 Her classmates don't do any work. T / F
3 Alice still likes her ex-boyfriend a lot. T / F
4 She and her ex-boyfriend are in the same year at school. T / F
5 Daniel likes Jane, but Jane is shy. T / F
6 Daniel always sits next to Jane. T / F

4 Discuss the questions.

• Which of the replies is best? Why?
• What do you think of the other replies?

Giving advice

5 Study the sentences and do the task.

> **should / ought to / needn't**
>
> You *should* talk to your friends.
> You *shouldn't* worry too much.
> You *ought* to wait and see.
> You *needn't* do anything right now.

Complete the rules with *good* and *necessary*.

• Use *should* or *ought to* to say it is _____ to do a thing. Note that they have the same meaning.
• Use *shouldn't* to say it isn't _____ to do a thing. Note that *oughtn't to* is also possible, but is not often used.
• Use *needn't* to say that it isn't _____ to do a thing.

6 Complete the sentences with *should, ought to, shouldn't* or *needn't*. Sometimes more than one option is possible.

1 Tom knows about the party. We _____ tell him.
2 It's very late. You _____ go home now.
3 He needs some exercise. He _____ drive everywhere.
4 She's got a fantastic voice. She _____ sing in a band.
5 I'm not hungry. You _____ make any lunch for me.
6 You _____ say bad things about your friends.

7 PAIRWORK Discuss your week.

> 💬 *This week I ought to study for the exam, but I needn't start today. And I should phone my grandmother.*

8a Invent a problem. Write a letter to an agony column.

Dear Zoe ...

8b GROUPWORK Give your letter to a member of the group. Write a reply to the letter you receive. Read out the letters and replies. Discuss them.

Teen worries

Zoe Mills can help you!
Just ask.....

Dear Zoe,
I really enjoy school and I'm good at most subjects but I've got one big problem. My friends aren't interested in studying and they never do any work. They just copy my work. They copy my answers in class and they copy my homework too. When I say I'm not happy about it, they are horrible to me. They say friends ought to share things. I don't know what to do.

Lucy

and you'll see......
you're not alone!

Zoe, Zoe, *ZOE!*
HELP!! My ex-boyfriend goes to my school. We aren't in the same year but we often see each other. I still have strong feelings for him but I don't know how he feels. Do you think I should speak to him? What should I say?

Alice, Manchester

Dear _____,
She obviously likes you and I'm sure you needn't worry too much about being cool. Why don't you ask her for her email address? Then you can ask her out in an email. That gives you time to plan what you say. Good luck!

Zoe

Dear _____,
I know you've got strong feelings about your ex, but you should wait and see in this situation. Think about your past relationship with your ex. Are you well-suited to each other or are there some big problems there? Talk to your friends about your feelings. Sometimes people get back together and they are happy, but often they just break up again.

Zoe

Dear Miss Mills,
My problem is that I'm shy. There's this girl in my class. I really like her, and I think she likes me because she often sits next to me. I'd like to go out with her. But I don't know how to ask her out in a cool way. Please help me.

Daniel, Leeds

Dear _____,
Congratulations on being such a good student, and I'm sorry you are having problems with your friends. You should talk to someone about this situation because it isn't fair on you. This could be a member of your family or a teacher. Your friends don't have to know about this. But I think maybe you should look for new friends!

Zoe

Using articles

9 **P** **Read the article. Circle T (True) or F (False).**

1 Jump Up Internet Camp is a holiday camp. T / F
2 The boys at the Mokcheon camp are drug addicts. T / F
3 Internet addiction is a health problem. T / F
4 People in South Korea love online games. T / F
5 90% of South Koreans have an Internet connection. T / F
6 At the Mokcheon camp, the teenagers play exciting Internet games. T / F
7 At the Mokcheon camp, you aren't allowed to use your mobile phone. T / F
8 At the moment, Internet addiction is only a problem in South Korea. T / F

10 **Study the rules. Circle definite articles and underline indefinite articles in the text.**

Articles

- Use the indefinite article, *a* or *an*, the first time you mention a thing. It tells us the thing is not known to the listener and it is not unique:

  ...teenage boys are staying at a camp. (= first mention of the camp; it isn't unique, there are lots of camps)

- Use the definite article, *the* the second time you mention a thing and when the listener knows about it:

  The camp is called 'Jump Up Internet Rescue School'. (= second mention of the camp)

  The country is Internet mad. (= we know which country, i.e. South Korea)

- Also use *the* for something unique or specific in its context.

  At the Mokcheon camp. (= there is only one)

Word **expander**   NO ARTICLE

The following common phrases don't have an article. You need to memorise them.

- at home | at school | at work | at university
- in hospital | in prison | in bed
- by bus | by train | by plane | by car
- on foot

INTERNET ADDICTS

The Internet, addiction, and government solutions. How harmful is serious surfing?

MOKCHEON, SOUTH KOREA It's the summer holidays and a group of teenage boys are staying at a camp in a village south of the capital, Seoul. The camp is called 'Jump Up Internet Rescue School'. But it isn't a holiday camp! The boys are doing military-style activities, and their instructors are very strict. These boys aren't soldiers, criminals or drug addicts. They suffer from a new and dangerous health problem. Their problem is Internet addiction!

EPIDEMIC South Korea is very Internet-friendly. Over 90% of the population have fast, cheap Internet access at home. The country is Internet-mad and playing online games is the favourite national sport. The result is an epidemic of Internet addiction, especially among young people.

LEAVING THE VIRTUAL WORLD The government has programmes to help Internet addicts. At the Mokcheon camp, teenage boys have to leave the virtual world and learn to live and interact with others in the real world. They don't play games online, they do exciting sports and activities such as horse-riding. They mustn't use computers at the camp and they can only use mobile phones for one hour per day. One boy, aged 15, says, 'At home I usually spend about 17 hours per day online. I sometimes play all night and then I miss school. My life at the camp is very different – but I like it.'

WORLDWIDE PROBLEM Internet addiction isn't only a problem in South Korea. The problem is worldwide. Many teenagers and adults are spending over two hours per day online. What about you? Maybe it's time to turn off your computer and get real!

RANDOM Fact *The first ever Internet addiction clinic in the USA cost $15,000 for 45 days. And it hasn't got an internet connection.*

Modal verb *should* / Modal form *ought to*

1 Study the rules.

- *Should* and *ought to* have the same meaning.
  I should read this book. = I ought to read this book.
- *Should* is a modal verb – a verb that expresses the attitude of the speaker.
- *Ought* uses *to* after the verb.
  He ought to study English.
- You can use *ought to* in negatives and questions, but it is more common to use *should*.
  They oughtn't to park there. (They shouldn't park there.)
  Ought we to do this exercise? (Should we do this exercise?)
- With *ought to*, remember to use *to* in short answers.
  Do you read English books? I ought to. NOT I ought.
- Use *should / shouldn't* or *ought to* when you want to give advice or to say that a thing is / isn't a good idea.
  There are black clouds. You ought to take an umbrella with you.
  You shouldn't smoke. It's bad for your health.

2 Write sentences with *should, shouldn't* or *ought to* using these expressions.

buy a new one | go to bed late | eat so much | buy new things so often | have something to eat | study more

1 **A** I'm so hungry.
  B You_____
2 **A** My laptop is so slow.
  B You_____
3 **A** Tom is putting on weight.
  B He_____
4 **A** I spend too much money on clothes.
  B You_____
5 **A** I'm scared about my English test.
  B You_____
6 **A** I can't get up in the mornings.
  B You_____

Modal form *needn't*

3 Study the rules. Then rewrite the sentences using *needn't*.

- *Needn't* is the negative form of the verb *need*. It is not used very much in American English.
- Use it to say a thing is not necessary. It often means the same as *don't have to*.

1 It isn't necessary for you to finish your homework tonight.
  You needn't finish your homework tonight.
2 We don't have to buy any drinks for the party.
3 It isn't necessary for your dad to drive us to the station.
4 They don't have to worry about the exam.
5 It isn't necessary for us to hurry because it's only four o'clock.
6 You don't have to bring your guitar tomorrow.

Articles

4 Match sentences a–k with rules 1–8.

a 3 Can you see me in *the morning*?
b ☐ Tom's dad is *a dentist*.
c ☐ *Love* is the most important thing.
d ☐ Rachel really loves *football*.
e ☐ *London* is my favourite city.
f ☐ He is learning to play *the guitar*.
g ☐ Have you been to *the USA*?
h ☐ *Italian* is my favourite language.
i ☐ *Cats* are popular pets.
j ☐ See you on *Tuesday*!
k ☐ *Internet addiction* is common.

- Use *the*
  [1]with the names of musical instruments.
  [2]with place names that contain the word *Republic*, *State* or *Union*.
  [3]with the words *morning, afternoon, evening*, (but not *night*).
- Use *a / an*
  [4]with jobs.
- Use no article
  [5]with languages, sports, colours, days of the week, months, seasons and years.
  [6]with abstract nouns.
  [7]with plural and uncountable nouns referring to things in general.
  [8]with institutions, place names, activities, school subjects and possessive adjectives.

5 Complete the sentences with *the, a/an* or - (for no article).

1 I often play _____ volleyball with my friends.
2 I hate _____ black.
3 He's practising _____ piano.
4 Daniel is allergic to _____ pollen.
5 The UK is a member of _____ European Union.
6 My sister wants to be _____ architect.
7 Can you come to my house in _____ morning?
8 I think _____ intelligence is less important than _____ good looks.
9 Please tidy up. Take these cups to _____ kitchen.
10 I think _____ Spanish is a beautiful language.
11 I go horse-riding on _____ Wednesdays.
12 My brother lives in _____ United States.
13 Bea's ill. We need _____ doctor.

6 ⇄ **Workbook pp 190-195; CD-ROM**

FILE

ASKING FOR DIRECTIONS

- Excuse me.
- Is there a... near here?
- Where's the...?
- Can you tell me where the... is?
- Can you tell me the way to the...?

GIVING DIRECTIONS

- Go left / right / straight on.
- Turn left / right.
- Take the first / second on the left / right.
- Go past... the traffic lights, etc.
- Go down / Cross Queen Street, etc.
- You can't miss it!
- It's on the corner of...

Vocabulary: places and prepositions

1 🔊 **Look at the map and match the words with the places. Then listen and check.**

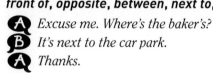

☐ post office	☐ town hall	☐ newsagent's
☐ police station	☐ car park	☐ baker's
☐ florist's	☐ greengrocer's	☐ butcher's
☐ chemist's	☐ stationer's	☐ sports centre
☐ fire station	☐ train station	☐ bus station
☐ library	☐ restaurant	☐ petrol station

2 **PAIRWORK Ask and answer questions about the map. Use *in front of*, *opposite*, *between*, *next to*, *near*, *behind*.**

Ⓐ *Excuse me. Where's the baker's?*
Ⓑ *It's next to the car park.*
Ⓐ *Thanks.*

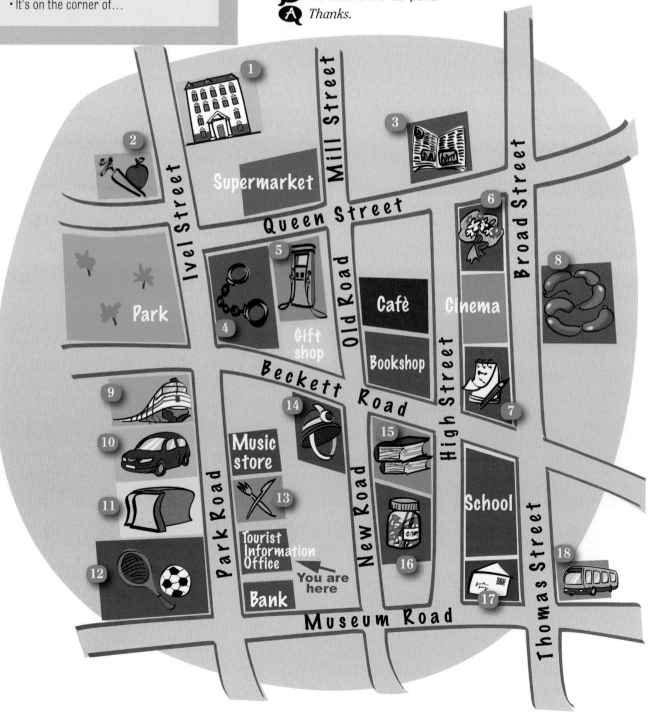

3 🔊47 **Match the pictures with the prepositions. Then listen and check.**

☐ across   ☐ over   ☒ towards
☐ out of   ☐ away from   ☐ along
☐ through   ☐ past   ☐ into

① ② ③

④ ⑤ ⑥

⑦ ⑧ ⑨

4a Look at the map on page 80. You are at the tourist information office. Complete the dialogues.

1 A Excuse me, can you tell me where the cinema is?
  B Yes, of course. Turn right, go ¹ _____ on, then take the first on the ² _____.
  A OK.
  B Go down this road and take the second on the left.
  A The second on the left?
  B That's right. Go along that road and it's on the right, ³ _____ the stationer's and the florist's. Is that clear?
  A Yes, thank you.

2 A Excuse me, can you tell me the ⁴ _____ to the post office?
  B The post office? Turn left, then ⁵ _____ the first on the left. ⁶ _____ down this road then take the second on the left. It's ⁷ _____ the corner, ⁸ _____ _____ the school. You can't miss it.
  A Thanks.

3 A Excuse me, is there a bus station ⁹ _____ here?
  B Yes … ¹⁰ _____ right then take the first on the right. ¹¹ _____ down this road and take the third on the right. The bus station's ¹² _____ the left, ¹³ _____ the post office. OK?
  A Yes, thank you very much.
  B Not at all.

4b 🔊48 **Listen and check.**

5 🔊49 **Visitors are asking directions at the Tourist Information Office. Look at the map, listen and write the name of the places.**

1 _____   3 _____
2 _____   4 _____

6 ROLE PLAY Work in pairs.
  • One student is at the Tourist Information Office, the other is a tourist.
  • Use the map to ask for and give directions. Use expressions from the *File*.
  • Swap roles.

  Ⓐ (Ask for directions to a place.)
  Excuse me. How do I get to the stationer's?
  Ⓑ (Give directions.)
  Turn right, go straight on…
  Ⓐ (Show that you are following.)
  I see… OK… Uh huh…

7a Read *Get into Culture* and do the task.

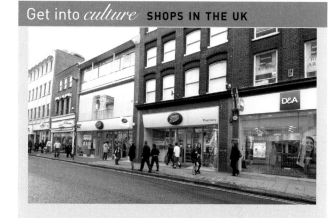

Get into *culture* SHOPS IN THE UK

In the UK many tourists notice that you see the same shops in all towns. In fact, British people often use a specific shop name. For example they say: *I'm going to HMV* rather than *I'm going to a music shop*. Here are some of the most common shops you see.

WHSmith (Smiths)   newspapers, magazines, stationery, books

HMV   music, computer games, DVDs, and videos

Boots, Superdrug   medicine, perfume, cosmetics, household goods

Tesco, Sainsbury's, Waitrose   supermarkets

Top Shop, Gap, Next, Primark   clothes shops

Waterstone's   book shop

• What are the most common shops in your country?
• Do you see the same shops in all towns in your country?

7b 🔊50 **Listen and repeat the names.**

8 ➡️ **LINKS Real communication pp 10–11**

AGE LIMITS

Listening

1a 🔊 **P Listen to Alesha and Justin researching age limits on the Internet. Complete the data file.**

Data file: UK Age limits	Age
get married with parents' consent	
join the army	
get a part-time job	
vote in an election	
learn to drive	
buy a lottery ticket	
change your name	
get a tattoo	

1b What about your country? Are the age limits the same?

Reading and speaking

2a Read the introduction to the text. What do these numbers refer to?

fifty-nine / thirty-one / eighteen / sixteen

2b Read the opinions in the text and decide if they are for or against voting at 16. Write F or A in the boxes.

2c What are the arguments for and against? Make notes.

For	Against
are aware of politics	aren't affected by
	politics

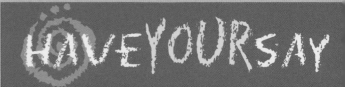

HAVE YOUR SAY

WEATHER	NEWS	LIVE-ON-AIR	HOME

SHOULD 16 YEAR OLDS BE ALLOWED TO VOTE?

In the UK a study showed that 59% of young people have little interest in politics and only 31% felt it was necessary to vote. Although 18 is the most common minimum voting age around the world, the UK is worried. They would like to get young people interested in politics. They think lowering the voting age to 16 would help.

What do our readers think? Here are some quotes from our debate room:

1 ☐ **DAMIEN:** As a 16 year old, I think that young people are as aware of politics as adults.

2 ☐ **MUTYA:** Most young people are still at school so they aren't affected by politics. They don't own a home, they don't pay bills, etc.

3 ☐ **SHANE:** The government allows 16 year olds to leave school, get a job and get married, so they should be allowed to vote.

SURVEY SERVICE FOR 'STUDIO ONE' LISTENERS

4 ☐ **JAY:** No way! Put the voting age up to 25. Teenagers just want to vote for girl or boy bands and DJs. Political voting is about more than The X Factor.

5 ☐ **MARTIN:** As a teacher, I say NO, NO, NO! Young people don't understand the realities of life.

6 ☐ **SEAN:** We are the future. Shouldn't we have a say in shaping it? Young people are interested in politics.

7 ☐ **JANINE:** Keep the voting age at 18, but raise the other limits such as driving, getting married and joining the army. They should all be at 18.

8 ☐ **SARAH:** 16 year olds must pay taxes, but they can't vote. It's not fair. And it's not democratic.

9 ☐ **MATT:** The age limit should remain the same. 18 is the right age. It is an age of independence, when you start working.

10 ☐ **IZZY:** I work with young people. They can lack self-confidence, but they have a knowledge of the outside world. And a lot of them have jobs. We have a lot to learn from them. They have fresh uncynical ideas. They ought to vote.

Pronunciation /ʊ/ /ɔ/

3a 🔊 52 **Listen and repeat.**

/ʊ/   should, good, put, book

/ɔ/   ought, short, four, sport

3b 🔊 53 **Listen and repeat.**

1   Sean's daughter ought to book her holiday.
2   Jordan should buy some shorts.
3   People should do sport.
4   You ought to shut that door!

Speaking

4   GROUPWORK Debate this proposal: *Young people in this country should vote at 16.*

1   Divide your group into two sides: *For* and *Against*.
2   Each side makes notes of all the reasons.
3   Debate the statement for at least three minutes. Use expressions from *Skills for life*.

Skills FOR life   HOW TO DEBATE

• Take turns to speak in favour or against the proposal. Give reasons for your opinions.
  I agree with the proposal. Young people ought to be allowed to vote at 16 because…
  I disagree with the proposal. Young people shouldn't be allowed to vote at 16 because…
  I think that…
  I don't think that…
  In my opinion, …
• Vote on the proposal. Has the debate changed anyone's opinion?

Writing

5   P T What do you think? Write a chat room contribution on the following proposals.

Young people should be allowed to…
• learn to drive at 15
• go hunting at 14
• leave school at 18
• get married at 14
• have tattoos at 12

I think / don't think young people should…
They ought to…
In my opinion, they…

6 🔊 54 **LINKS Go to page 63 and listen to** *Three Little Birds.*

FILE

DESCRIBING A PICTURE

Describing what you see in a picture is very good language practice. It makes you flexible and able to deal with conversation topics. You need good vocabulary and the correct grammatical structures. You also talk in the exam about the theme of the photos, e.g. holidays, reading, work, etc.

Towards PET Paper 3 Speaking, Parts 3 and 4

Tips

1 Start with a summary. *The picture shows / is an outdoor scene / is a view of...*
2 Then give general information. *It looks like a hot summer's day..., There are about six people doing...*
3 Finally, describe the picture in detail. *Two people are talking and a woman is drinking a cup of coffee...*

Useful language

- *There is / are. There are two cars in the picture.*
- Present continuous. *A woman is sitting in the...*
- Prepositions. *There's a hill behind the village.*
- Descriptive adjectives. *It's a nice, big house.*
- Speculation. *Maybe... / Perhaps... / I think...*
- Verbs *look* and *look like. The people look happy. It looks like the Caribbean.*
- Position, e.g. *on the left, on the right, in the background, in the foreground*
- General description. *We can see...*

1 PAIRWORK Look at the photos with your partner. Make notes under these headings:

Opening summary
General / background information
Details

2a P PAIRWORK Each student describes one of the pictures to the other one.

2b Give feedback to your partner on his or her description. Then swap pictures and try again.

3 P PAIRWORK Discuss the questions.

What types of things can you find on the Internet and in bookshops? What are the differences between reading a book and reading on the Internet? What are the advantages and the disadvantages of the two ways of getting information?

4 T Write up your description.

5 **LINKS Exam listening p11**

FILE

UNDERSTANDING FACTUAL INFORMATION

We often have to read information about products in order to buy the correct one. It is important to be able to read something and find factual information. In this activity, you have to read descriptions of some people, and match them with appropriate goods, books, holidays, etc.

Towards PET Paper 1 Reading, Part 2

Tips

- Read the information about the people carefully. Underline essential information.
- Read about the CDs and do the easiest matches.
- Then read both sets of texts again to check your matches.
- Finally, use all the information to make your final decisions.
- Be careful of 'false matches'. They are there to check you are reading the information carefully.
- Just because you see the same key words in two texts doesn't mean that they match.
- In the exam there are five descriptions of people and eight texts, so there are always three that don't match.

1 **P** **Debbie wants to buy some Christmas presents. Read about her friends and family. Decide which CD would be most suitable for each person. Write the letter in the box.**

1 ☐ Callum is 17 years old. He reads all the music magazines and always has an mp3 player plugged into his ear. He likes listening to all kinds of new music but he doesn't like rap.

2 ☐ Lee is 16 years old. He wears gangsta clothes: baggy trousers and a beanie hat. He's cool, man. His favourite singers are Kanye West and 50 Cent. He hates dance.

3 ☐ Kelly is 20 years old. She cares a lot about green issues and she is a member of Friends of the Earth. She doesn't listen to much chart music but she has got a big collection of music from different cultures.

4 ☐ Tara is 15 years old. She spends her weekends with her friends. On Saturday night they all watch a music talent competition on TV together. They get really excited about the competitors and they vote for their favourites.

5 ☐ Tim is 45 years old. He's got a son of 15. Tim thinks he's so cool, but his son doesn't agree. Tim likes all the old rock bands and doesn't even know the difference between dance and hip hop.

Best buys for Xmas

A Classics from the rock world. Police, Rod Stewart, Rolling Stones, The Who. All the great rock classics you remember rocking to!

B Do you want Saturday night to last for ever? Tune in to the best of techno from Manchester's *Squelch* DJs.

C A compilation of tracks from the best new bands and singers including The Killers, Stereophonics and The Script. This great album features newcomers and songs from the indie, dance and rock world.

D Top names in the world music scene from Africa, South America and Australasia come together in a musical celebration of cultural diversity. A must-have for all lovers of world music. AND 10% from every sale goes towards the protection of the world's rainforests.

E All the best dance hits from the charts. Two CD set with all the latest tunes to get you on your feet!

F Are you one of the 8 million who wouldn't miss an episode of *The X Factor* for anything? Relive the dreams of some of your favourite performers.

G Classic love songs from the world's favourite singers including Frank Sinatra and Dean Martin.

H Get the beat from the street. Rap classics all on one album. So put on your Gangsta gear and get rapping.

LANGUAGE CHECK

1 Choose the correct words.

1 You ___ eat more vegetables. They're good for you.
   a) ought   b) should   c) allowed   d) need
2 We ___ eat in the classroom. It's a school rule.
   a) don't have to   c) needn't
   b) aren't allowed to   d) oughtn't
3 Visitors ___ take their shoes off at the entrance.
   a) must   b) have   c) allow   d) ought
4 Passengers ___ smoke on the plane. It's forbidden.
   a) needn't   c) don't have to
   b) shouldn't   d) mustn't
5 Do you ___ to go to bed early on school nights?
   a) ought   b) should   c) must   d) have

2 Write *a, an, the* or – *(no article)*.

1 Can you play ___ basketball?
2 He usually has a shower in ___ morning.
3 Ben Affleck is ___ excellent actor.
4 I'm learning to play ___ piano.
5 Most countries in ___ European Union use the euro.

TOTAL: ____/10

3 Complete the table with the shops.

Item	Shop
bread	1 _____
meat	2 _____
newspaper	3 _____
medicine	4 _____
paper and pens	5 _____

4 Find the parts of a computer.

1 suoem   m_____
2 bdroyake   k_____
3 ritoonm   m_____
4 rrnetpi   p_____
5 necsre   s_____

TOTAL: ____/10

5 Follow the instructions in brackets and complete the dialogue.

A I'm hungry. [1] *[Make a suggestion]*
  Shall we go to the shops and get some food?
B Yes, [2]*[Reply]* _____.
  I'd like some chocolate.
A [3]*[Agree]* _____.
  Where can we get some?
B I think they sell chocolate in the newsagent's, or [4]*[Make a suggestion]*
  _____ cycle to the supermarket?
A [5]*[Express preference]*
  _____ cycle to the supermarket. [6]*[Ask for an opinion]*
  _____?
B Yeah, let's do that.

6 Circle the correct words.

A Excuse me! Can you tell me the [1]*road / way* to the sports centre, please?
B Yes, it's easy to get to from here. [2]*Take / Turn* the first right and go [3]*straight / across* on. Go [4]*past / over* a big hotel on your left and it's on the [5]*turning / corner*. You can't miss it.

TOTAL: ____/10

7 Write a paragraph about the rules for Internet safety. You can include:

• personal information
• passwords
• public/private areas in chatrooms
• online bullying
• meeting new online friends

TOTAL: ____/10

TOTAL: ____/40

 LINKS Interculture pp 26-29; CLIL (Civic Studies) pp 52-53

A2 Key objectives

Grammar past simple; past time expressions; modal verb *could*; *was / were able to*; *had to*

Functions talking about the past; describing people; talking about obligation; telling a story

Vocabulary jobs; physical appearance; personality; adventure

Get started

1 CD3 2 **Match the jobs with the pictures. Then listen and check.**

☐ actor / actress   ☐ mechanic

☐ dentist   ☐ film director

☐ artist   ☐ butcher

☐ lorry driver   ☐ pharmacist

☐ waiter / waitress   ☐ singer

☐ businessman / woman   ☐ bank clerk

☐ psychologist   ☐ farmer

☐ flight attendant

☐ cashier

☐ surveyor

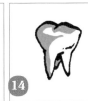

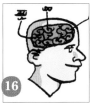

---

x

CAREER CORNER

What career would be right for you? Well first things first! What skills and qualities do you need in different jobs? Perhaps you have to...

be good with people	be organised
be fit and strong	be musical
speak a foreign language	
be physically strong	be patient
be good at maths	be creative
be practical	be good with animals
understand people	
be good at managing people	
be good at IT	have a good voice
look smart	be a good teamworker
be a good problem-solver	
have a good memory	
be good at drawing	

Knowing your skills and qualities can help you find the right career.

2a **PAIRWORK** Read Career Corner. Say what skills and qualities you need for three of the jobs above.

🗨 *A flight attendant has to be good with people, practical and...*

2b **PAIRWORK** Ask and answer about the skills and qualities in Career Corner. Think of an ideal job for your partner. See page 18 for more jobs.

🅐 *Can you speak a foreign language?*
🅑 *Yes, and I'm creative.*
🅐 *I think you should be a...*

3 **GAME** Work in groups. Play *What's my line?* Choose a job. Mime an activity to your group. The group can ask ten questions.

🅐 *Do you have to work in an office?*
🅑 *No, I don't.*
🅐 *Do you have to be good with animals?*
🅑 *Yes, I do.*
🅐 *Are you a farmer?*

Unit 9

Life's like that

Unit objectives

Grammar past simple of *be*; past simple regular; past time expressions

Functions talking about the past; describing people

Vocabulary physical appearance; personality

Warm up

1 PAIRWORK Discuss the questions.

- Your friend promises to do something, but doesn't do it. How do you feel? What do you say?
- You promise to do something for a friend, but you don't want to do it. What excuse do you make?

Comprehension

2a 🔊 **Listen and read *Who's that girl*? Circle T (True), F (False) or DS (Doesn't say).**

1 Charlie and Jack are talking about the gig. T / F / DS
2 Charlie enjoys babysitting his little brother. T / F / DS
3 Rose wasn't at the gig. T / F / DS
4 Jack is a good singer. T / F / DS
5 Mia is angry with Rose. T / F / DS
6 Rose's accident was in the park. T / F / DS

2b PAIRWORK Can you remember the story so far? Number the events in the correct order and add details.

☐ They all go to a concert at the Zodiac.
☐ They're really excited!
☐ Rose comes to a rehearsal and she has a great voice.
☐ He likes their music and offers them a gig.
☐ Rose misses the gig and Jack has to sing.
☐ Charlie, Jack and Mia make a new friend called Rose.
☐ Rose and Mia are nearly late and have to run.
☐ The band plays for the manager of the Zodiac.
☐ Mia and Jack invite Rose to sing in their band.

Talking about the past

3 Study the sentences and do the task.

> **Past simple of *be***
>
> *I was at home.*
> *Rose wasn't at the gig.*
> *The other bands were good.*
> *Were you good?*
>
> **Complete the rules with *questions, was (not)* or *were (not)*.**
>
> - To form the past simple of *be* use _____ with *I/he/she/it* and _____ with *we/you/they*.
> - Invert the order of the words to form _____ with the past simple of *be*.

4 Find more examples of the past simple of *be* in the dialogue.

5 Complete the sentences with the correct form of *be*.

1 In 1990, my sister ___was___ twelve.
2 He _____ happy last night. He was very sad.
3 When _____ your friends in Madrid?
4 You _____ really nice yesterday.
5 This morning we _____ very hungry.
6 I _____ on the Internet for five hours!

6 Write questions and short answers.

1 I was very tired last night.
   Were you very tired last night? Yes, I was.
2 Vishak and Yasmin weren't hungry.
   Were Vishak and Yasmin hungry? No, they weren't.
3 Debbie wasn't at school this morning.
4 They were my best friends last year.
5 He wasn't angry yesterday.
6 Frank Sinatra was American.
7 I wasn't there.
8 We were out last night.

7 P T PAIRWORK Ask and answer the questions.

Where were you last weekend?

Where were you last night?

Where were you on Sunday morning?

Where were you last summer?

Where was your best friend at the weekend?

Where was your best friend yesterday?

Who was your favourite singer when you were 11?

What was your favourite food when you were 8?

What was your favourite game when you were young?

Who's that girl?
Episode 7

It's the morning after the gig. Jack meets Charlie at school.

JACK Hi, Charlie. Are you OK?

CHARLIE Yeah, not bad. But I'm sorry I wasn't at the Zodiac last night. I was at home with my little brother. Babysitting. He was such a pain. But tell me, how was the gig?

JACK There were loads of people in the audience. And the other bands were OK.

CHARLIE But what about your band? Were you good? And how was Rose? Was she brilliant?

JACK Rose wasn't at the gig.

CHARLIE What?

JACK She was at home.

CHARLIE Who was the singer? Was it Mia?

JACK No, it wasn't. It was me.

CHARLIE But you can't sing, man!

JACK Thanks, Charlie. I know.

CHARLIE What was wrong with Rose?

JACK There was an accident or something.

CHARLIE An accident?

JACK Yeah. In the park. You can guess the reason.

CHARLIE Running?

JACK That's right. She never thinks about the band first! She only thinks about her stupid running. So she was in bed last night with a bad leg while we were on stage. I'm really fed up with her. She's bad news.

CHARLIE But you really like her, Jack.

JACK Not now. She's history!

REAL TALK ... such a pain.   ... or something.   fed up   She's bad news.   She's history.

8 Read the email and complete the sentences with the correct word.

1 Rose's email is to _____.
2 She supports a _____ called Wateraid.
3 The charity helps people in the _____ world.
4 Rose is organising a _____ to raise money for charity.
5 She advertised the marathon on the _____.
6 She can't walk now because of an _____.

9 Study the sentences and do the tasks.

Past simple regular: positive

I discovered Wateraid.

Lots of people emailed me.

Complete the rule.

• Add _____ to the end of the verb to make the past simple of regular verbs.

Past simple regular: questions and negatives

I didn't explain things properly.

Did Jack perform the songs OK?
Yes, he did. / No, he didn't.

What did Rose organise?

Complete the rules with *No, did* or *did not (didn't).*

• Use _____ + subject + the base form of the verb for questions.
• Use subject + _____ + the base form of verb for negative sentences.
• Use *Yes/*_____ + subject + *did (not)* for short answers.

10 Answer the questions with short answers.

1 Did Charlie phone Rose yesterday?
2 Did Rose explain things properly on the phone?
3 Did Rose discover Wateraid last month?
4 Did Rose talk to students in America?
5 Did a lot of people see the advertisement on the Net?
6 Did they phone Rose?

11 Complete the sentences with the past simple of the verbs in brackets.

1 I _played_ tennis with Rachel yesterday. (play)
2 Sara's brother _____ what happened. (explain)
3 John _____ his driving test four times. (fail)
4 We _____ the film. We were too tired. (not watch)
5 Yesterday I _____ my dad with his work. (help)
6 The train _____ on time. (not arrive)
7 I _____ the gig last night. (enjoy)
8 My parents _____ yesterday. (not work)

| weekly timetable | mail.mailbox.com | liveblog | news-sport |

Sorry RETURN TO INBOX

☀ To Charlie **from Rose**   SEE DETAILS TODAY 12:45 REPLY

Hi Charlie

Thanks for your phone call yesterday. I'm sorry I was so upset. I didn't explain things properly. I know I messed up their gig last night. I'm so, so sorry. Did Jack perform the songs OK? What did Mia say to you?

The thing is, I discovered Wateraid last year. It's a charity that helps people in the developing world. Then I talked to students in Africa and learned all about their problems. I wanted to help them. I wanted to change things.

Two months ago, I started to organise a marathon. I wanted to raise money for the charity. I trained every day and worked really hard. I advertised the marathon on the Net. Lots of people emailed me and volunteered. I was very excited. The marathon is in two weeks! And then this accident! I can't walk now. I can't even stand up! So the gig was impossible. It's a disaster!

Can you say sorry to them for me? Please? I really care about them.

love
Rose

REAL TALK I'm so, so sorry. The thing is... messed up It's a disaster!

12 P T PAIRWORK Ask and answer questions.

Did you enjoy last weekend?

Did you watch TV last weekend?

Did you talk on the phone yesterday?

Did you text your friends last night?

Did you play a game last weekend?

Get the grammar

Past simple of *be*

1 Complete the table with *was, wasn't, were* or *weren't*.

Positive	Negative	Questions
I was	I wasn't	Was I?
You were	You _____	_____ you?
He/She/It _____	He/She/It _____	_____ he/she/it?
We/They were	We/They weren't	Were we/they?

Short answers: positive	Short answers: negative
Yes, I/he/she/it was.	No, I/he/she/it _____.
Yes, we/you/they _____.	No, we/you/they weren't.

2 Complete the sentences with the correct forms of the verb *be*.

1 **A** Who _____ J.F. Kennedy?
  B He _____ an American president.
2 **A** What _____ the film like?
  B It _____ very good. (not)
3 **A** _____ you at school yesterday?
  B No, I _____. I _____ ill.
4 **A** Where _____ you yesterday?
  B We _____ on the beach.

3 Write *Yes/No* questions and short answers.

1 Madonna was born in 1955. ☒
  Was Madonna born in 1955? No, she wasn't.
2 Carlos wasn't happy this morning. ☑
3 Your friends were not at the party. ☑
4 It wasn't cold yesterday. ☒
5 Her birthday was in May. ☑
6 Victoria's email wasn't very friendly. ☒

Past simple regular

4 Complete the table with *did* or *didn't*.

Positive	Negative
I/You/He/She helped Adam.	I/You/He/She didn't help.
It rained.	It _____ rain.
We/They stopped.	We/They _____ stop.

Questions	
Did I/you/he/she help?	Why did Rose stay home?
_____ it rain?	Where _____ the train stop?
_____ we/they stop?	When did they phone?

Short answers: positive	Short answers: negative
Yes, I/you/he/she/it/we/ did.	No, I/you/he/she/it/we/ they they didn't.

- Use the past simple to talk about actions that began and ended in the past.
- The past simple of regular verbs ends in _____.
- Use the same form for all persons.

Spelling: past simple

5 Study the rules.

- If the base form of a verb ends in -*e*, add -*d*:
  notice – noticed
- If the verb ends in a consonant + -*y*, change the -*y* to -*i* and add –*ed*:
  study – studied
- If a short verb ends in a single vowel + a single consonant, double the final consonant and add -*ed*:
  stop – stopped

For pronunciation see page 95.

6 Complete the sentences with the past simple form of the verb in brackets.

1 **A** _____ Megan _____ her mother? (help)
  B Yes, she did.
2 Kevin and Lauren _____ for their English test. (study)
3 We _____ to school today. (walk)
4 I _____ to the teacher. (not listen)
5 The car _____ at the traffic lights. (not stop)
6 Nick _____ hard last week. (work)
7 You _____ my email. (not answer)
8 When _____ your grandparents _____ house? (move)

Past time expressions

7 Study the rule.

- Use past time expressions at the beginning or at the end of sentences.
  Last weekend I watched a good film.
  I wasn't at home yesterday.

8 Put the expressions in time order.

last week | in 2001 | a week ago | two hours ago | last night | last year | five days ago | yesterday | this morning | last Saturday | last month | 20 years ago | an hour ago | yesterday morning

an hour ago, two hours ago…

9 Complete the sentences so that they are true for you.

1 During my holidays last year I was …
2 As a child I often played …
3 Two years ago I attended …
4 Last week I helped …
5 Some days ago I watched …
6 Last weekend I wanted to …
7 Last week I played …
8 Last night I talked to …

10 ↯ **Workbook pp 196-201; CD-ROM**

FILE

ASKING ABOUT A PERSON
• What's he / she like?

DESCRIBING MOOD
• I'm feeling sad.

DESCRIBING APPEARANCE
• He's tall.
• He's got red hair.
• She's got blue eyes.
• He's got a moustache.
• She wears glasses.

USING MODIFIERS
• She's quite short.
• He's very thin.
• They aren't very nice.

DESCRIBING PERSONALITY
• I'm quite hard-working.
• I'm a bit selfish.
• I can be generous.
• I tend to be quite friendly.

Anthony   Jessica   James   Tom   Ellie   Lucy

Vocabulary: physical appearance

1 🔊 **Look at the pictures and complete the descriptions with the names. Then listen and check.**

1 _____ is very tall and very well built.
2 _____ is short and plump.
3 _____ is tall and slim.
4 _____ is tall and extremely thin.
5 _____ is quite short and slim.
6 _____ is neither tall nor short, he's average build.

2 🔊 **Now look at their faces and complete the descriptions with the names and pronouns. Then listen and check.**

1 _____ has got long blonde hair, a round face, small nose and blue eyes. _____ wears her hair loose.
2 _____ is bald with a long face and brown eyes. _____ has got a moustache.
3 _____ has got short wavy brown hair and a beard. _____ has got a thin face with green eyes and an eyebrow piercing.
4 _____ has got medium-length wavy red hair, a chubby face, and a pierced ear. _____ is clean-shaven and wears glasses.
5 _____ has got dreadlocks. _____ has got greeny-blue eyes, and a small nose.
6 _____ has got pierced ears, curly black hair, and a stud in her lip. _____ wears her dreadlocks tied back.

3 Look at the categories. Make lists of useful words for describing people.

- face
- hair colour, length & shape, style
- eyes
- ornaments
- height
- build

Hair is an uncountable noun (always singular). *Moustache* is always singular. *Glasses* is always plural.

4 GAME Write a description of yourself. Don't write your name. Use the *File* and the words above to help you. Stick the descriptions on the board and number them. Can the class guess who is who?

Identifying people

5 ⑥ P Megan and Abigail are describing their boyfriends, Zachary and Nicholas. Listen, look at the picture and identify them.

☐ Zachary   ☐ Nicholas

6 PAIRWORK Student A describes a family friend. Student B asks questions. Then he / she describes the person back to Student A. Has he / she got a good memory?

 My friend is slim.
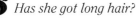 *Has she got long hair?*
Ⓐ *No, not really. It's quite short.*

Vocabulary: personality

7a Look at the adjectives and check that you understand them.

patient | unselfish | friendly | thoughtful | generous | outgoing | hard-working | reliable | funny | imaginative | loyal | sensitive | sincere | decisive

Word **expander**   OPPOSITES

When you learn new adjectives and verbs, learn their opposites. This helps you build up your vocabulary. They are often formed with prefixes (*dis*, *im*, *in*, *un*, etc.) or suffixes (*less*, *ful*, etc.).

7b Match these words with their opposites in exercise 7a.

disloyal | impatient | indecisive | insensitive | insincere | lazy | mean | selfish | serious | shy | thoughtless | unfriendly | unimaginative | unreliable

8 T Write a description of yourself. Divide it into these paragraphs. Use the *File* to help you.

- Physical appearance
- Personality
- Present mood

9 Read *Get into Culture* and do the task.

Get into *culture*   BODY DECORATION

Many cultures decorate the body, and many British teenagers want to have tattoos or piercings. The most popular piercings are of the ears, nose, eyebrow, tongue and navel. Parents are often not very happy about these body decorations. There is no national age limit for body piercing, but some parts of London have rules, e.g. parental consent under the age of 16. But it can be painful – it is illegal in the UK to give an anaesthetic for a piercing! And in the UK it is illegal to give a tattoo to a teenager under the age of 18.

- **Do teenagers have tattoos or piercings in your country?**
- **What do your parents think about it?**

10 LINKS Real communication pp 12-13

Reading

1 PAIRWORK Look at the pictures. What are the people doing? Why?

2 Read the article and choose the best heading for each paragraph.

a ☐ What is flash mobbing?   c ☐ Flash mobbing today

b ☐ The history of flash mobbing   d ☐ A strange day in London

todaysnews@thebelfaststudent.news.ac

Flash mob craze

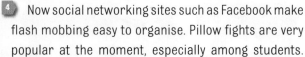

It's so cool! It's a form of art.

1 On February 18th 2008, London's Trafalgar Square was full of tourists and passers-by as usual. But at exactly 3.30 pm 1,000 people stopped moving – while taking a photo, drinking, talking on the phone, even kissing! Just like with a video freeze button. And then after five minutes they all started moving again.

2 From Rome to London, New York to Tokyo, flash mobbing is a new craze. It is a sudden gathering of people at the same place, at the same time. They all do the same strange activity and then quickly go away again. They get their information from Internet message boards, blogs, text messages and emails.

It's peaceful. You get to chill out. Enjoy the moment!

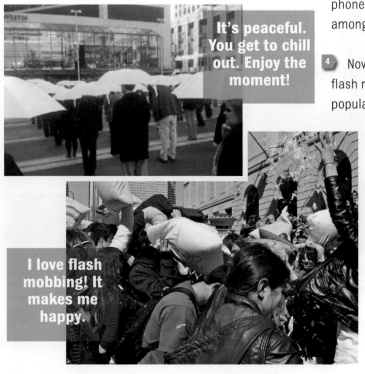

I love flash mobbing! It makes me happy.

3 It all started in 2003. On June 17th in New York, 150 people gathered around an expensive rug in a shop. They all wanted to buy it! But after ten minutes they all disappeared again. That was the first flash mob ever. In August of that year, in a street in Berlin, a group of people all shouted together 'yes, yes!' into their mobile phones. And in September, flash mobbers danced among commuters at a busy station in London.

4 Now social networking sites such as Facebook make flash mobbing easy to organise. Pillow fights are very popular at the moment, especially among students. There was a Worldwide Pillowfight Day on March 22nd 2008 in over 25 cities. About 5,000 people were in the New York event! In the summer of 2009 when Michael Jackson died, there were dance flash mobbing events all over the world. On July 8th at 5.30pm, in the middle of Central Station Stockholm, 300 people suddenly danced to the music of *Beat it!* Commuters were very surprised!

But why do people do it? There is no point to flash mobbing. It isn't political or commercial – flash mobbing is just fun.

3 **Read the article again and answer the questions. Choose the correct answer (a, b, c or d).**

1 Where was the first flash mob?

a London.   b Rome.   c Tokyo.   d New York.

2 What did flash mobbers do in London in September 2003?

a Stopped moving.   c Had a pillowfight.

b Danced.   d Shouted into their mobile phones.

3 How many flash mobbers were there in the New York pillowfight?

a 25,000.   b 1,000.   c 150.   d 5,000.

4 How are flash mobs organised?

a On social networking sites.   c On TV.

b By an office in New York.   d On the radio.

5 Why do people do flash mobbing?

a For political reasons.   c To enjoy themselves.

b Because it's clever.   d For commercial reasons.

4 **Make notes about each event.**

· Date + Time: February 18th 2008, 3.30 pm

· Where: Trafalgar Square, London

· How many: 1,000 people

· Event: stopped moving for 5 minutes

Listening

5a 🎧 **Read the information in the messages below. Then listen and complete the notes.**

5b P **Compare your answers with your partner. Then listen again and check.**

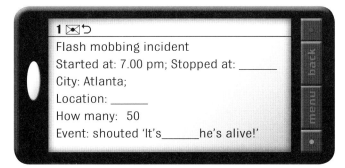

1 ✉↺

Flash mobbing incident
Started at: 7.00 pm; Stopped at: _____
City: Atlanta;
Location: _____
How many: 50
Event: shouted 'It's_____he's alive!'

back

menu

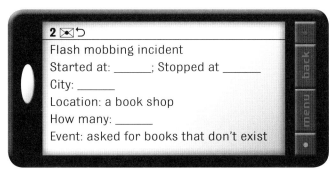

2 ✉↺

Flash mobbing incident
Started at: _____; Stopped at _____
City: _____
Location: a book shop
How many: _____
Event: asked for books that don't exist

back

menu

Pronunciation   /d/, /t/, /ɪd/

6a 🔊 **Study the rule. Then listen and repeat the words in the table.**

The final -ed of the past simple has three different pronunciations.

/t/ after /k/, /f/, /p/, /s/, /sh/, /tch/

/ɪd/ after /t/, /d/

/d/ after all the other sounds

/t/	/d/	/ɪd/
worked	listened	waited
watched	studied	decided
finished	played	visited

6b 🔊 **Complete the table above with these words. Then listen and check.**

talked | started | looked | washed | shouted | carried | lived | stopped | gathered | posted | divided | arrived | danced | asked

Speaking

7 **PAIRWORK Tell your partner about the incidents in exercise 5. You can add extra information.**

There was a flash mobbing incident in Atlanta yesterday. It was really funny. There were about 50 people....

Writing

8 P T **PAIRWORK Invent a flash mobbing incident. Then write a short newspaper article.**

Skills FOR life   PLANNING

When you write, you need to plan your work. Make rough notes: It will help you think of useful words and expressions and organise your ideas.

In exercise 8 make notes about:
• place
• time
• number of people
• what happened, etc.

Organise your article into paragraphs:
• Paragraph 1 When and where
• Paragraph 2 What happened and how long it lasted

RANDOM **Fact** *The average number of friends people have on Facebook is 120. But they only regularly contact eight of them!*

Unit objectives

Grammar past simple irregular; modal verb *could*; *was / were able to; had to, didn't have / need to*
Function talking about the past; obligation; telling a story
Vocabulary adventure; accidents

Warm up

1 **PAIRWORK Discuss the questions.**

- What skills and qualities does an explorer need?
- Do you know about any famous explorers?
- Would you like to be an explorer?

Comprehension

2 🔟 **Listen and read. Answer the questions.**

1 How far was the journey to the North Pole?
2 Why did Camilla go on the expedition?
3 How did she improve her strength for the expedition?
4 When did Camilla's back hurt?
5 What kind of food did they eat?
6 Why couldn't they rest at the end of the day?
7 What effect did the trip have on Camilla and her father?
8 What did Camilla fall in love with?

Talking about the past

3 **Study the sentences and do the tasks.**

Past simple irregular

Why did she go on the adventure?
Her back hurt, but she didn't give up.
She fell in love with the Arctic.

Look at the examples and complete the rules with *did* or *didn't*.

- Irregular verbs each have a special form for the past simple positive.
- Use _____ + subject + the base form for questions.
  NOT ~~Why did she went on the adventure?~~
- Use subject + _____ + the base form for negative sentences.
  NOT ~~She didn't gave up.~~

Circle the correct words to complete the rule.

- Irregular and regular verbs form questions and negative sentences in *the same way / a different way*.

Modal verb *could*

- Use *could* to talk about abilities in the past.
  She could develop her strength.
- Use *could* to describe a general possibility in the past.
  They could fall through the ice.
- Use *was(n't) / were(n't) able to* when somebody did / didn't do something difficult.
  At the end of the day they weren't able to rest because...

4 **Find and underline the positive form of these irregular verbs in the article.**

go | wear | hurt | know | eat | bring | fall

5 **Write the irregular past forms of these verbs.**

come | say | speak | spend | see | drive | fall | hear | meet | buy | find | get | run | have | hit | break

6 **Complete the sentences with the past simple form of the verbs in brackets.**

1 John _went_ to my class. (go)
2 She _____ three hours on the Internet this morning. (spend)
3 We _____ more than 600 kilometres yesterday. (not drive)
4 They _____ a lot of money last year. (lose)
5 She _____ her friends yesterday. (not meet)
6 I _____ to him last Friday. (speak)

7 **ROLEPLAY Work in pairs.**

- Go to LINKS page 61.
- Choose A or B.

Vocabulary: adventure

8 **Put these words from the article into the correct category.**

sledge | freezing | cold | tent | trek | attack | risk | expedition

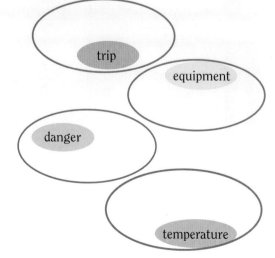

trip

equipment

danger

temperature

TEENAGER BREAKS NORTH POLE RECORD!

Do you enjoy a challenge? Could you survive in freezing conditions? Would you like to help the environment? For 15 year old Camilla Hempleman-Adams the answer was 'yes, yes, yes!'.

On 16th April 2008, she became the youngest British woman to ski to the North Pole.

What was the expedition and why did she go on it?

The expedition was an 80-mile trek to the North Pole in temperatures of between -40°C and -60°C. Camilla went on the trip with her father, the well-known adventurer David Hempleman-Adams, and a team of 11 others because she wanted to draw attention to climate change and the melting of the polar ice caps. They travelled on skis, pulling heavy sledges with their food and equipment.

How did she prepare for the adventure?

She pulled heavy sledges around a field every day, and she wore her big boots and Arctic wind suit. In that way she could develop her strength and prepare for the experience.

What were the worst things about the expedition?

It was very cold and her back hurt when she pulled the sledge, but she didn't give up. They couldn't ski easily on the rough uneven ice. They knew that there was a constant danger that they could fall through the ice into the freezing sea water or that polar bears could attack them. At the end of the day, they weren't able to rest because they had to put up the tents and make food. The dried food was disgusting and she only ate it because she needed the energy.

What were the best things about it?

There were lots of good things! It was a life-changing experience and it brought Camilla and her father very close. Camilla also fell in love with the beauty of the Arctic landscape and wants to return one day.

Talking about obligation (present and past)

9 🎧 **P Complete the article with these words. Then listen and check your answers.**

TEXT 1   boat | qualifications | wear | dead | awake | storms | dangerous | temperatures

TEXT 2   drivers | bike | practical | use | dangerous | exam | hours | letters

IT'S A TOUGH JOB!

**THIS WEEK WE SPEAK TO TWO PEOPLE ABOUT THEIR JOBS.
WHAT HAVE THEY GOT IN COMMON?
WELL THEY BOTH DO VERY DANGEROUS JOBS!**

1

I'm an Alaskan deep sea fisherwoman – it's a very dangerous job. OK, so I didn't need to get any ¹_____ and I didn't have to go to university, but I certainly had to learn a lot of skills. Our boat has very ²_____ machinery and we have to be very careful.

We also have to be very strong. We fish in the winter and there are subzero ³_____ and ten-metre-high waves! Sometimes we have to stay ⁴_____ for 20 hours! And we have to work during terrible ⁵_____.

Drowning is a real risk. So of course we have to ⁶_____ life jackets. Once I fell overboard and I had to swim back to the ⁷_____. I nearly died of cold. Without that life jacket I would be ⁸_____. Are you asking why I do it? Well, when the catch is good I get excellent pay.

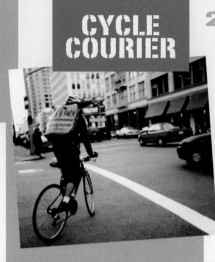

CYCLE COURIER

DEEP SEA FISHERWOMAN

2

I'm a cycle courier in London. I have to deliver urgent ⁹_____ and parcels. You have to be super-fit to cycle for ¹⁰_____ a day and you have to be able to cycle very fast.

I had to buy a good ¹¹_____, a bike lock, a bag, a helmet and waterproof clothes. I didn't need to ¹²_____ my mobile phone – the company gave me a two-way radio. I had to study the streets of London too! Yes, I actually had to do a written ¹³_____ during my job interview!

The things I don't like? Well... I had to learn how to change a tyre... and I'm not ¹⁴_____. And I absolutely hate the cold and wet.

You know, being a courier is a ¹⁵_____ job – you have to ride on busy roads, and ¹⁶_____ in London are crazy! But at the end of the day I'm tired but happy.

---

10 Read the article again and circle the correct answers.

1 *Deep sea fisherwomen / Cycle couriers* have to be very strong.

2 Deep sea fisherwomen don't have to *learn a lot of skills / go to university*.

3 Deep sea fisherwomen have to be careful because of the dangerous *machinery / drivers*.

4 The deep sea fisherwoman once had to swim back to the *beach / boat*.

5 Cycle couriers have to deliver letters and *parcels / presents*.

6 The cycle courier had to buy a *mobile phone / bike*.

7 The cycle courier *had to / didn't have to* take an exam.

8 Cycle couriers have to ride on *quiet / busy* roads.

11 Study the sentences and do the task. Then underline the sentences in the article with *had to* and *didn't have / need to*.

> *had to, didn't have / need to*
>
> I *didn't need to* get any qualifications.
> I *had to* learn a lot of skills.
>
> **Complete the rules with *had to* and *didn't have / need to*.**
>
> • Use _____ to say that it was necessary or important to do something.
>
> • Use _____ to say that it was not necessary to do something.

12 PAIRWORK Imagine you did a job last year. Choose from: shop assistant, waiter, babysitter. Say what you had to / didn't have to do.

Get the grammar

Past simple: verb formation

1 Complete the table. Use the list of irregular verbs on page 247 to help you.

Regular verbs		Irregular verbs	
want	wanted	drive	
start		go	
prepare		lose	
pull		find	
stop		eat	
travel		hurt	
train		give	
select		make	
test		do	
need		put	
complete		know	
marry		choose	
copy		forget	

Past simple irregular

2 Study the sentences then circle the correct words to complete the rules.

My mother drove to work this morning.
It took them a long time to reach the North Pole.
During the journey, they ate dried food.

- When you form the past simple of irregular verbs, you use *the same form / a different form* for each person.
We didn't see him yesterday.
Did you eat alone? Yes, I did./No, I didn't.

- The negative and question forms and short answers in the past simple of irregular verbs are formed in *the same way as / a different way from* those of regular verbs.

3 Write questions and answers in the past simple.

1 you / meet / Jo / last week (☒ / two weeks ago)
Did you meet Jo last week?
No, I didn't. I met her two weeks ago.
2 they / drink / coffee / for breakfast (☑)
3 he / write / you / letter (☒ / send email)
4 I / tell you about my new job (☑)
5 Clarissa / fail / her test (☒ / get the answers right)
6 you / buy / a shirt (☒ / buy jumper)
7 Hannah / choose / a present / for Bob (☑)
8 we / send / a postcard / to Ann (☑)
9 you / drive / to / London (☒ / take the train)
10 Ben / make / dinner (☒ / Paula)

4 Complete the email with the past form of the verbs in brackets.

weekly timetable	mail.mailbox.com	liveblog	news-sport

✱ To JJB from Simon SEE DETAILS TODAY 12:45 REPLY

Hi Jonathan,
I'm back from Turkey. I ¹_____ (go) with my mother on her business trip. It ²_____ (be) really great. We ³_____ (stay) in Istanbul for a few days first. My mother ⁴_____ (not have) much time to go sightseeing, so I ⁵_____ (go) out a lot on my own. I ⁶_____ (see) some great places. What I ⁷_____ (love) most was the Bazaar, a huge covered market. I ⁸_____ (get) a cool leather jacket for just over £60! After Istanbul we ⁹_____ (travel) to Izmir, a lovely town on the sea. Mum ¹⁰_____ (visit) a business partner there. His daughter Cari ¹¹_____ (show) me lots of great places. We ¹²_____ (have) a lot of fun!! No, I ¹³_____ (not fall) in love – Cari's boyfriend was always with us!
Cheers, Simon

Modal verb *could*

5 Complete the sentences with *could* or *couldn't* and the verb in brackets so that they are true for you.

1 When I was five I _____. (swim)
2 I _____ fast when I was young. (run)
3 I _____ a bike when I was ten. (ride)
4 My mum _____ English when she was young. (speak)
5 I _____ all the questions in our last English test. (answer)
6 I _____ the piano last year. (play)

had to, didn't have / need to

6 Study the rules and the sentences. Then complete the sentences with *had to* or *didn't have / need to*.

- Use *had to* to talk about a past obligation.
- Use *didn't have / need to* to express the lack of an obligation in the past.
We had to walk all the way.
She didn't have to ask her parents.

1 There were no taxis. We _____ walk home.
2 She had a lot of time. She _____ hurry.
3 Chris _____ sell his car. He needed money for the operation.
4 John wasn't at home when we arrived. We _____ wait for him.
5 He was ill. He _____ stay in bed for a few days.

7 **Workbook pp 202-207;CD-ROM**

Real communication
ANECDOTES

FILE **TELLING A STORY**

OPENING
- Guess what happened to me.
- I had an embarrassing experience.
- One day… • A few weeks ago…
- Last week… • When I was about thirteen…

CONTINUING
- Then…
- So…
- But…
- Guess what happened next!

SHOWING INTEREST
- Really? • Did you? • Were you?

RESPONDING WITH ANOTHER STORY
- That reminds me of the time I…

2 Coco the clown

A few weeks ago, my older sister, Alex, invited some friends round to watch a DVD. Well, she has this gorgeous friend, called Oliver, and I wanted to impress him. So I put on my best jeans and top and lots of make up. But I didn't realise that my blue eye make up was all over my face. I looked like Coco the clown! I made such a fool of myself.

1 Coffee break!

I really fancied this girl. One day I saw her in the local café and I invited her to have a coffee with me. But as I sat down I spilt the coffee all over my chair. I didn't dare tell her because I was too embarrassed. So I sat down in it. We chatted, but all I could think about was the coffee in my pants! Then she had to go. But I couldn't get up to go with her. So I just sat there as she left the café! It was so awful!

Telling a story

1 🔢 Listen to and read the stories. Then put them in order of embarrassment, in your opinion, on the Blushometer. You decide. How embarrassing are the stories?

BLUSHOMETER

It certainly wasn't my coolest moment! I was getting very hot! Boiling point!

Word expander **ACCIDENTS**

Complete the sentences with these words in the past simple.

spill | break | drop | hit | fall over | knock over

The dog <u>knocked over</u> the vase with its tail.
A boy at the party _____ his drink all over my new jacket.
I _____ my mobile phone on the floor and it _____.
My sister _____ in the street and _____ her head.

4a **PAIRWORK** Read the next story and think about what words go in the gaps. What do you think the last sentence could be?

4b Listen and complete the story. Did you guess correctly?

It was a Friday after school and I was really [1]_____. So I went to [2]_____ in front of the TV. My friends Dylan and Brian put mayonnaise and ketchup all over my [3]_____. Then they took a [4]_____ with Dylan's mobile phone. And guess what they did! They [5]_____ it to all our friends. Of course, I didn't know. And when I went to the youth club that evening, all my friends [6]_____ at me. I didn't understand until they [7]_____ me the photo. [8]_____ _____ _____ _____.

5 **P T PAIRWORK** Cover up the page and tell one of the stories from exercise 1 again. Start like this.

A friend of mine had a really embarrassing experience. He / She…

6a Write a mind map about an embarrassing experience that happened to you or someone else. You don't have to use real names!

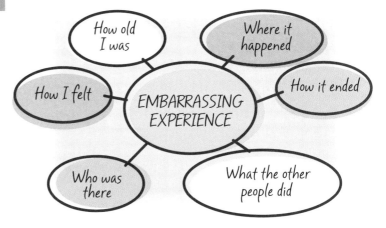

6b **P T ROLE PLAY Work in threes.**
- Tell your stories.
- Use the File to help you.

7 LINKS Real communication pp 12-13

3 Strawberry blushes

I want to tell you about the most embarrassing thing that ever happened. It was when I was about thirteen years old. I bought some strawberry bubble bath in a glass bottle. Then I met a friend and as we chatted the bottle hit against the door. It broke and the bubble bath went all over the floor. It was terrible! I went really red! The shop assistant was really angry with me.

2 **Read the stories again and find the past simple of these verbs.**

sit down | spill | can | leave | put on | make | buy | meet

3 **Choose the best final sentences for the stories.**

a I never go to that shop now.

b And I never told my mum what happened.

c And my sister didn't tell me, of course.

d The girl never spoke to me again.

e He didn't do that again in a hurry, I can tell you.

THE Quiz OF THE Century

Speaking and reading

1a PAIRWORK Discuss the questions.

- Do you watch any TV quiz programmes? Why? / Why not?
- Why do you like / don't you like them?
- Which is the best / worst TV quiz?

1b GROUPWORK Read and answer the quiz questions. You must try to agree!

What do you think is the answer to number 1?

Skills FOR life AGREEING AND DISAGREEING

To give your opinion:
I think it's... I'm pretty sure that...
Could it be...? Perhaps it's... I'd guess...
To check what someone else thinks:
Are you sure? Do you agree?
To express agreement or disagreement:
I agree. I don't agree.

Listening

2 🔊14 **Listen to a TV quiz show and check your answers. Did you do better than Jess, the contestant?**

Writing

3 PAIRWORK Write five past tense quiz questions on any subject you like.

When did Keanu Reeves star in the film Matrix?

Pronunciation SENTENCE STRESS

4a 🔊15 **Listen and repeat. Stress the underlined words.**

<u>When</u> did Marco <u>Polo</u> go to <u>China</u>?
<u>What</u> were the <u>names</u> of the <u>Beatles</u>?

4b Underline the stressed words.

1 Who was the youngest president of the USA?
2 When did Kurt Cobain die?
3 Who designed the dome of St Peter's in Rome?
4 Who invented the espresso machine?

4c 🔊16 **Listen and check. Then listen and repeat.**

5 GAME Take it in turns to ask another team your quiz questions from exercise 3. You have 30 seconds to agree on the answer. See which team gets the most correct answers.

1 **How high did Orville Wright go in the first powered flight in 1903?**
  a 3 metres
  b 20 metres
  c 30 metres

2 **What did Laszlo and Georg Biro invent in 1938?**
  a the pocket calculator
  b the ballpoint pen
  c air conditioning

3 **When did Einstein present his Theory of Relativity?**
  a 1905
  b 1920
  c 1935

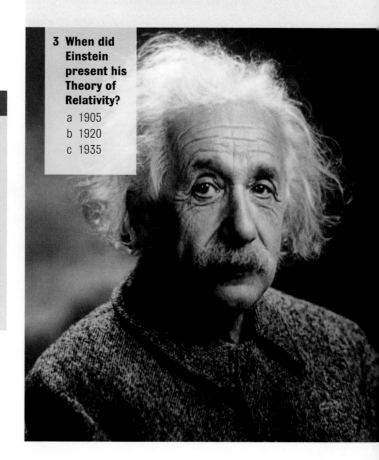

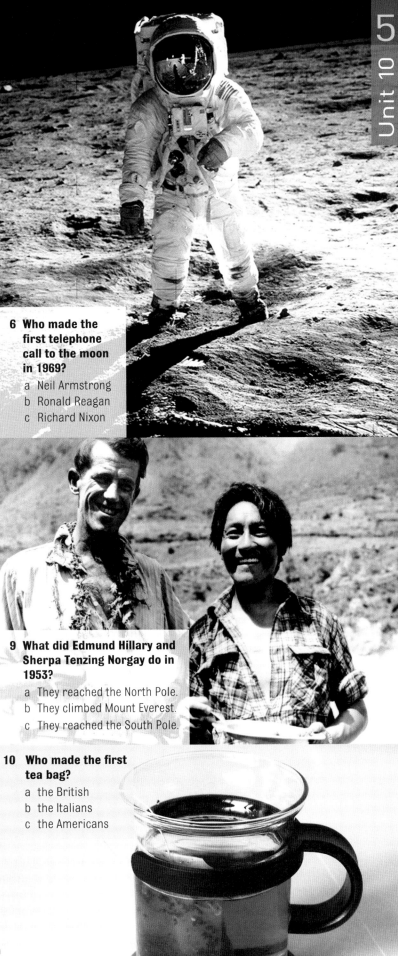

4 Which science fiction blockbuster came out in 1977?
- a Close Encounters of the Third Kind
- b ET the Extra-Terrestrial
- c Star Wars

5 When did black people in South Africa vote for the first time?
  a 1980   b 1986   c 1994

6 Who made the first telephone call to the moon in 1969?
- a Neil Armstrong
- b Ronald Reagan
- c Richard Nixon

7 Which cartoon character first appeared in 1928?
- a Bugs Bunny
- b Snoopy
- c Mickey Mouse

8 Who starred in the film Titanic in 1997?
- a Leonardo DiCaprio and Kate Winslet
- b Leonardo DiCaprio and Gwyneth Paltrow
- c Matt Damon and Kate Winslet

9 What did Edmund Hillary and Sherpa Tenzing Norgay do in 1953?
- a They reached the North Pole.
- b They climbed Mount Everest.
- c They reached the South Pole.

10 Who made the first tea bag?
- a the British
- b the Italians
- c the Americans

FILE

WRITING A STORY

We often write a story in a letter or email about something that has happened to us. There are several ways to prepare for this skill. You should make a point of regularly practising writing about things that have happened to you, as homework or work for your Portfolio. You should also read simplified versions of English stories for inspiration.

Towards PET Paper 1 Reading and Writing, Writing Part 3
Trinity ISE 1 Portfolio

Tips
- Organise the layout of the story in note form before you start writing.
- Try to achieve a clear, logical structure which is easy for readers to follow.
- At the same time, bring your story to life with varied, vivid and accurate vocabulary. You can use a dictionary.
- Use linking words, e.g. *and, but, so, then* etc.

Useful language
- Use *said* to report someone's exact words.
  'I'm hungry,' he said.
  She said, *'Hello, I'm pleased to meet you.'*

1 PAIRWORK Write a story. Choose A or B and brainstorm ideas for a story of about 100 words.

   A A story with the title: *How I met my best friend.*

   B A story that begins: *When the phone rang, I was really scared.*

2a Read Story A and put these sentences in the right places.

I was so happy. | He swam to me and helped me to relax. |
I was very hot so I went swimming. | I was really scared.

A

How I met my best friend

This is the story of how I met my friend Stefano. It was a sunny day and I was at the beach with my family. ¹ I swam a long way and then I got into trouble. I shouted for help but my parents couldn't hear me. ² Then I heard a boy shout 'It's OK! I'm coming.' It was Stefano. ³ Then we swam back to the beach together. ⁴ And after that he became my best friend.

2b Read Story B and choose the best word or phrase for each gap.

1	a quiet	b stupid	c loud
2	a lawyer	b doctor	c thief
3	a working	b dancing	c sleeping
4	a phone	b door	c question
5	a the police	b the pizza company	c Peter
6	a mother	b brother	c dog

B

When the phone rang, I was really scared. It made a very ¹_____ noise. But why was I scared? You have to understand – I'm a professional ²_____. It was midnight, it wasn't my house, and the family were upstairs ³_____. I had to think quickly. I decided to answer the ⁴_____. I heard a man's voice. The man said, 'It's ⁵_____.' I felt sick. Then he said, 'I believe there's a thief in your house.' 'Thank you, officer,' I said, 'but that's my ⁶_____. He forgot his key and had to get in through the window.'

3 P T Now write one of these stories, using about 100 words. Plan the story in note form before you start.

- A story that begins: *He woke up at 8 o'clock. He was late for work.*
- A story with the title: *A really brilliant day out*

1 🎧 **P Listen to the television review and choose the correct answer, a, b or c, to complete the sentences.**

1 The final of the UK Top Talent Competition is decided by
   a the judges.
   b public vote.
   c the theatre audience.

2 Jean Stanton surprised the audience in the final because
   a she didn't look very glamorous.
   b she sang a different type of song.
   c she couldn't remember her words.

3 During the ten weeks of the competition, Tom and Mimi
   a fell in love.
   b broke up and got back together.
   c changed their hair colour.

4 Lisa Coren is
   a Tom and Mimi's choreographer.
   b a dance champion.
   c one of the judges.

5 Preston Smith has inspired lots of people
   a to take violin lessons.
   b to listen to classical music.
   c to join an orchestra.

6 In the final, Preston Smith
   a played a jazz piece on the violin.
   b made a few mistakes.
   c waved to his mum in the audience

2 **LINKS Exam Listening p 13**

LANGUAGE CHECK

1 Complete the sentences in the past simple.

1 _____ (I/be) at home yesterday evening.

2 _____ (they/go) to the cinema last night?

3 _____ (We/not be) in the classroom this morning.

4 _____ (you/see) the programme about bullying yesterday?

5 _____ (we/eat) all the food in the fridge.

2 Choose the correct words.

1 Sarah ____ to Turkey on holiday last year.
   a) was   b) were   c) went   d) did go

2 I ____ walk home because the bus didn't arrive.
   a) could   b) did   c) have to   d) had to

3 When they were four years old they ____ write their names.
   a) could   b) can   c) do   d) did

4 Chris ____ in love with Marina.
   a) didn't fall   b) didn't fell   c) hadn't fall   d) wasn't fall

5 Did you ____ your mother's birthday present yesterday?
   a) chose   b) choose   c) choosed   d) chosed

TOTAL: ____/10

3 Complete the list of personality adjectives with their opposites.

	adjective	opposite
1	patient	_____
2	_____	mean
3	loyal	_____
4	_____	funny
5	hard-working	_____

4 Complete the jobs.

1 He/She works on a plane: f _ _ _ _ _ a _ _ _ _ _ _ _ _

2 She works in a restaurant: w _ _ _ _ _ _ _

3 He is in films: a _ _ _ _

4 He/She repairs cars: m _ _ _ _ _ _ _

5 He/She knows about the mind: p _ _ _ _ _ _ _ _ _ _ _

TOTAL: ____/10

5 Complete the questions and answer them about you.

A   hair / like? _____

YOU _____

A   tall or short? _____

YOU _____

A   colour / eyes? _____

YOU _____

A   glasses? _____

YOU _____

A   piercings? _____

YOU _____

TOTAL: ____/10

6 PAIRWORK Ask and answer questions about your last holiday.

- where / go ?
- who / go with?
- what / do ?
- hot ?
- enjoy ?

TOTAL: ____/10

TOTAL: ____/40

 LINKS Interculture pp 30-33; Story pp 42-43; CLIL (History) pp 54-55; DVD Confessions

106

Grammar comparatives; qualifiers; superlatives; question tags
Functions going to the doctor; asking for confirmation
Vocabulary weather; parts of the body; houses; places

Module 6
One world

Get started CLIL

1 (18) **Match the words and pictures. Then listen and check.**

- ☐ thunder and lightning
- ☐ hail
- ☐ sunshine / sunny
- ☐ wind / windy
- ☐ snow / snowy
- ☐ cloud / cloudy
- ☐ fog / foggy
- ☐ storm / stormy
- ☐ frost / frosty
- ☐ rain / rainy

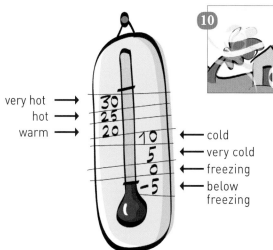

very hot →
hot →
warm →

← cold
← very cold
← freezing
← below freezing

2 **PAIRWORK Ask and answer questions about the weather.**

A *What's the weather like today?*
B *It's sunny and warm.*
A *What was the weather like yesterday?*
B *It rained and it was stormy.*

3a **What do you think the weather is like in these places in December?**

Cairo, Egypt | Geneva, Switzerland | Toronto, Canada | Mumbai, India

3b (19) **Listen and complete the weather guide. Did you guess correctly?**

☀ DECEMBER AROUND THE WORLD ☀

Thinking of going on holiday? *What's the weather like around the world this month?*

Cairo, Egypt – It is warm and ¹_____ and it rains a bit. At night the temperature is about 8 or 9 degrees. There are often sandstorms with high ²_____.

Geneva, Switzerland – It is often beautiful and sunny although it can be ³_____ and ⁴_____. It is very cold – temperatures can go as low as -10. There is a lot of ⁵_____.

Toronto, Canada – It is extremely ⁶_____ with temperatures often below zero. It is snowy. The temperatures feel low because of the wind. It often ⁷_____.

Mumbai, India – It is ⁸_____ during the day, but the nights are cold in December. It isn't the rainy season and it doesn't ⁹_____ a lot, although it can be ¹⁰_____.

107

Unit 11
Health

Unit objectives

Grammar comparative adjectives; *as... as...*, *more / less than*; qualifiers: *a lot, a bit, a little, enough, really, fairly, too*; comparative adverbs

Functions making comparisons; qualifying what you say; going to the doctor

Vocabulary parts of the body; illnesses

Warm up

1 Look at the photos on page 109 and answer the questions.

1 Do you think Mia is angry with Rose about the gig? Why? / Why not?

2 What do you think is on the piece of paper Charlie is holding?

Comprehension

2 🎧20 Listen and read *Who's that girl?* Circle the correct words.

1 Rose *can / can't walk* today.

2 Rose *is / isn't* sorry about the gig.

3 Mia is *happy / sorry* Rose couldn't run in the marathon.

4 Charlie wrote a poem last *week / night*.

5 Jack and Charlie want to use the song to get money for *charity / the band*.

6 Rose sings very *well / badly*.

Making comparisons

3 Study the rules and the sentences.

> ### Comparative adjectives
>
> - Add *-er* to adjectives of one syllable, and adjectives ending in *-y*.
>   *Mia's voice is stronger than Jack's.*
>   (*strong ⇨ stronger*)
>
> - If the adjective ends in a consonant + *-y*, change the *-y* to *-i* and add *-er*.
>   *Jack is a lot happier today.* (*happy ⇨ happier*)
>
> - Use *more* with adjectives of two or more syllables.
>   *Rose's voice is more beautiful than Jack's voice.*
>   (*beautiful ⇨ more beautiful*)
>
> - Some common adjectives are irregular.
>   *Is your leg better?* (*good ⇨ better*)
>   *My leg was worse yesterday.* (*bad ⇨ worse*)
>
> - Use *than* to make a comparison.
>   *The marathon was more important than the gig.*
>
> - Use *as... as* when two things are the same.
>   *Our gig was as important as the marathon.*

4 Complete the sentences with the correct form of the adjectives in brackets.

1 The Empire State building is <u>taller</u> than the Eiffel Tower. (tall)

2 This laptop is _____ than my old one. (expensive)

3 This exercise is _____ than the first one. (difficult)

4 Jane's sister is _____ than Jane. (friendly)

5 My old mobile phone is _____ than my new one! (good)

6 Do you think London is as _____ as New York? (interesting)

5 PAIRWORK Compare the two people or things. Use these phrases, or use *as... as...* .

better / worse than   more / less attractive than
easier / more difficult than   more / less exciting than
healthier / less healthy than

I think Cristiano Ronaldo is a better footballer than Wayne Rooney.

> **Wayne Rooney / Cristiano Ronaldo**
>
> **Beyoncé / Estelle**
>
> **Rome / Milan**
>
> **skiing / climbing**
>
> **fast food / home cooking**
>
> **English / my language**

Who's that girl?
Episode 8

1 *Mia and Rose are chatting in Rose's garden.*

MIA How do you feel today, Rose? Is your leg better?

ROSE Well, it's less painful now. It was a lot worse yesterday, but the doctor gave me some painkillers. I can walk now!

MIA That's great.

ROSE But I feel so bad about you and Jack. The gig was as important as the marathon. And I messed them both up.

MIA Don't be silly! The marathon was more important than the gig. I'm sorry you couldn't run in it.

ROSE Thanks, Mia. That's really sweet.

MIA Hey, there's Jack and Charlie.

2 *Jack is a lot happier today. But why is he carrying his guitar? And what's Charlie holding?*

CHARLIE OK girls, we have a plan. I wrote a poem last night.

MIA You wrote a poem? Weird!

CHARLIE And this morning, Jack wrote a song with my words.

MIA So what's the plan?

CHARLIE Well, we film our new song... about the charity Wateraid. We put it on our website. Then we contact our friends. They pay to download it, and we give the money to the charity! So you can still make a difference, Rose.

ROSE Wow. That's a fantastic idea!

JACK And this is the song. Just to give you an idea. Now, I know you've got a better voice than me, Rose...

MIA Better? Her voice is stronger, sexier, more beautiful, more...

JACK OK, I get the point! Anyway, the song goes like this.

REAL TALK Don't be silly! Weird! I get the point! Anyway, ...

Who's that girl?
Episode 9

Two hours later...

MIA So what do you think of the song, Rose?

ROSE I think it's brilliant. You guys are too good to me! I was feeling so depressed about the marathon and stuff... but I feel a bit better now! I just hope my voice is good enough for the song.

MIA Good enough? You've got an amazing voice! You sing better than Lily Allen!

ROSE And what about Charlie? I didn't know he could write poems. He's a star!

MIA Yeah, definitely, he's a lot more sensitive than I thought. It was a big surprise.

ROSE I know! I mean, he's a funny guy, but he's really talented, too!

MIA And he's good-looking.

ROSE Mia! Do you fancy him?

MIA Charlie? No... well, maybe a bit. Do you think he fancies me?

ROSE I've got a fairly good idea!

REAL TALK

Do you fancy him?
He's a star!
Yeah, definitely.
I've got a fairly good idea!

Qualifying what you say

6 🔊 21 **P Listen and read *Who's that girl?* Circle T (True) or F (False) or DS if it doesn't say.**

1 Mia really likes the song. T / F / DS
2 Rose is still depressed about the marathon. T / F / DS
3 Mia starts talking about Charlie. T / F / DS
4 Rose and Mia were surprised by Charlie's poem. T / F / DS
5 Rose thinks Charlie is funny but not talented. T / F / DS
6 Mia fancies Charlie a bit. T / F / DS

7 Study the sentences and do the task.

> **Qualifiers: *a lot, a bit, a little, enough, really, fairly, too***
>
> • Qualifiers are words which intensify or soften an adjective.
>   *You're too good to me.*
>   *He's a lot more sensitive.*
>   *I hope my voice is good enough.*
>   *He's really talented.*
>   *I feel a bit better now.*
>   *I've got a fairly good idea.*
>
> **Complete the rules with *in front of* and *after*.**
>
> • Put *really, fairly, too* _____ the adjective.
> • Put *a lot, a bit, a little* _____ the comparative form of the adjective.
> • Put *enough* _____ the adjective.

8 Write the words in the correct order.

1 getting / it's / here / in / hot / too
   It's getting too hot in here.
2 him / well / know / I / fairly
3 a bit / think / you / nervous / are / I
4 am / hungry / really / I
5 car / she / drive / old / not / is / enough / to / a
6 book / better / his / new / a lot / think / I / is

9 P T Complete the sentences so they are true for you. Then compare your ideas with a partner.

> I get a bit nervous when...

> I think it's really unfair that...

> I'm too old to...

> I'm not old enough to...

> I'm a lot better at... ing than at... ing.

> A person who knows me fairly well is...

Comparative adjectives

1 Read the rules and complete the examples.

- Add -er to adjectives of one-syllable. (But only -r if the adjective ends in -e.)
  warm – <u>warmer</u>   old – _____   nice – _____
  large – _____
- Double the consonant if the adjective ends in a single vowel + a single consonant (except -r, -w or -x).
  big – <u>bigger</u>   hot – _____
  yellow – _____   clever – _____
- If the adjective ends in a consonant + -y, change the -y to -i and add -er.
  happy – <u>happier</u>
  lazy – _____   lively – _____
- Use more to form the comparative of other adjectives of two syllables and adjectives with more than two syllables.
  helpful – <u>more helpful</u>   attractive – _____
- Use the following irregular comparatives.
  _____ – better   _____ – worse
  _____ – further / farther

2a Write the comparative form of these adjectives.

1 new _____
2 crazy _____
3 interesting _____
4 funny _____
5 bad _____
6 sad _____
7 wide _____
8 good _____
9 unhappy _____
10 silly _____
11 ambitious _____
12 strange _____
13 intelligent _____
14 sweet _____

2b Write a true comparative sentence for each adjective.
My mobile is newer than yours.

Making comparisons

3 Study the rules and the sentences.

- When you make a comparison between two things or people:
  ◦ use the comparative form of the adjective + than.
  ◦ use as + adjective + as to say that they are the same.
  London is bigger than Paris.
  He thinks tennis is as boring as golf.
- You can use less + adjective + than to express a minor comparison of adjectives and adverbs.
  Her latest novel is less interesting than her other books.
- You can use the comparative form of an adjective in front of a noun.
  She is a better actress than Dan.

4 Complete the sentences. Make comparisons using the adjective in brackets and more, less and than where necessary.

1 That mobile phone is _____ mine, but I think it is much nicer. (expensive)
2 I think Paris is _____ Amsterdam. I love walking along the river Seine. (pretty)
3 Joanne is two years _____ Jane. (old)
4 Cooking is _____ cleaning. You can eat the food you cook! (interesting)
5 Today the weather is even _____ yesterday. (bad)
6 I think we need a _____ car _____ this one. (big)
7 Dolphins are _____ sharks. They don't attack humans. (dangerous)
8 He is a _____ footballer _____ me. He scores a goal in every match. (good)

5 Write eight sentences comparing Huw and Sam. Use the information in the chart and these adjectives.
tall | old | good | bad | expensive

	Height	Age	Maths	Art	Mobile phone
Huw	1m 75	15	93%	34%	€55
Sam	1m 65	18	68%	78%	€75

Comparative adverbs

6 Study the sentences and rules and complete the examples.

We want everyone to drive more carefully.
Kevin can add up faster than a computer.
Her daughter types better than she does.

- Use more in front of most adverbs ending in -ly.
  angrily – more angrily
- Add -er to these irregular adverbs.
  fast – <u>faster</u>   high – _____   hard – _____
- Use the following irregular comparatives for these adverbs.
  well – better   badly - worse

7 Complete the sentences with comparative adverbs. Use the adjectives in brackets.

1 I always work _____ in the morning than in the evening. (fast)
2 Please listen _____ this time. (attentive)
3 Cindy speaks English much _____ than me. (good)
4 Can you please check _____ than last time? (careful)
5 She speaks Spanish _____ than French. (fluent)
6 I have to work _____ than last year. (hard)

8 ➦ **Workbook pp 208-213; CD-ROM**

FILE

GIVING ADVICE	**DOCTOR: QUESTIONS**	**PATIENT: ANSWERS**
• Why don't you…?	• What's the problem / matter?	• I feel really ill.
• You'd better…	• When did it start?	• I've got a sore throat, etc.
• You should…	• How did it happen?	• It started two days ago.
	• Can you move it?	• I fell over.
	• Are you coughing / being sick, etc.?	• I can't move my arm.
	• Have you got a temperature?	• I'm coughing all night.

Vocabulary: parts of the body, illnesses

1 (22) **Label the picture. Then listen and check.**

head | forehead | chin | neck | shoulder |
arm | elbow | hand | finger | wrist | chest |
back | hip | leg | knee | foot | toe | heel

2a (23) **Complete the sentences with these words. Then listen and check.**

pain | sore throat | headache | earache |
stomach ache | toothache | hurt | feel sick

The hypochondriac's lament

I feel terrible. I can't think clearly because I've got an awful ¹_____. I've got ²_____ so I can't hear. I can't talk because I've got such a bad ³_____. Hot and cold drinks are painful because of my ⁴_____. I can't eat because I've got ⁵_____ and anyway, just the smell of food makes me ⁶_____. And then yesterday I went running. I fell over and ⁷_____ my foot and so today I've got a really bad ⁸_____ in my foot.

2b What's wrong with these people? Write advice.

1 *She's got toothache. She should go to the dentist.*

Going to the doctor CLIL

3 (24) **Listen and complete the sentences.**

medicine | stay in bed | prescription | temperature | coughing | sore throat | problem

DOCTOR   What's the [1]_____?
PATIENT   I've got a horrible [2]_____ and earache.
DOCTOR   When did it start?
PATIENT   A few days ago but it's much worse now.
DOCTOR   Are you [3]_____ much?
PATIENT   I'm coughing all night. It's terrible.
DOCTOR   Have you got a [4]_____?
PATIENT   Yes, I have. It's about 38°.
DOCTOR   Well, why don't you [5]_____ for the next two days? You should feel better by then. And take this [6]_____. Here's the [7]_____.

4 (25) **P Listen to the doctor's next patient and answer the questions.**

1   What's the matter?
2   What happened?
3   What does the doctor do to the patient?
4   What does the doctor advise?

Word expander   FALSE FRIENDS

Some common expressions can be false friends.

the doctor *examines* you NOT *visits*
you have a *blood test* NOT *analysis*
you have a *temperature* NOT *fever* (fever is a symptom of a very high temperature)
the doctor gives you *a prescription* NOT *a recipe*

5 **Listen again and tick ☑ what the doctor instructs the patient to do.**

☐ lie on the couch   ☐ roll up your sleeve
☐ have a blood test   ☐ breathe deeply
☐ open your mouth   ☐ look over there

6 **ROLE PLAY Work in groups.**

• **Act out similar dialogues to exercises 3 and 4.**
• **Use expressions from the *File*.**

7 **LINKS Real communication pp 14-15**

8 **Read *Get into Culture* and do the task.**

Get into *culture*   UK HEALTH STATISTICS

• 26% of people over 16 smoke.
• 25% of people over 16 drink more than a safe amount of alcohol.
• 23% of adults are obese. This makes Britons the most obese adults in Europe.

On a typical day in the UK

• 750,000 people visit the doctor.
• Pharmacists sell half a million prescriptions.
• 8,000 ambulances make emergency journeys.
• 2,000 babies are born.

What about in your country?
Do some research on the Internet. Write a comparison between health in the UK and health in your country.

One man's dream

Can one ordinary person persuade world leaders to stop war? That was the dream of the young British film-maker, Jeremy Gilley. He wanted the United Nations (UN) to create an annual international day of peace. For one day he wanted to stop all the guns in the world – a global ceasefire.

What did he do? It wasn't easy – he spent all his time campaigning. In 1999 he created the organisation Peace One Day (POD). At first no one wanted to listen, but Gilley is a great communicator. He travelled all over the world and went to war zones, including the Middle East.

He made a short film about his idea and showed it to world leaders. Eventually he won the support of many people including Nelson Mandela and the Dalai Lama; organisations such as the Arab League; and celebrities such as David Beckham, Angelina Jolie, Jude Law and Mohammed Ali.

It was a difficult two years. Jeremy had lots of problems, but in 2001, after many meetings, he won the support of the UN.

They decided to make 21st September an International Day of Peace – a day of global ceasefire and non-violence.

He also wanted to communicate his message to ordinary people all over the world. On his journey he met thousands of school children, students and victims of war. He showed them his first documentary, Peace One Day, and gave talks.

People die of diseases in war zones because it's too dangerous for doctors and nurses to go there. So in 2007 the actor Jude Law went with Jeremy to Afghanistan, talked to tribal leaders, and organised a huge polio vaccination campaign for Peace Day. As a result, nurses gave vaccinations to 1.4 million children.

Although there isn't a global ceasefire on Peace Day at the moment, there are thousands of projects to help people in war zones, to raise money and communicate the importance of peace. By 2007, 100 million people were active on Peace Day in 192 countries with health campaigns, peace walks, films and music events.

Reading

1 GROUPWORK Discuss these quotes about war and peace. Choose one you agree with and one you disagree with. Tell the class.

There never was a good war or bad peace.

It is always possible to forgive.

War creates hunger and poverty.

Peace is an impossible dream.

We make war so we can live in peace.

War resolves nothing. Winning a war is as bad as losing a war.

2 Read the article and complete the fact file.

> **F**
> **A** **PEACE ONE DAY**
> **C**
> **T** Founded in <u>1999</u> by <u>Jeremy Gilley</u>   .
> **F** Date of UN Peace Day: _____
> **I** Title of his documentary film: _____
> **L** Number of countries involved in 2007: _____
> **E** Number of people involved: _____
>   What Jeremy did to achieve his objective: _____
>   What happens on Peace Day now: _____

3 Read the article again and find other words that go with these verbs.

spend money, <u>spend time</u>; win a prize, _____;
have fun, _____; make a cake, _____;
give lessons, _____, _____

> ### Word **expander**   CONNECTORS
>
> **When you speak and write, remember to connect your ideas together with words such as:**
> also | but | because | so | as a result | although
> **Find and underline sentences containing these words in the article.**

Listening

4a 📷26 Listen to three students talking about what they did for Peace Day this year. Which project did they do? Write 1, 2 and 3 in the correct boxes.

☐ a marathon run
☐ a class friendship project
☐ a peace walk
☐ a sale of books, CDs and DVDs
☐ a lunch party
☐ a class peace painting

4b Listen again and circle the correct facts.

STUDENT 1 they made quite a lot of money / they didn't make much money

STUDENT 2 the painting was small / the painting was big

STUDENT 3 they talked to their friends / they talked to people they don't know well

> ### Pronunciation   /w/, /v/, /f/, /r/
>
> **5a 📷27 Listen and repeat.**
> /w/ **w**ar | **w**orld | **w**in | **w**ant
> /v/ **v**iolence | **v**accination | e**v**entually | **v**ictim
> /f/ **f**ilm | ceasefire | **f**antastic | **f**riendly
> /r/ c**r**eated | g**r**eat | celeb**r**ity | dange**r**ous

5b 📷28 Underline the letters with the sounds in these charities. Then listen and repeat.
Oxfam | UNICEF | Save the Children | British Heart Foundation | War on Want | World Wide Fund | Cancer Research | British Red Cross

Speaking and writing

6a PAIRWORK Discuss what your class could do for Peace Day. Choose one of the projects from exercise 4 or think of your own project.

6b Plan the project in note form:
Title , Aims , Preparation , What happens on the day

6c T GROUPWORK Present your ideas to the class.

7 Write your opinion of what Jeremy Gilley did.

> **RANDOM Fact** Every minute 2 people are killed in a conflict around the world.

Unit 12

Places

Unit objectives

Grammar: superlatives; question tags
Function: talking about the best; asking for confirmation
Vocabulary: houses; landscape; countries

Warm up

1 **GROUPWORK** Think of places in the world that have extreme living conditions. Use these ideas:

very crowded | very dry | very wet | very cold | very hot | very high

Comprehension CLIL

2a 🔊 **29** Scan the article on page 117 and complete the headings. Then listen and check.

the coldest | the hottest | the most crowded | the driest | the highest | the wettest

2b Read the article and answer the questions.

1 Where is it difficult to make tea?
2 Where is it difficult to be alone?
3 Where is it possible to keep food very cold?
4 Where does the rainy season last about six months?
5 Where is it best to get up early?
6 Where is a good place for astronomers?

3 Can you match the photos with the places?

Talking about the best

4 Study the sentences and do the task.

> **Superlative adjectives**
>
> *That's the coldest place on Earth.*
> *The best cure for altitude sickness is coca leaves.*
> *It's the world's purest air.*
> *The mercury rises... at the hottest time of the day.*
>
> • Use the following irregular forms:
>   good – better – the best
>   bad – worse – the worst
>   little – less – the least
>   much (many) – more – the most
>   far – further (farther) – the furthest (farthest)
>
> **Find and underline examples of the superlative in the article.**

5 **PAIRWORK** Ask and answer about places and people in your country.

hottest region | best singer | longest river | most famous actor | most beautiful city | tallest building

A *Which is the hottest region in (country)?*
B *I'm not sure. Is it...?*

EXTREME EARTH

place

Imagine a place four times colder than your freezer. That's the coldest place on Earth. It's Yakutia in Siberia where temperatures fall to as low as minus 50°C. Hi-tech clothing doesn't help there. The best way to keep warm is with animal fur.

place

You can't go out without a plastic raincoat in Mawsynram, north-east India, where it rains day and night for weeks. Then it's the wettest place in the world. However, it's incredibly dry from May to October — people walk kilometres to get drinking water!

place

Did you know that the best cure for altitude sickness is coca leaves and lemon juice? Well, this is common knowledge in La Paz, Bolivia, because they live 3½ km above sea level. It's the highest place in the world. Hot drinks are a little cooler here because water boils at a lower temperature!

place

It doesn't rain very often in the Atacama Desert in Chile, the driest place in the world. In fact, it rained in 1971 for the first time in 400 years! People get water from the fog. And it's a perfect place for studying the stars. 'It's the world's purest air,' says one astronomer. 'There's nothing between you and Mars.'

place

In Mali, West Africa, mercury rises halfway to boiling point at the hottest times of the day. That's an incredible 50°C! It's the hottest place in the world. The people here have to get up early before it gets too hot. Traditionally, they wear cotton robes because these protect them from the heat.

place

How crowded is the place where you live? In Mong Kok, Hong Kong, there are 165,000 people per square kilometre. It's the most crowded place in the world. Apartment blocks fill the sky, there are shops on the pavement and it's difficult to walk in the streets. It's like a scene from *Bladerunner*.

Asking for confirmation

6 🔊 **Listen and complete the dialogue.**

Who's that girl?
Episode 10

Two days later...

CHARLIE You _____ the new song with Rose today, didn't you?

JACK Yes, I did.

CHARLIE You _____ her voice, don't you?

JACK Yeah, of course.

CHARLIE She _____ sing really well, can't she?

JACK Yeah...

CHARLIE And you _____ another rehearsal today, have you? But you can't see Rose tomorrow because she has to see the doctor.

JACK What's up, Charlie? Why are you asking all these questions? And how do you know all this?

CHARLIE Mia told me.

JACK Mia? Oh, I get it. Mia _____ to you a lot, doesn't she?

CHARLIE Erm... yeah.

JACK And _____ pretty, isn't she?

CHARLIE What are you saying, Jack?

JACK What am I saying, Charlie? You and Mia are an item, aren't you?

CHARLIE I guess so!

REAL TALK   What's up?   I get it.   an item

---

7 **Study the sentences and do the task.**

Question tags

You practised the new song, didn't you?

You like her voice, don't you?

- Use negative questions with _____ sentences.
- Use positive questions with _____ sentences.

- Use *be* with the verb *be* and the present continuous.
- Use *have* with *have got*.
- Use the corresponding modal with *can*, *could*, *must*, *should*, *will*, etc.
- Use *do / does* with the present simple.
- Use *did* with the past simple.

Complete the rules with *negative* and *affirmative*.

---

8 **Complete the sentences with question tags.**

1   You got home late last night, *didn't you*?

2   I shouldn't eat so much meat, _____?

3   She's got a nice house in the countryside, _____?

4   We weren't rude, _____?

5   He can't help me, _____?

9 **PAIRWORK Check ten facts about your partner, using question tags.**

Ⓐ *You're fourteen, aren't you?*

Ⓑ *Yes, I am. / No, I'm not. I'm fifteen.*

Ⓐ *Your surname's..., isn't it?*

Ⓐ *You live in...., don't you?*

Get the grammar

Superlative adjectives

1 Read the rules and complete the lists.

- Add -est to adjectives of one-syllable (but only -st if the adjective ends in -e.)
- Double the consonant if the adjective ends with a single vowel + a single consonant (except -r, -w or -x).
  soft – softer - softest
  young – younger – _____
  wide – wider – _____
  safe – safer – _____
  fat – fatter – _____
  thin – thinner – _____
  yellow – yellower – _____
  clever – cleverer – _____
- If the adjective ends in a consonant + -y, change the -y to -i and add -est.
  happy – happier – happiest
  friendly – friendlier – _____
  NB *silly – sillier – silliest*
- Use *most* to form the superlative of other adjectives of two syllables and all adjectives with more than two syllables.
  interesting – more interesting – most interesting
  careful – _____ – _____
- Use the following irregular superlatives for some adjectives.
  good – better – best
  bad – worse – worst
  far – further/farther – furthest / farthest
  little – less – least
  much – more – most
- Usually *the* is used in front of the superlative form of an adjective.
  Carol is the fastest swimmer in our class.
  This is the most beautiful flower in the garden.
  The end of the book was the most interesting part.

2 Write the superlative form of these adjectives.
1 strong _____   6 wet _____
2 bad _____   7 light_____
3 comfortable _____   8 good _____
4 funny _____   9 heavy_____
5 intelligent _____   10 busy_____

3 Write the sentences with correct superlative forms.
1 Seville / hot city in Spain.
  Seville is the hottest city in Spain.
2 Maths / difficult subject.
3 Ian / nice boy in the class.
4 Amy Winehouse / good British singer.
5 My mum / fast swimmer in our family.
6 Robert / bad driver in the world!

4 Complete the sentences with the superlative form of the adjectives in brackets.
1 I've never read a more interesting book.
  It's the most interesting book I ever read. (interesting)
2 All the students in my class are shorter than Will.
  Will is _____ student in my class. (tall)
3 This steak is really excellent!
  It's _____ steak you can get. (good)
4 Jane really likes Nick.
  She thinks he is _____ boy in the world. (attractive).
5 All my classmates are better than me at Maths.
  I'm _____ in the class at Maths. (bad)
6 My father is very tolerant.
  He's _____ father you can imagine. (tolerant)
7 Sally is very sweet. She's _____ person I know. (friendly)
8 I loved *Space Invaders*! It was _____ film ever. (crazy)

Question tags

5 Study the sentences and the rules, then circle the correct words.

  You're French, aren't you?
  They've got a big car, haven't they?
- Use a question tag to ask for confirmation of a fact or opinion.
- Check that the pronoun, tense and auxiliary in the question tag are the same as those in the main clause.

1 People shouldn't drink and drive, *should / shouldn't* they?
2 You liked the band, *did / didn't* you?
3 It's Kate's birthday tomorrow, *is / isn't* it?
4 Elephants are the largest mammals, *aren't / are* they?
5 We can eat at your house, *can't / can* we?
6 Angelina Jolie was brilliant in the film, *was / wasn't* she?

6 Complete the sentences with question tags.
1 Your brother is in the USA, _____?
2 You don't know my girlfriend, _____?
3 Her parents have got a new house, _____?
4 Mr Wren died in that house, _____?
5 They're visiting Paris in May, _____?
6 You can juggle, _____?
7 You are Kate's brother, _____?
8 You've got a new mobile phone, _____?
9 We mustn't make a noise, _____?
10 You'd like a cup of tea, _____?

7 Workbook pp 214-219; CD-ROM

FILE

DESCRIBING HOUSES

- It's got…
- There is / are…
- It's got a nice…
- There's a lovely…
- The nicest room is…
- It's very light / roomy / welcoming / cosy / modern
- It's rather dark / cluttered / old-fashioned
- It needs decorating.

HESITATING	GENERALISING
… um…	… sort of…
… oh…	… kind of…
… er…	

Vocabulary: houses

1 **31 Match the words and pictures. Then listen and check.**

- ☐ kitchen sink
- ☐ washing machine
- ☐ armchair
- ☐ dishwasher
- ☐ bedside table
- ☐ chest of drawers
- ☐ coffee table
- ☐ cupboard
- ☐ cooker
- ☐ toilet
- ☐ basin
- ☐ wardrobe
- ☐ bath
- ☐ bookcase
- ☐ TV
- ☐ table
- ☐ chair
- ☐ bed
- ☐ sofa

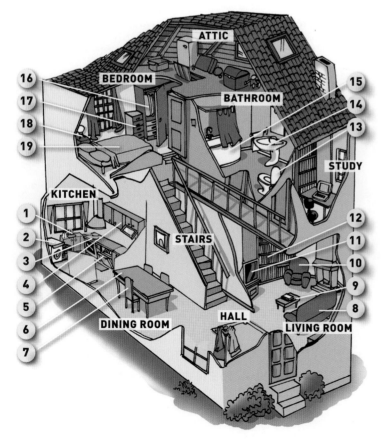

2 **32 P Listen and tick ☑ the two apartments described.**

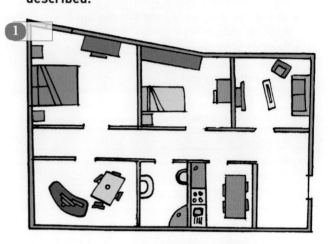

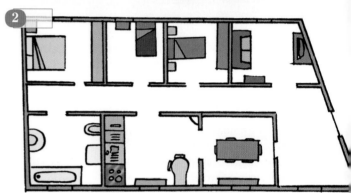

3a **33 Read and complete the description. Then listen and check.**

bedroom | hall | dining room | study | bathroom

What's your house like?

Well, it's on three floors. Downstairs there's a
¹_____ and a living room and, um, a dining
room and a kitchen. And, er, the kitchen and the
²_____ are quite light because they get the sun.
Upstairs there's a ³_____, a bedroom and a nice
⁴_____. Oh, and on the top floor there's a spare
⁵_____ and a smaller en-suite bathroom.

3b **Underline the "hesitating" words the speaker uses.**

4a P T **PAIRWORK** Describe your house to your partner. Use the words and expressions from the *File*.

4b Are you a good listener? Draw a plan of your partner's house and describe it back.

Vocabulary: landscape

5 Tick ☑ the words you find in the adverts.

☐ hills	☐ beach	☐ garage
☐ lake	☐ country	☐ docks
☐ mountains	☐ seaside	☐ river
☐ wood	☐ garden	☐ city centre

House adverts

6 P **Read the adverts and decide which house is best for each person below.**

1 Taylor wants to stay in the countryside this summer. A big group of friends wants to celebrate his birthday.

2 Debbie loves the country and walking. She likes traditional things. She has two children.

3 Owen is a photographer and needs to be in town for his job. He lives on his own and would like to be close to pubs, restaurants and shops.

4 Lisa is a fashion designer. She works from home and needs an office space. She also entertains a lot in the summer.

7 T **Write a paragraph about your dream house.**

8 Read *Get into Culture* and do the task.

Get into *culture* THE AVERAGE BRITISH HOME

The average home in the UK has 2.4 people living in it. About 15% of people live on their own. 80% of British people live in a house rather than an apartment. 27% of British families don't have a car; 45% have one car, and 29% have two or more cars.

8 million homes have a cat and 7 million have a dog.

What about your country?

9 ③④ **LINKS** Go to page 63 and listen to *Our House.*

10 **LINKS** Real communication pp 14-15

House Search

A

To rent. Beautiful cottage in the countryside surrounded by gentle hills. Near the shops and main railway station. Three bedrooms, two living rooms, old fireplaces and very large traditional kitchen. Near the lake for walks.

B

Lovely big detached house in the country. Within easy reach of the airport. 5 km from a beautiful beach and 10 minute walk from shops. Consists of five bedrooms, two living rooms, dining room and fully-fitted kitchen. Beautiful views. Extensive gardens.

C

Terraced town house in attractive part of town. Five minutes from the station and shops. Luxurious décor. Three bedrooms, a living room, dining room, study, kitchen and two bathrooms. Modern garden with barbecue.

D

Apartment in the heart of a new development. Views of the docks and river. A step away from the most lively part of the city centre. One designer bedroom, spacious open plan living room and fully-fitted kitchen, bathroom. Garage.

WORLD HERITAGE SITES

What do the Grand Canyon, the cities of Venice and Brasilia, Chinese panda sanctuaries, tropical rainforests in Sumatra, and the archaeological site of Machu Picchu in Peru have in common? Well, they are all UNESCO World Heritage Sites – places of 'outstanding universal value'. And there are hundreds of these sites to discover around the world.

A Do you like beautiful views?

Check out the spectacular landscape of Tongariro National Park in New Zealand with its lakes, forests and active volcanoes. It is also a spiritual centre for the Maori people. You can even go on a *Lord of the Rings* tour!

B Are cities more your cup of tea?

Admire the temples, gardens and buildings of the ancient city of Kyoto, Japan. Or go 2,850m above sea level in the Andes to Quito, the capital of Ecuador. It is the best-preserved historic city in Latin America, and you can see views of volcanoes while you drink your coffee!

C Do you love a challenge?

Walk 100km of the Route of Santiago de Compostela in France and Spain. It was important in medieval times and it is still one of the most important pilgrimage sites in Europe. There are 1,800 buildings to admire along the route too!

D Are you an animal lover?

Go whale watching in Baja California. It's one of the longest and wildest peninsulas in the world. The sanctuary of El Vizcaino is home to whales, seals, sea lions and turtles. Or see elephants and tigers in the wonderful Thungyai-Huai Kha Khaeng wildlife sanctuaries of Thailand.

E Are you keen on caves?

Visit the amazing salt mines of Wieliczka in Poland, or the Škocjan caves in Slovenia with one of the world's largest underground chambers. And don't forget the prehistoric cave paintings in the Vézère Valley in France.

F Or is archaeology more your thing?

Hidden in the jungle of Guatemala is Tikal, one of the largest Mayan archaeological sites. Or in Mexico go to the incredible temples and pyramids of Chichen Itza. Get there early and see the sun rise over the ruins.

Vocabulary: countries

1 **PAIRWORK** Find these countries on the maps. Then listen and check.

- ☐ New Zealand
- ☐ the USA
- ☐ France
- ☐ Slovenia
- ☐ Poland
- ☐ Thailand
- ☐ Guatemala
- ☑ Japan
- ☐ Ecuador
- ☐ Mexico

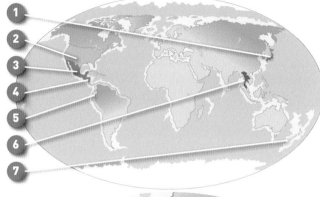

Reading and speaking CLIL

2 Scan the website article and match the photos with the descriptions.

3a Try to match the places with the countries. Then read the article and check your answers.

1	Tongariro National Park	a	the USA
2	Škocjan caves	b	Mexico
3	Mayan ruins of Chichen Itza	c	New Zealand
4	the city of Kyoto	d	Poland
5	the city of Quito	e	Thailand
6	Baja California	f	Guatemala
7	salt mines of Wieliczcka	g	Japan
8	cave paintings,Vézère Valley	h	Ecuador
9	Mayan ruins of Tikal	i	Slovenia
10	Thungyai-Huai Kha Khaeng	j	France

3b Read the article again. Where can you see...

- • active volcanoes
- • temples
- • animals
- • cave paintings
- • interesting buildings

4 **P T GROUPWORK** You are arranging an ideal school trip. Choose one of the places. Tell the class why you have chosen your site. Have a class vote.

Word expander   IMPLICIT SUPERLATIVES

Some adjectives, e.g. *spectacular, wonderful, amazing, incredible* add colour. They are already superlative – don't add *very*.
    NOT ~~The building is very spectacular.~~
You can add the adverb *absolutely* to show enthusiasm.
The view was absolutely wonderful!

Pronunciation   SHOWING ENTHUSIASM

5 **36** Listen and repeat the sentences.

1 Venice is an absolutely incredible place!
2 This painting is absolutely beautiful!
3 The food is fantastic!
4 There are lots of wonderful buildings!
5 The gondolas are amazing!

Listening CLIL

6a **37** Listen and answer the questions.

1 What is on the Cambodian national flag?
2 Why didn't tourists visit Cambodia in the past?
3 What does Jorani's mother do?
4 Why is there a water problem at Siem Reap?
5 Why is it dangerous if there isn't enough water?

Jorani lives in Angkor, Cambodia, close to the World Heritage Site Angkor Wat temples. They were built in the 12th century, and have an amazing location in the jungle.

6b Listen again. What do you think is Jorani's attitude to Angkor Wat?

Writing

7 Write a short article about a World Heritage Site in your country. Include this information.

Name | Location | Type of site | What you can see and do

FILE

WRITING LETTERS

Although letters have a similar structure to emails, there are more rules to follow. It is important to know how to lay out and write a simple letter. And although we now write more emails, letter-writing is still a skill that can be useful in daily life.

Towards PET, Paper 1, Reading and Writing, Writing Part 3, Trinity ISE I (Writing task)

Tips
It is important to put the following in the correct order and position:
– address
– date
– opening greeting
– body of letter
– closing salutation
– your name
Divide the body of the letter up into paragraphs.

Useful language
Dear (name),
Thanks for your letter. / I'm writing to ask / tell you...
14th January 2009
Write back soon.
Love / Lots of love / Yours, (name)

1 GROUPWORK Discuss the questions.

- What are the differences between emails and letters?
- What are the similarities?
- Why write a letter instead of an email?
- Do you prefer emails or letters? Why? / Why not?

2 Match the sections of the letter a–f with the diagram.

- a date
- b body of letter
- c closing salutation
- d opening greeting
- e name
- f address

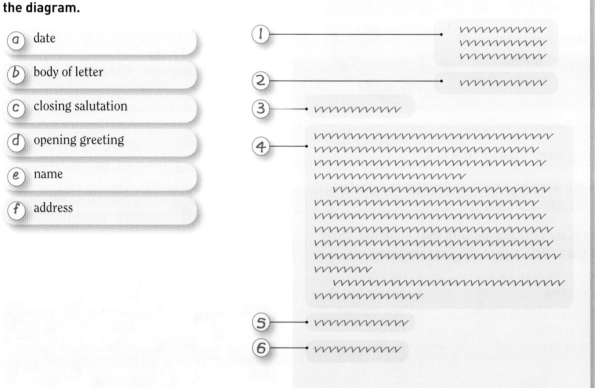

3 P T Write a letter to a penfriend, inviting him or her to stay with you. Follow the instructions below.

- Don't forget the address, date and opening salutation.
- Say why you are writing (= to invite your friend to stay with you).
- Describe the place / area to give them an idea of it.
- Describe what you and your penfriend can do during his / her visit.
- Write a closing sentence (you hope your friend can come / ask him / her to write back soon).
- Don't forget the closing salutation and signature.

4 LINKS Exam Listening p15

FILE

MULTIPLE CHOICE OPTIONS

Understanding the exact meaning of vocabulary and grammar in a text helps with your reading skills. So this is part of the Cambridge PET and Trinity exams.

There are ways you can practise and develop this skill, including filling in the gaps in a text.

Towards PET Paper 1, Reading and Writing, Reading Part 5

Tips

- Read the text to the end first. This helps you understand the type of text and the vocabulary and grammar it uses.
- Before you look at the multiple-choice options, think about what type of word it must be: an adjective, noun, main verb, auxiliary verb, etc.
- Follow the patterns in the text. For instance, if all the verbs are in the past tense, choose the past tense.

1 First read the article and find the words and expressions that mean the following.

1 an Irish sport
2 very busy
3 relax
4 most fashionable
5 go directly to
6 don't make a mistake

2 P Read the article again and circle the correct word for each space.

	a	b	c	d
1	time	population	living	people
2	seeing	saw	see	sees
3	capital	biggest	example	part
4	do	did	need	can
5	school	town	architecture	furniture
6	than	eldest	older	oldest
7	narrow	traffic	rain	sure
8	it	there	possibly	so
9	are	doing	liking	talk
10	a	an	some	the

Ireland
a young country

Ireland is a young country. In fact, over 40% of the ¹_____ is under 25. In the rest of 'old' Europe, that figure is 25%. So, let's go to the land of the young, and ²_____ what's on offer.

Dublin is the ³_____ of the Republic of Ireland. It's on the east coast and it's the city where Guinness, a dark beer, comes from. You ⁴_____ walk along the River Liffey, see the Book of Kells in Trinity College, look at the lovely ⁵_____ of Merrion Square (that's where Oscar Wilde lived), and visit places James Joyce wrote about in Dubliners and Ulysses. But to find the hippest, trendiest places, go straight to Temple Bar. It's one of the ⁶_____ parts of the city, but it's where young people hang out in its restaurants, pubs and clubs.

Galway is the centre of the action on the west coast. With its ⁷_____ streets and old stone buildings, it still looks a bit like a medieval fishing port – but don't be fooled. Galway is the liveliest city on the west coast of Ireland, and ⁸_____ the loudest! Students from the university keep the city buzzing. There's a jazz festival in February, an arts festival in July and pubs and discos the whole year! It's a good place to hear Irish, too.

Cork is Ireland's second city – and the home of Murphy's, Ireland's other great beer. On the south coast, it's a great place for all kinds of sports such as rugby, football and the Irish game of hurling. The Irish ⁹_____ a lot about craic. This is a Gaelic word and means 'good times and good talk'. Go to the Blarney Castle and kiss ¹⁰_____ famous Blarney Stone to get the gift of brilliant conversation.

LANGUAGE CHECK

LANGUAGE I CAN NOW COMPARE / QUALIFY / USE QUESTION TAGS

1 Choose the correct words.

1 Our new car is ____ than our old car.
   a) small   b) smallest   c) more small   d) smaller

2 Enjoying your work is ____ important as passing exams.
   a) as   b) than   c) more   d) too

3 The pain in my foot was ____ yesterday than it is today.
   a) badder   b) worser   c) worse   d) worst

4 Who is ____ popular teacher at your school?
   a) the most   b) the more   c) the too   d) most

5 Erica is ____ good at tennis.
   a) a lot   b) a bit   c) enough   d) really

6 The Maths exam was ____ easier this year.
   a) fairly   b) too   c) a bit   d) really

7 Nick is the ____ person in our class.
   a) funny   b) funnier
   c) more funny   d) funniest

8 Your name is Samantha, ____?
   a) isn't it   b) aren't you
   c) is it   d) is she

9 The visitors didn't go to the museum, ____?
   a) didn't they   b) weren't they
   c) did it   d) did they

10 We're watching the new film tonight, ____?
   a) don't we   b) aren't we
   c) isn't it   d) can't we

TOTAL: ____/10

VOCABULARY I CAN NOW TALK ABOUT WEATHER / PARTS OF THE BODY / HOUSES

2 Complete with weather words.

In a storm there is often [1] t_____
and [2] l_____.
When it is [3] f_____, you can't see
well.
I love [4] s_____ because I love skiing.
It was very hot and [5] s_____ on our
holiday in Egypt.

3 Complete the table.

Kitchen: cooker, [1] w_ _ _ _ _ _ m _ _ _ _ _ _, [2] d_ _ _ _ _ _ _ _ _

Living room: bookcase, [3] c_ _ _ _ _ t_ _ _ _, [4] a_ _ _ _ _ _ _

Bedroom: bed, [5] c_ _ _ _ of d_ _ _ _ _ _

TOTAL: ____/10

COMMUNICATION I CAN NOW GO TO THE DOCTOR / DESCRIBE HOUSES

4 Complete the dialogue with these words.

medicine | stomache ache | feel | start | can't | temperature | better | should | doctor | worse

DOCTOR Hello, Eva. [1] __What's__ the problem?
EVA I feel really ill and I've got a [2] _____.
DOCTOR I see. When did it [3] _____?
EVA Two days ago, but it's much [4] _____ now.
DOCTOR Oh dear, and have you got a [5] _____?
EVA Yes, I have. I [6] _____ quite hot.
DOCTOR I think you've got flu. You [7] _____ stay in bed for two or three days.

EVA But I've got an exam tomorrow.
DOCTOR You [8] _____ go to school with flu. I can write a note for you.
EVA OK, [9] _____. Should I take any [10] _____?
DOCTOR Not at the moment. Come back in three days if you don't feel [11] _____.

TOTAL: ____/10

---

5 PAIRWORK Ask and answer questions about your house. Include these things:

- how many floors / rooms ?
- what / living room like ?
- biggest room ?
- spare room ?
- furniture / your bedroom ?

TOTAL: ____/10

TOTAL: ____/40

 LINKS Interculture pp 34-35; CLIL (Earth science) pp 56-57; DVD Homes

Grammar present continuous for future; *be going to*; present perfect

Functions talking about the future; making and accepting invitations; talking about experiences; ordering food

Vocabulary holidays; food

Module 7
Experiences

Get started

1 **PAIRWORK Read the article and tick** ☑ **three things you would like to do.**

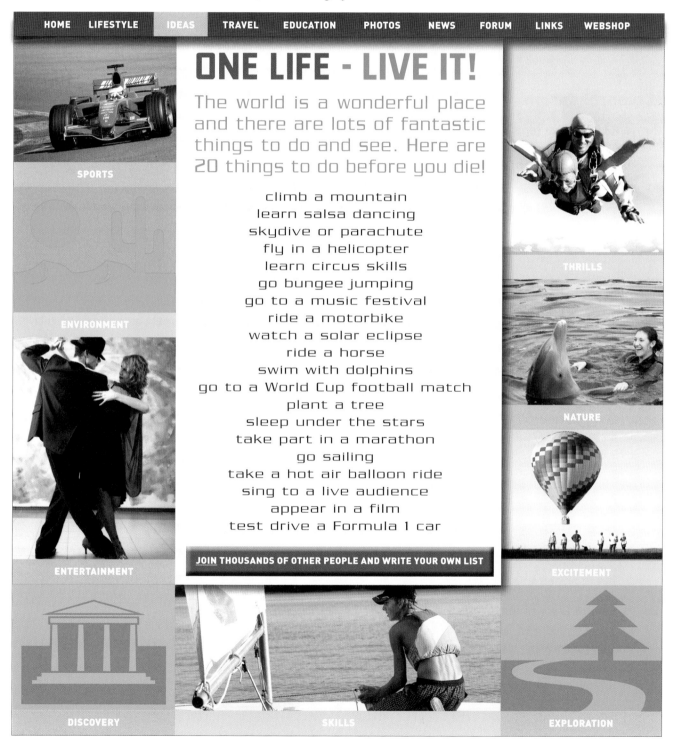

HOME   LIFESTYLE   IDEAS   TRAVEL   EDUCATION   PHOTOS   NEWS   FORUM   LINKS   WEBSHOP

SPORTS

ENVIRONMENT

ENTERTAINMENT

THRILLS

NATURE

EXCITEMENT

ONE LIFE - LIVE IT!

The world is a wonderful place and there are lots of fantastic things to do and see. Here are 20 things to do before you die!

climb a mountain
learn salsa dancing
skydive or parachute
fly in a helicopter
learn circus skills
go bungee jumping
go to a music festival
ride a motorbike
watch a solar eclipse
ride a horse
swim with dolphins
go to a World Cup football match
plant a tree
sleep under the stars
take part in a marathon
go sailing
take a hot air balloon ride
sing to a live audience
appear in a film
test drive a Formula 1 car

JOIN THOUSANDS OF OTHER PEOPLE AND WRITE YOUR OWN LIST

DISCOVERY   SKILLS   EXPLORATION

2a **GROUPWORK Think of four more things to do before you die. Make a poster. Use these categories.**

Activities and sport   Flying and driving   Creative and entertainment
Travel and holidays   Nature and animals   Education and learning

2b **Tell the class your choices. Have a class vote for the top three experiences.**

Unit 13

Plans

Unit objectives

Grammar present continuous for future; *be going to*
Functions talking about the future; making and accepting invitations
Vocabulary holidays; food

Warm up

1 PAIRWORK Look at the photo on page 129 and answer the questions.

Charlie has some news for the band.
1 Do you think it's good or bad?
2 What do you think it could be?

Comprehension

2a 38 P Listen and read *Who's that girl?* and answer the questions. Choose the correct answer (a, b, c or d).

1 Who has got plans for Saturday?
  a Mia   b Charlie   c Jack   d Rose

2 Why do Jack, Rose, Mia and Charlie have to get up early?
  a Because they have band practice.
  b Because they're going to a restaurant.
  c Because they have a meeting.
  d Because they always do on Saturdays.

3 Who is paying for lunch?
  a Charlie   b Jack
  c A music producer   d Yellow Fish

4 How does the producer know about Yellow Fish?
  a He loves their music.
  b He's got a link to their website.
  c He emails them.
  d He saw their concert.

5 What do Rose, Jack and Mia think of Charlie's plan?
  a They're embarrassed.
  b They're angry.
  c They're upset.
  d They're delighted.

2b PAIRWORK Discuss these questions.

• Do you think Charlie is a good businessman? Why? / Why not?
• Do you think it is important for the band to have a website? Why? / Why not?

Talking about the future

3 Study the rules and do the tasks.

Present continuous for future

• Use the present continuous to talk about plans already made for the future.

What are you doing on Saturday?

We're going to London on Saturday morning.

Do you remember the other situations when you use the present continuous?

• Use expressions of future time with the present continuous to specify the future moment, eg

this evening | tonight | next week | next month

Underline other examples of the present continuous in *Who's that girl?*

4 Complete the sentences with the present continuous form of the verbs in brackets.

1 I'm spending_____ my summer holidays in Spain. (spend)
2 My friends _____ rugby at the weekend. (play)
3 I can't come to your party. I _____ on holiday tomorrow. (go)
4 The champion's league final _____ on the 18th July. (take place)
5 You _____ Mei Ling at 10.30 and Marvin at 11.00. (see)
6 Michael and Tim _____ a presentation tomorrow. (give)

5a Copy and complete the table. Make notes about what you are doing on some evenings this week.

this evening:
tomorrow evening:
.... evening:
.... evening:
.... evening:

5b PAIRWORK Ask and answer questions.

Ⓐ *What are you doing this evening?*
Ⓑ *I'm...*

Who's that girl?
Episode ...

Charlie has some news.

CHARLIE What are you doing on Saturday?

MIA Er, nothing special.

JACK I haven't got any plans.

ROSE Me neither.

CHARLIE Good. Because we're going to London on Saturday morning.

MIA We?

CHARLIE That's right.

JACK Why are we going to London, Charlie?

CHARLIE Because we're meeting a music producer.

JACK A music producer?

CHARLIE That's what I said. We're seeing him at 11 o'clock at the studio – so you have to get up early. And then we're having lunch together in a cool restaurant. And he's paying!

JACK Hang on. I don't get it. Why are we meeting a music producer?

CHARLIE Because he loves Yellow Fish, Jack. He loves our sound!

JACK How does he know about us?

CHARLIE Well, I just thought, we've got a great song, we're a good band... and there are lots of music producers out there. Let's give it a go! So, I sent emails to lots of them and gave them a link to our website. And now this guy wants to meet us!

JACK Hey, man! That's amazing!

ROSE You're a genius, Charlie.

MIA You're my hero!

REAL TALK That's what I said.
I don't get it.
Let's give it a go.

I'm going to......
before I'm old!!!!

This week three teenagers in Liverpool tell us about their future plans. You decide, are they over-ambitious?

Danielle 15

Sophie 17

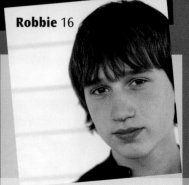

Robbie 16

	Danielle	Sophie	Robbie
Before I'm **20** *I'm going to...*	★ learn to ride a motorbike ★ go to fashion college ★ meet a great guy	★ have a huge 18th birthday party! ★ learn to drive ★ take flying lessons	★ go to university ★ design a new computer game ★ make a lot of money
Before I'm **30** *I'm going to see...*	🦋 New York 🦋 Easter Island 🦋 the jungle in Guatemala	🦋 the cockpit of a jet from the pilot's seat 🦋 Graceland 🦋 Kenya	🦋 the Golden Gate Bridge 🦋 the Statue of Liberty 🦋 the Sydney Opera House
Before I'm **40** *I'm going to buy...*	🐱 a Harley Davidson bike 🐱 a flight into space 🐱 100 pairs of shoes (I love shoes!!!)	🐱 a swimming pool 🐱 my own helicopter 🐱 a house for my 12 dogs, my 7 cats and my 4 children	🐱 toys for an orphanage 🐱 a place to live for the homeless in London 🐱 a school for street children in Brazil

6a 🔊39 **Cover the text and photos above and listen. Write *Danielle*, *Sophie* and *Robbie*.**

1 Who is going to see the USA and Australia? *Robbie*
2 Who is going to study fashion?
3 Who is going to have a big family?
4 Who is going to be a pilot?
5 Who is going to do charity work?
6 Who is going to ride a motorbike?

6b Read and check. Whose ideas do you think are the best?

7 Study the sentences and complete the rule.

> **be going to**
>
> *I'm going to buy a Harley Davidson motorbike.*
> *She's going to see New York.*
>
> • Use *be* + _____ + verb for intentions and predictions for the future.

8 Write sentences using *be going to*.

1 my mum/spend some time / Australia / summer
   My mum is going to spend some time in Australia in the summer.
2 my friend and I / buy new bikes / tomorrow
3 David / watch a new DVD / tonight
4 I / stay with a friend / Sunday
5 Carol and Anna / invite 10 people / Saturday evening
6 you / fly to Rome / next Wednesday

9 PAIRWORK Ask and answer about what you are going to do before you are 20, 30 and 40.

10 PAIRWORK Ask and answer questions.

💬 *What are you going to do this evening / next weekend / next week / tomorrow morning?*

Get the grammar

Present continuous for future

1 Match sentences a–c with rules 1–3.

a ☐ *Sandy and Kevin are going on holiday with us in the summer.*

b ☐ *Look! Tony's rollerblading for the first time!*

c ☐ *I'm studying French, Spanish and German this year.*

1 Use the present continuous to say what is happening at the time you are talking.

2 Use the present continuous to talk about temporary actions or situations.

3 Use the present continuous to talk about plans that have already been made and things already organised for the future.

2 Look at Amber's diary for next week and write sentences about her plans.

Amber is meeting Alison to work on a science project on Monday.

MONDAY
meet Alison to work on science project

TUESDAY
buy present for Richard

WEDNESDAY
study for Maths test

THURSDAY
go shopping with Jenny

FRIDAY
go to Richard's party

SATURDAY
stay at home, write emails, read

SUNDAY
visit granny with mum

---

3 Write sentences about your plans or fixed arrangements for next week.

1 On Monday…

2 On Wednesday evening…

3 On Thursday afternoon…

4 On Saturday…

be going to

4 Study the sentences and the rules.

- Use *be going to* to talk about intentions for the future.
- Use *be going to* to make predictions when you know (or can see) at present that something is about to happen.
  My bike is very dirty. I'm going to clean it.
  Look at the clouds. It's going to rain soon.
- **NB** Use the present continuous to talk about plans that have already been made.
  We're playing tennis on Sunday.

5 Write three intentions for the weekend.

I'm going to invite some friends over on Saturday.

6 Write questions and short answers.

1 I'm going to move to Belgium next month. ☑
Are you going to move to Belgium next month?
Yes, I am.

2 They're going to build a new bridge next year. ☒

3 We're going to have dinner in a restaurant tonight. ☒

4 He's going to install a new printer on Friday. ☑

5 She's going to have a party next week. ☑

6 It's going to be a lovely day. ☒

7 I'm going to study Arabic next year. ☑

8 We're going to buy a new TV soon. ☒

Present continuous v *be going to*

7 Study the sentences and complete the rules with *be going to* or the *present continuous*.

I'm seeing Michelle at nine o'clock tonight.
My room is very untidy. I'm going to tidy it.
Look at that car! It's going to crash.
It's ten to three. She's going to ring me soon.
I'm going to visit my aunt this weekend.
We are leaving at four o'clock.

- *be going to* and the present continuous are often interchangeable.
- Use _____ to talk about future plans that have already been made.
- Use _____ to make predictions when you know (or can see) now that something is about to happen.

8 Complete the sentences with the correct form of the verbs in brackets – present continuous or *be going to*.

1 I _____ Anthony later. I want to talk to him about this. (ring)

2 Eminem _____ a concert in London next Tuesday. (give)

3 They're so angry. They _____ an argument when they get home. (have)

4 I _____ Kate in London next weekend. (see)

5 He's driving too fast. He _____ an accident. (cause)

6 We _____ tennis at four o'clock. (play)

7 Jake failed his exams. He _____ harder next year! (study)

8 I had a busy day. I _____ well. (sleep)

9 Martin and Emily _____ to an exhibition at Tate Modern on Sunday. (go)

10 Watch out! You _____ that steak! (burn)

9 ⮌ Workbook pp 220-225; CD-ROM

FILE

INVITING
- Are you free on…?
- What are you doing on…?
- Would you like to come….?

ACCEPTING INVITATIONS
- Thanks. I'd love to.

SUGGESTIONS AND OFFERS
- How about …-ing?
- Shall I / we….?
- Why don't we…?
- Can I help at all?

APOLOGIES
- I'm afraid I can't.
- I'm really sorry.
- I'm so sorry.

ACCEPTING APOLOGIES
- That's OK.
- Don't worry.
- It's not a problem.

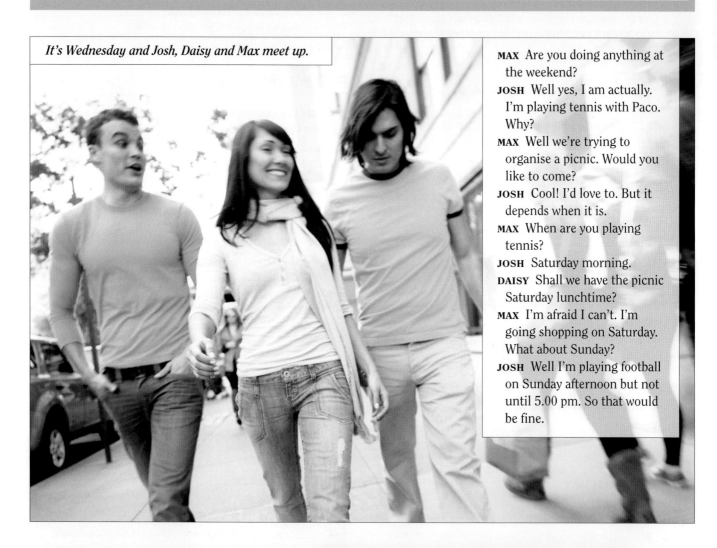

It's Wednesday and Josh, Daisy and Max meet up.

MAX Are you doing anything at the weekend?

JOSH Well yes, I am actually. I'm playing tennis with Paco. Why?

MAX Well we're trying to organise a picnic. Would you like to come?

JOSH Cool! I'd love to. But it depends when it is.

MAX When are you playing tennis?

JOSH Saturday morning.

DAISY Shall we have the picnic Saturday lunchtime?

MAX I'm afraid I can't. I'm going shopping on Saturday. What about Sunday?

JOSH Well I'm playing football on Sunday afternoon but not until 5.00 pm. So that would be fine.

Arranging a picnic

1 🔊40 **Listen and read the dialogue. Answer the questions.**

1 When is Josh playing tennis?
2 When is he playing football?
3 When do the friends agree to have a picnic?

2 🔊41 **Listen and write the correct name for each activity.**

1 organising the drinks _____
2 going to the supermarket _____
3 going to a piano lesson _____
4 bringing a dessert _____

Word **expander** BRING | TAKE

- Use the verb *bring* when the movement is towards where the speaker or the hearer is (or will be):
  I'll bring my CD player to your house for the party.
  Hafsa is bringing her dog to school tomorrow.

- Use the verb *take* when the movement is towards any other place:
  I'll take my dictionary when I go on holiday.
  We took our dog to the vet yesterday.

Organising a barbecue

3 **P ROLE PLAY Work in groups of four.**
- Discuss and arrange a barbecue.
- Use expressions from the *File*.

1 ✉↺ ©

Subject: barbecue
Would you like to come to a bbq at 12.30 on Saturday at my house? Give me a call if you can so we can arrange it. ☺

STUDENT A Invite the others to the barbecue.

STUDENT B You would like to go, but you've got a driving lesson at 12.00 pm.

STUDENT C You think it's a great idea. Offer to do the shopping.

STUDENT D Suggest that you all write a shopping list.

4a **P ROLE PLAY Work in pairs.**
- You want to meet your friend for an hour on Saturday.
- Your diary is here, your friend's diary is in LINKS page 61.
- Ask and answer questions to find out when you can meet.

Saturday morning
9 – 10 am go shopping with Lizzie
10 – 11 am
11 – 12 am meet Alice and Steve to discuss project for school
lunchtime
12 – 2 pm lunch at Riverside Café with Chris
afternoon
2 – 3 pm
3 – 5 pm at home: write emails, read and do Internet research for school project
5 – 6 pm
evening
7 – 10 pm go to the cinema with Chris

Ⓐ *What are you doing on Saturday morning?*
Ⓑ *I'm going to a guitar lesson from 10.00 to 11.00, but I'm free before that. Can we meet then?*
Ⓐ *I'm afraid I'm not. I'm going shopping.*

4b **GAME Test your partner's memory. Ask questions.**

Ⓐ *What am I doing on Saturday between 9:00 and 10:00 am?*
Ⓑ *You're meeting someone.*
Ⓐ *That's wrong.*
Ⓑ *Ah, I think I remember. You're going shopping with…*

5 **Write four sentences about what you are really doing on Saturday.**

6 **Read *Get into Culture* and do the task.**

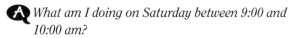

Get into *culture* **BARBECUES**

Barbecues are very popular in the UK in the summer. People invite friends to their gardens at lunchtime or in the early evening. They usually barbecue hamburgers, steak, sausages and vegetables. There are vegetarian sausages and hamburgers too. In the summer, shops sell lots of barbecue equipment and chairs, tables and umbrellas for the garden.

Do many people have barbecues in your country? Are they a popular form of entertainment?

7 **LINKS Real communication pp 16-17**

Reading CLIL

1 PAIRWORK Ask and answer the questions.
1 Where are you going to go for your next holiday?
2 What are you going to do?
3 What's your ideal holiday?
4 Is it different from your next holiday?

2a Scan the advertisements and answer the questions.
1 Where can you do lots of outdoor activities while staying on an island?
2 Where can you study art or learn to cook?
3 Where can you get fit and relax on an activity holiday in the mountains?
4 Where can you stay in a famous city and do exciting things every day?
5 Where can you stay in a famous city, go to galleries and learn about art?
6 Where can you relax and sunbathe, play tennis and listen to music?

2b PAIRWORK Decide which holidays are:

the most interesting | the most boring | the most exciting | the least expensive | the most expensive | the most relaxing | the most educational

Vocabulary: holidays

3a PAIRWORK Complete the mind map with these words and phrases. Add more things to the lists.

book your accommodation | ski suit | passport | swimming costume | international driving licence | pack your suitcase | sun cream | buy a guidebook | ticket | vaccination documents | get currency

3b 🔊42 Listen and check your answers.

Listening

4a 🔊43 Listen to four teenagers. Match them with the correct advertisement.
☐ Adam   ☐ Henry   ☐ Flora   ☐ Emma

4b Listen again and make notes on each person.
• Who is he / she going with?
• How does he / she feel about the holiday?
• What is he / she going to do?

Skills FOR *life* — MAKING NOTES AS YOU LISTEN

When you listen you don't have to write down all the words that you hear. You should only make a note of the main points. Here are some suggestions.
• Don't write in complete sentences.
• Leave out pronouns, adjectives, articles, verbs or prepositions if possible.

For example, if you hear *'Sheila is going to go to the seaside for her holiday in June'* you can write this note:
Sheila seaside holiday June.

Speaking and writing

Pronunciation   *GOING TO*

5 🔊44 Listen and look at the underlined words. What happens to them?
1 I'm going <u>to</u> play tennis tomorrow.
2 What are you going <u>to</u> do tonight?
3 Steve isn't going <u>to</u> watch TV.
4 They're going <u>to</u> buy a DVD.

6a PAIRWORK Plan a ten-day train trip around Europe. Think about the questions.

Where are you going to go? Why? What are you going to see/do/eat?

6b T Give a talk to the class about your trip.

6c P T Write out your holiday plan.

Next summer we're going to travel round Europe by train. We're going to go to Paris first and stay there for two days. I'm going to go on a boat trip on the Seine, but Alex is going to visit the Louvre museum. Boring!

7 🔊45 Go to LINKS page 64 and listen to *Holiday*.

SUMMER IS COMING

TIME TO PLAN YOUR HOLIDAY!

▲ FRENCH VILLAS (frenchfunvillas.co.uk)

Villa Croix des Gardes, Cannes. Sleeps 6. Sunbathe by the huge pool, have a barbecue in the garden, or escape to the basement games room with table tennis and table football. Satellite TV included plus music system in living room. Tennis courts nearby plus fantastic views of the sea. £1,000 per week.

▲ ACTIVITY HOLIDAYS (startwalking.co.uk)

Get away from the stress of everyday life and go walking, fishing or cycling in the lovely Black Forest of Germany. Accommodation in farm houses (family rooms). A healthy holiday for all the family. Only £500 per person per week.

▲ CITY BREAKS (cityculture.co.uk)

A seven-day intensive cultural break in London. Visit the British, Science and V&A museums. Study the world's greatest paintings at the National Gallery and the Royal Academy. Guided tours with special lectures. City centre hotel. A holiday and an education all in one! £600 per person.

▲ ROMANTIC SPAIN (romanticspain.co.uk)

A relaxing two-week holiday near the beautiful city of Granada. A place to read, dream and relax. Courses in conversational Spanish, painting and cookery in the peaceful countryside. £550 per person all inclusive.

▲ ADVENTURE HOLIDAYS (adventurehols.co.uk)

This summer, why not go mountain biking, trekking, horse riding, rafting, and water-skiing on a beautiful Greek island? Enjoy the sun, sea and mountains, and have the most exciting time of your life! £400 per week excluding flights.

▲ AUSTRALIA (visitOz.co.uk)

The best holiday of your life. Two weeks in Sydney in a city-centre three-star hotel. Views of Sydney Harbour Bridge and the Opera House. Ride on a Harley Davidson along the coast. Go to the coolest restaurants, discos and clubs. £1,500 per person including flights.

CHECK OUT OUR GREAT HOLIDAY OFFERS **BOOK TODAY**

Have you ever eaten a curry?

Unit objectives

Grammar: present perfect, present perfect with *for / since*; prepositions of place and movement
Function: talking about experiences; ordering food
Vocabulary: food; past participles

Have you ever been to...
⊙ the UK?
⊙ a football match?
⊙ a music festival?
⊙ a theme park?

Warm up

1 PAIRWORK Look at the pictures on these pages. What can you see?

Comprehension

2a PAIRWORK Ask and answer the questions in the quiz.

Ⓐ *Have you ever been to the UK?*
Ⓑ *Yes, I have. / No, I haven't.*

2b Count up your answers and check your score.

Talking about experiences

3 Study the rules and do the task.

Present perfect

• Use the present perfect to talk about experiences without saying when they happened.
Have you ever eaten a kebab?
I've been to a football match.
I haven't milked a cow (or *I've never milked a cow.*)

Complete the rules with *have / has* and past participle.

• Form the present perfect positive with the subject + _____ + past participle.

• Form the present perfect negative with the subject + *have / has + not +* _____.

• Form questions in the present perfect with _____ + subject (+ *ever*) + _____.

NB When you are giving details about your experiences, e.g. when and where something happened, use the past simple.
I've been to Ireland. I went last year.

4 Find the past participles of these verbs in the quiz. Which ones are regular?

eat | drink | see | grow | win | ride | read | cook | sleep | pick

5a PAIRWORK Give more information about each question.

Ⓐ *I've never been to a music festival. I'd really like to go.*
Ⓑ *I've slept in a tent. It was last summer on holiday by the sea.*

5b Swap partners. Tell your new partner about your first partner's answers.

Eduardo hasn't ever won a prize but he's seen a famous person.

6 T Write more quiz questions. Ask a partner your questions.

Have you ever eaten...
⊙ a curry?
⊙ Thai food?
⊙ a kebab?
⊙ Japanese food?

Have you ever...
- ⊙ won a prize?
- ⊙ ridden a horse?
- ⊙ slept in a tent?
- ⊙ read a Harry Potter book?

IT'S FOR REAL

Have you ever seen...
- ⊙ a famous person?
- ⊙ a balloon festival?
- ⊙ an elephant?
- ⊙ a waterfall?

Have you ever...
- ⊙ been to a farm?
- ⊙ picked fruit from a tree?
- ⊙ milked a cow or a goat?
- ⊙ grown vegetables?

Have you ever drunk...
- ⊙ a smoothie?
- ⊙ a vanilla-flavoured Coke?
- ⊙ iced tea?
- ⊙ vegetable juice?

Have you ever cooked...?
- ⊙ an omelette?
- ⊙ spaghetti?
- ⊙ a pizza?
- ⊙ a cake?

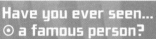

Score (one point for each Yes answer)

22–28 Wow! Is there anything you haven't done?

16–21 Well done! You're a very adventurous person!

8–15 Hey, not bad. You aren't afraid of new things!

0–7 Don't worry! There's plenty of time to catch up!

WELCOME TO
Rose's blog

most recent post older

HOME PROFILE BLOG PHOTOS FRIENDS EVENTS

Hi there! What an amazing time! Things have been crazy since we moved here to Brighton. We've lived here for six months now – and my life has really changed. I've got new friends. I'm in a band. We've collected lots of money for my favourite charity (in fact, we've collected over £500 since Monday). And… I'm in love! ☺ ☺ ☺

Jack's been my 'official' boyfriend for three weeks now. We see each other every day and we send texts the whole time. He's sent me five texts since seven o'clock this morning– and it's still only eleven o'clock!

What other news is there?
Oh yeah. I nearly forgot (ha ha!). Last Saturday we met a music producer in London. His name's Alec James and he's a really nice guy. He's successful, too. And he wants us to record an album of our own songs! The first Yellow Fish CD ever! We're going to be famous (maybe)! LOL

7 Read Rose's blog and write short answers to the questions.

1 How long has Rose lived in Brighton?
2 How much money has the band collected since Monday?
3 How does Rose describe Jack?
4 How often do Rose and Jack see each other?
5 How many texts has Jack sent this morning?
6 When did Rose and the band meet Alec James?

8 Study the rules and do the task.

Present perfect with *for / since*

• Use the present perfect with *for / since* to say how long something has lasted or when it started.
Jack's been my boyfriend for three weeks.
He's sent me five texts since seven o'clock.

Complete the rules with *for* or *since*.

• Use _____ + a period of time.
• Use _____ + a specific date or point in time.

9 Write sentences in the present perfect with *for* or *since*.

1 Katie / live / in Manchester / five years
  Katie's lived in Manchester for five years.
2 I / have / this coat / last October
3 My uncle / work / in a bank / three months
4 I / love / cartoons / I was young
5 They / have / a cat / 2006
6 James / not read / a book / five years

10 PAIRWORK Ask and answer questions using *for* or *since*.

How long have you…
• been at this school?
• lived in your house / apartment?
• had your present hairstyle?
• had your mobile phone?

Ⓐ *How long have you been at this school?*
Ⓑ *For two years.*

Present perfect

1 Study the rules and the sentences. Then complete the table.

- Use the present perfect to talk about past actions when the exact moment is not important.
  Justin has been to New York three times.
- Use the present perfect to talk about all your experiences up to now.
  I've never been to the USA.
- Use *ever* in questions with the present perfect to find out if something has happened before.
  Have you ever talked to a famous person?

Positive	I/You/We/They	have	eaten.
	He/She/It	has	eaten.
Negative	I/You/We/They	haven't	_____.
	He/She/It	_____	eaten.
Questions	Have	I/you/we/they	eaten?
	_____	he/she/it	eaten?

Short answers		
Positive	Yes, I/you/we/they	have.
	Yes, he/she/it	_____.
Negative	No, I/you/we/they	haven't.
	No, he/she/it	_____.

2 Match the questions and answers.

1 ☐ Have you seen *The Lord of the Rings*?
2 ☐ Has your friend ever been to Canada?
3 ☐ Have you ever eaten alligator steak?
4 ☐ Have you seen the cat?
5 ☐ Have you eaten?
6 ☐ Has Peter come home?

a No, I haven't, and I don't want to!
b Yes, I've had a hamburger.
c Yes, I have – it's in the garden.
d No, he hasn't. I think he's still at school.
e Yes, I have – all three parts.
f Yes, she has. Vancouver.

Past participles

3 Read the rules and write the past participles.

The past participles of regular verbs, and some irregular verbs, have the same form as the past simple.
- regular verbs add *-ed* to the base form. *wash – washed*
- verbs ending in *-e* add *-d* to the base form. *like – liked*
- verbs ending in *-y* change *-y* to *-i* and add *-ed* to the base form. *cry – cried*
- verbs ending in a consonant after a short vowel double the consonant. *fit – fitted*

Base form	Past participle	Base form	Past participle
watch		study	
collect		see	
work		write	
eat		stop	
live		go	

Present perfect with *for / since*

4 Complete the table with these expressions.

an hour | I was little | 2001 | ten years | a week | yesterday | a long time | March | the whole day | this morning

for + a period of time ...	*since* + a specific time ...

5 Write six sentences about yourself and your family using the present perfect with *for* or *since*.

1 We've had our car for six months.

Prepositions of place and movement

6 Study the prepositional phrases and then complete the rules with *in, at* and *to*.

in the kitchen	*in Green Street*
in Leicester Square	*in London*
in the UK	*at the bus stop*
at school	*at the restaurant*
go to Manchester	*go to the airport*

- Use _____ to say where someone or something is eg a room, a shop, a street, a square, a town, a country or a continent.
- Use _____ to refer to a specific point or to the function of a building, eg a school, a restaurant, the dentist's, etc.
- Use _____ to talk about direction.
- Use: *at home, in a book, in the sun.*

7 Complete the sentences with the correct prepositions.

1 She is not _____ home. She's still _____ school.
2 Let's meet _____ the station at four.
3 Jane is _____ the doctor's _____ the centre of town.
4 The cathedral is _____ the main square.
5 I'd like to go _____ England this summer. I want to study English _____ a college.
6 The British Museum is _____ Trafalgar Square.
7 There are a lot of beautiful places _____ the USA.
8 Shall we meet _____ the bus stop?
9 I met my husband _____ Times Square, New York.
10 Excuse me. When's the next train _____ Stratford?

8 **Workbook pp 226-231; CD-ROM**

Real communication
EATING OUT

Vocabulary: food

1 GROUPWORK What are the possible ingredients of these three dishes?

eggs | mushrooms | cabbage | tomatoes | onions | carrots | pasta | courgettes | cheese | potatoes | rice | aubergines | peppers | garlic

tomatoes

tomato pasta

vegetable soup

Spanish omelette

cabbage

eggs

Ordering in a sandwich bar

2a 46 Complete the dialogue with these words. Then listen and check your answers.

can | white | here | all | please | help | baguette | large

2b PAIRWORK Practise the dialogue. Order different things from the menu.

Mega
SANDWICH BAR

Choice of freshly-made fillings in a white or brown bread sandwich, or a freshly baked baguette.
(Baguette + 30p)

Sandwiches		Drinks		
Cheese and tomato	£2.00	Mineral water		£1.00
Houmous and salad	£2.00	Cans of drink		85p
Tuna mayo	£2.20	Orange juice		£1.10
Mozzarella and sun-dried tomato	£2.50	Filter coffee	SMALL	£1.40
			LARGE	£1.60
Chicken tikka	£2.50	Cappuccino	SMALL	£1.70
BLT (Bacon, lettuce and tomato)	£2.50		LARGE	£2.00
		Espresso		£1.60
Prawn mayonnaise	£2.60	Americano		£1.60
Ham and mustard	£2.60	Hot chocolate		£1.90

SERVER Can I help you?
DEV Can I have a tuna mayo sandwich, please?
SERVER Sure, brown or [1]_____ bread?
DEV White, please.
SERVER Is that [2]_____?
SHIRIN Oh, I'll have a chicken tikka [3]_____, please.
SERVER Sure. Any drinks?
DEV Oh, a cappuccino, [4]_____.
SERVER [5]_____ or small?
DEV Um... small, please.
SHIRIN And a [6]_____ of cola for me, please.
SERVER Cans are in the drinks fridge. [7]_____ yourself.
SHIRIN Thanks.
SERVER [8]_____ you are. That's £7.55.

Modal verb *will*   Use *I'll have...* when you order something in a restaurant or a bar.

Eating out in a restaurant

3 Read the menu and answer the questions.

1 Which items are: fish dishes | meat dishes | vegetarian dishes?

2 Which dishes are: roast | grilled | toasted | fried?

3 What is the difference between these cooking methods?

4 Read *Get into Culture* and do the task.

5 🔊 **P Listen to the customers and make a note of what they order from the menu.**

1 Roger and Jenny   2 Lisa and Jack

3 Shaun and Zoe   4 Maria and Simone

6 🔊 **Complete these sentences from the dialogues. Then listen and check.**

1 I think I'll _____ the prawns and avocado.

2 And what would you _____ for your main course?

3 **A** How _____ you like your steak sir?
  B Medium, please.

4 And I'd _____ a Carlsberg beer.

5 _____ else?

6 No that's _____ thank you.

7 _____ you like to order now?

8 I'd like to have fish. _____ is the fish today?

9 _____ coffees?

7 ROLEPLAY Work in groups of three.

• Two students are customers and one student is the waiter.

• Order food and drink from the menu.

• Use the expressions from the *File* and exercise 6.

t.a.s.t.e.
MENU OF THE DAY

STARTERS ALL AT £4.50

Soup of the day

Prawns and avocado

Mozzarella, tomato and basil salad

Grilled wild mushrooms
on speciality toasted bread

MAIN COURSES ALL AT £10.50
(except the fish)

Fisherman's pie
(fish and seafood with cheese topping)

Roast lamb
with traditional roast vegetables

Scotch sirloin steak
with a choice of sauces

E.A.T. vegetarian salad
(roast peppers, pine nuts,
artichokes and parmesan)

Fish in season (see the blackboard)

Grilled chicken breast with herb butter

SIDE DISHES ALL AT £3.50

fried mushrooms

chips

mixed salad

fresh vegetables

DESSERTS ALL AT £4.90

lemon tart

banana cream pie

rich dark chocolate cake

DRINKS

Mineral water large bottle £3.00

Beer £3.50

Red house wine a bottle £11.00

White house wine a bottle £11.00

Coffee £2.50

8 **LINKS Real communication pp 16–17**

FOOD...
YOUR CONFESSIONS!

What is your absolutely favourite food?
Chocolate.
Where is the strangest place you have ever eaten?
In front of an elegant clothes shop.
What's the most revolting food you've ever eaten?
Octopus.
What should you never do at the dining table?
Eat in a hurry.

What is your absolutely favourite food?
Spaghetti with tomato sauce.
Where is the strangest place you have ever eaten?
Sitting on the floor near the fridge.
What's the most revolting food you've ever eaten?
Grilled snails.
What should you never do at the dining table?
Speak with your mouth full.

What is your absolutely favourite food?
Popcorn.
Where is the strangest place you have ever eaten?
In a swimming pool.
What's the most revolting food you've ever eaten?
Liquorice.
What should you never do at the dining table?
Keep your mobile phone by your plate.

What is your absolutely favourite food?
Chicken and mayonnaise.
Where is the strangest place you have ever eaten?
At the top of the Empire State building.
What's the most revolting food you've ever eaten?
Meat.
What should you never do at the dining table?
Put your elbows on the table.

Reading and speaking

1 GROUPWORK In groups of three, look at these words and check the ones you don't know in a dictionary. Then discuss your opinions.

prawns | ice cream | tripe | olives | pizza | snails | liquorice | pasta | octopus | hamburgers | liver | spinach | steak | chocolate | yoghurt | nuts | beans | cake

A *I love octopus. I think it's delicious!*
B *Do you? I hate it. I think it's disgusting.*
C *Actually, I've never had octopus.*

2 Read the article and answer the questions. Who...

1 has eaten in the strangest place? _____
2 hates a food that you quite like? _____
3 likes a food that you don't really like? _____
4 talks about a habit that you don't like? _____

3 PAIRWORK Ask and answer the questions in the article.

Listening CLIL

4a 49 P Study the Eatwell Plate. Then listen to the radio broadcast. Number the food groups in the order you hear them.

☐ Fruit and vegetables
☐ Bread, rice, potatoes, pasta and other starchy foods
☐ Milk and dairy products
☐ Food and drink high in fat and/or sugar
☐ Meat, fish, eggs, beans and other non-dairy sources of protein

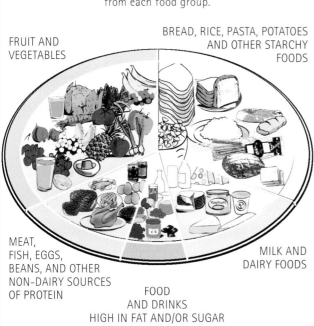

THE EATWELL PLATE
Use the eatwell plate to help you get the right balance. It shows how much of what you eat should come from each food group.

FRUIT AND VEGETABLES

BREAD, RICE, PASTA, POTATOES AND OTHER STARCHY FOODS

MEAT, FISH, EGGS, BEANS, AND OTHER NON-DAIRY SOURCES OF PROTEIN

FOOD AND DRINKS HIGH IN FAT AND/OR SUGAR

MILK AND DAIRY FOODS

4b Listen again and circle the correct words.

1 Low carbohydrate diets are usually high in *protein / fat*.
2 Most people today need to eat *more / fewer* carbohydrates.
3 We need *five / eight* portions of fruit and vegetables every day.
4 Milk and dairy products are good for the *heart / bones*.
5 People should eat more *meat / fish*.
6 You *should / shouldn't* eat olive oil, avocadoes, nuts and seeds.

4c What is your diet like? Make a list of what you have eaten in the last two days. Write each item under one of the five food groups.

Pronunciation CONSONANTS WITH /r/

5 50 /r/ is a soft sound in English. Listen and repeat the words.

1 fresh fruit
2 breakfast bread
3 grilled grated
4 strawberry scrambled
5 tripe trout
6 croissant cream
7 prawn apricot

Writing

6 P T Write a 100–200 word composition about the Mediterranean diet. Do some research on the Internet or in the library.

Skills FOR life WRITING A COMPOSITION

• Collect all your ideas.

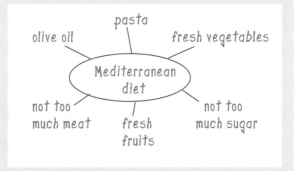

olive oil
pasta
fresh vegetables
Mediterranean diet
not too much meat
fresh fruits
not too much sugar

• Do some research on the topic in books and on the Internet.
• Write an outline for the composition:
PARA 1: introduction: what the Mediterranean diet is
PARA 2: why it is a healthy diet
PARA 3: some typical dishes
PARA 4: conclusion
• Write the composition. Check the grammar and spelling.

FILE

MAINTAINING A CONVERSATION

When you are chatting, the conversation quickly moves from one topic to another. So you need to be able to find new words easily and develop strategies to explain what you mean. You also need to develop a good general vocabulary of everyday words.

Towards PET Paper 3 Speaking, Part 4
Trinity ISE The Interview conversation phase

Tips

In preparation for the discussion parts of the exam, check that:
• you have enough words, and in enough variety, for each topic.
• you can use a range of tenses and pass from one to the other.
• you can ask different types of questions and use interrogative pronouns and adverbs.

Useful language

TAKING TIME
Um... / Er... / Let me think... / Hold on a second...

VAGUE LANGUAGE
stuff, thing, I mean, sort of, you know

EXPLANATION
They're the things you wear on your hands when it's cold. It's the person who bakes cakes. It's the shop where you buy newspapers.

APOLOGY
I'm sorry I can't remember / I don't know the word.

1 **PAIRWORK Add a question to each word field. Try to use different tenses in your questions.**

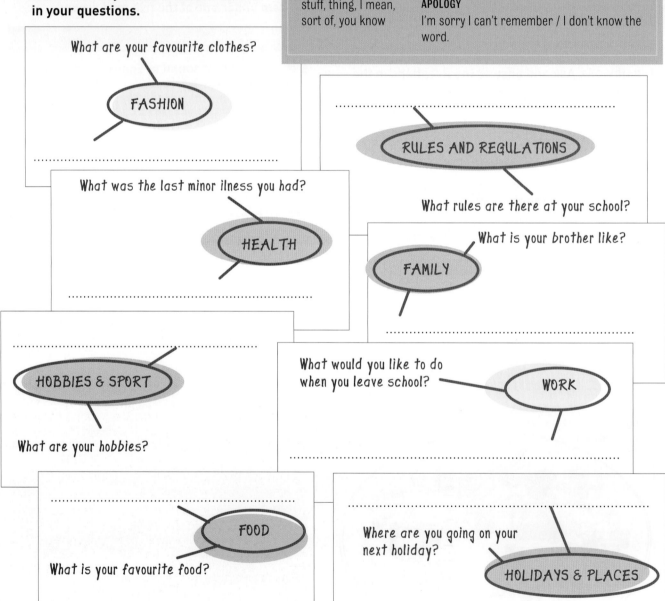

What are your favourite clothes?
FASHION

....
RULES AND REGULATIONS

What was the last minor ilness you had?
HEALTH

What rules are there at your school?

What is your brother like?
FAMILY

HOBBIES & SPORT

What are your hobbies?

What would you like to do when you leave school?
WORK

FOOD

What is your favourite food?

Where are you going on your next holiday?
HOLIDAYS & PLACES

2 **P T GROUPWORK Try to maintain a conversation for two minutes!**

A *What are your favourite clothes?*
B *I like wearing jeans and trainers. I never wear hats.*

FILE

LISTENING FOR SPECIFIC INFORMATION

When we listen we often have to identify what is being discussed, eg in a radio announcement, a conversation in a shop, a long speech, etc. In the Cambridge PET exam you have to listen to some short recordings and identify the correct picture out of three pictures for each question.

Towards PET Paper 2 Listening, Part 1

Tips

BEFORE YOU LISTEN
• Look at the pictures and think about which words you will probably hear.

WHILE YOU LISTEN
• The first time you listen, identify the key words and see if you can eliminate one or even two of the three pictures.
• Don't worry about understanding everything you hear.
• The second time you hear the recording, listen to confirm what you think is correct.

---

1 🔊 **P Listen and choose the correct picture and put a tick ☑ in the box.**

1 Where did the girl leave her mobile phone?

2 What did the man buy in the shop?

3 What do they order?

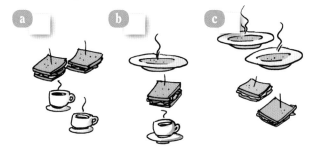

4 What is the weather going to be like tomorrow?

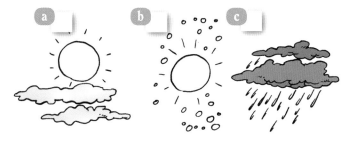

5 What is the gate and time of the flight?

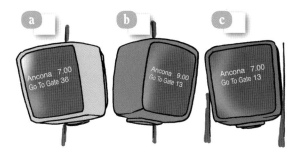

6 What clothes is the girl wearing?

7 What are they doing at the weekend?

2 ➡️ **LINKS Exam Listening p 17**

LANGUAGE CHECK

1 Look at Lucy's diary for next week. Complete and answer the questions.

> **MONDAY**
> Meet Gemma for lunch ☑
> **TUESDAY**
> Go to tennis lesson ☒
> do science homework with Ian ☑
> **WEDNESDAY**
> Jack arrives home ☑
> practising song for the concert ☒
> **THURSDAY**
> Mum and Dad buying new computer ☑

1 On Monday is Lucy _meeting / going to meet Gemma for lunch? Yes, she is._ _____

2 On Tuesday is Lucy _____ _____

3 On Tuesday are Lucy and Ian _____ _____

4 On Wednesday is Jack _____ _____

5 On Wednesday is Lucy _____ _____

6 On Thursday are Lucy's parents _____ _____

2 Choose the correct words.

1 _____ you been to Greece?
  a) Do   b) Has   c) Have   d) Are

2 Has she ever _____ octopus?
  a) ate   b) eaten c) eating d) eated

3 I've _____ done a parachute jump.
  a) never b) ever c) not   d) haven't

4 'Have they ordered their food?' 'Yes, _____.'
  a) they did   c) they do
  b) they are   d) they have

5 He's studied Russian _____ six years.
  a) the   b) ago   c) for   d) since

TOTAL: ____/10

---

3 Complete the holiday words.

1 the place where you stay – a_ _ _ _ _ _ _ _ _ _ _
2 you need this to travel – t_ _ _ _ _
3 you need this to go to a different country – p_ _ _ _ _ _ _
4 you put this on your face when it is very sunny – s_ _ c_ _ _ _
5 you can get this at the bank – c_ _ _ _ _ _

4 Complete the menu items.

1 hroumosm _____ omelette
2 blateevge _____ soup
3 nwapr _____ sandwich
4 mootta _____ pasta
5 cecnikh _____ tikka baguette

TOTAL: ____/10

---

5 Circle the correct words to complete the dialogues.

1 A Can I [1] *serve / help* you?
  B Yes. I'd [2] *like / have* a tuna mayo sandwich, please.
  A [3] *Anything / Any* to drink?
  B No, that's [4] *else / all*, thanks.
  A OK. [5] *Help / Take* yourself to salad from the salad bar.

2 A [6] *Would / Can* you like to come out for a meal?
  B Yes, I'd love [7] *it / to*.
  A Great. Are you [8] *free / OK* on Friday evening?
  B I'm [9] *sorry / afraid*. It's my brother's birthday.
  A It's not a [10] *problem / worry*. What about Saturday?

TOTAL: ____/10

6 PAIRWORK Ask and answer questions about your plans for next year. Include these things:

- subjects / study ?
- exams / take ?
- free-time activities ?
- where / holiday ?
- exciting experiences / looking forward to ?

TOTAL: ____/10

TOTAL: ____/40

 LINKS Interculture pp 36-37; Story pp 44-45; CLIL (Biology) pp 58-59; DVD Food

FOR REAL
elementary
Martyn Hobbs and Julia Starr Keddle
with Rob Nicholas
Workbook

Contents

Grammar reference

Present simple

Positive		
I/You	speak	
He/She/It	speaks	Italian.
We/You/They	speak	

Negative full form				
I/You	do			
He/She/It	does	not	speak	French.
We/You/They	do			

short form			
I/You	don't		
He/She/It	doesn't	speak	French.
We/You/They	don't		

- The present simple positive for *I, you, we* and *they* is the same as the base form.
- Form the present simple positive for *he, she* and *it* by adding *-s* to the base form.
- Form the present simple negative with:
  subject (*I, you, we, they*) + *do not / don't* + base form
  subject (*he, she, it*) + *does not / doesn't* + base form

Usage

Use the present simple to talk about:
- actions in our daily routine
  She goes to school every day.
  They don't study English on Tuesdays.
- likes or dislikes
  We like chocolate.
  She doesn't like pizza.
- facts that are always true
  Italians drink a lot of coffee.
  He doesn't go to school with me.

Questions			
Do	I/you		
Does	he/she/it	go	to a gym?
Do	we/you/they		

Positive short answers		
Yes,	I/you	do.
Yes,	he/she/it	does.
Yes,	we/you/they	do.

Negative short answers		
No,	I/you	don't.
No,	he/she/it	doesn't.
No,	we/you/they	don't.

- Form present simple questions with:
  do + subject (*I, you, we, they*) + base form
  does + subject (*he, she, it*) + base form
- Form present simple positive short answers with:
  Yes, I / you / we / they + do.
  Yes, he / she / it + does.
- Form present simple negative short answers with:
  No, I / you / we / they + don't.
  No, he / she / it + doesn't.

like, love, etc. + *-ing* form

- Form the *-ing* form, (the gerund), by adding *-ing* to the base form.
  walk ⟶ walking
  play ⟶ playing
  Note the following spelling rules.
- If the verb ends in *-e*, omit the final *-e* before adding *-ing*.
  dance ⟶ dancing
  ride ⟶ riding
- If the verb ends in a single consonant after a single stressed vowel, double the consonant before adding *-ing*.
  jog ⟶ jogging
  swim ⟶ swimming
- If the verb ends in the consonant *l* after a single vowel (stressed or unstressed), double the *l*.
  travel ⟶ travelling
- If the verb ends in *-y*, just add *-ing*. But if the verb ends in *-ie* change the *ie* into *-ying*.
  try ⟶ trying
  lie ⟶ lying

Usage

• Use the -ing form after verbs of preference like *love*, *like* and *hate*.

  I love singing.
  We don't like jogging.

So do I. / Neither do I.

	Agree	Disagree
I love music.	So do I.	I don't.
I don't like sport.	Neither do I.	I do.

To express agreement or to say *Me too / Me neither* use:

• *So do I* after a positive sentence
  I love taking photos. – So do I.
• *Neither do I* after a negative sentence
  She doesn't speak Chinese. – Neither do I.

To express disagreement use:

• *I don't* after a positive sentence
  I understand French. – I don't.
• *I do* after a negative sentence
  He doesn't love dogs. – I do.

Modal verb *can*

Positive

I/You/He/She/It/We/They	can	dance.

Negative

I/You/He/She/It/We/They	can't	dance.

Questions

Can	I/you/he/she/it/we/they	dance?

Positive short answers

Yes,	I/you/he/she/it/we/they	can.

Negative short answers

No,	I/you/he/she/it/we/they	can't.

Can is a modal verb. Remember, modal verbs:

• don't take -s when the subject is *he*, *she* or *it*
  He can ski. NOT ~~He cans ski.~~
• are followed by the base form
  We can sing well.
• form the negative by adding *not* + base form
  He can't drive.
• go before the subject in questions
  Can you play an instrument?

Usage

• Use *can* to talk about being able to do something.
  They can dance quite well.
  We can't understand what he's saying.

Word list

The words in grey appear in the unit, but are not in the vocabulary sections.

Sports

athletics	rugby
basketball	running
canoeing	sailing
cycling	skiing
diving	skydiving
football	surfing
golf	swimming
gymnastics	table tennis
hockey	tennis
judo	volleyball
karate	waterskiing
riding	windsurfing

Hobbies and interests

acting in plays	playing computer games
collecting things	reading books
drawing	taking photos
painting pictures	writing poetry / stories / blogs
playing an instrument	

Musical instruments

clarinet	keyboards
drums	piano
guitar	violin

Films

action film	musical
cartoon	romantic film
comedy	science fiction film
fantasy film	teen movie
horror film	thriller

Vocabulary

Sports

1 Write the letters in the correct order to make sports.

1 **stingyscam** is very difficult – I can't do it. _gymnastics_

2 When I'm on holiday by the sea, I always go
   dwinfinrugs. w_____

3 **latchetis** is an Olympic sport. a_____

4 My brother likes **ydivsinkg** – but I don't want to jump
   out of a plane! s_____

5 I like **wignimms** in the sea. s_____

6 I try to go **irnugnn** two or three times a week.
   r_____

7 China has got a lot of really good **bleat nestin** players.
   t_____

2 Write the sports.

1 I hit the ball over a net with my hands. __volleyball__
2 I love scoring goals. f_____
3 I run really fast with the ball in my hands. r_____
4 This is exciting when the boat goes really fast!
   s_____
5 I like riding on very quiet roads – I don't like busy
   roads. c_____
6 I like doing this when there is lots of snow.
   s_____

Hobbies and interests

3 Complete the sentences with the correct verbs.

1 My brother likes _____ in plays.
2 My favourite activity is _____ books.
3 I enjoy _____ pictures.
4 My sister enjoys _____ her blog.
5 My friends and I like _____ computer games.
6 My dad likes _____ photos.
7 My best friend likes _____ stamps and postcards.
8 My favourite hobby is _____ football.

Films

4 Complete the sentences with the correct film type.

1 __Thrillers__ , like *Hancock*, are great!
2 I don't like _____ – they're frightening.
3 My brother always watches _____ about
   space and monsters.
4 We laugh when we watch _____ because
   they're funny!
5 I'm a teenager, so _____ are perfect for me!
6 My sister watches _____ about people who
   are in love.
7 My dad likes _____ – and he sings along!
8 My favourite _____ are *Mickey Mouse* and
   Dora the Explorer.

Grammar

Present simple

1 Complete the sentences with the correct form of these verbs. Check your spelling.

fly	go	~~wash~~	have	do	watch

1 Susi __washes__ her hair every day.
2 Sally _____ a small plane at weekends.
3 Ben _____ his homework at night.
4 Chris _____ TV every day.
5 Marta _____ tennis lessons on Tuesdays.
6 Paolo _____ on skiing holidays in Switzerland.

2 Complete the sentences with the correct form of the verbs in brackets.

1 Joe __likes__ (like) playing the guitar. He
   _____ (not speak) Chinese, but he _____
   (speak) German and French.
2 Olivia _____ (study) at university. She
   _____ (go) out with her friends at the weekend.
   They _____ (like) dancing, but they _____
   (not sing) karaoke!
3 Naomi _____ (come) from Canada. She
   _____ (play) the piano and she _____
   (practise) every day.
4 Lewis _____ (be) a marathon runner. He
   _____ (not have) a lot of free time, but he
   _____ (windsurf) and plays the drums.

3 Correct the statements about the people in exercise 2. Write one negative sentence and one positive sentence.

1 Joe speaks Spanish.
   He __doesn't speak Spanish__.
   He __speaks German and French__.
2 Olivia and her friends like playing the guitar.
   They _____.
   They _____.
3 Naomi comes from Australia.
   She _____.
   She _____.
4 Lewis plays the piano.
   He _____.
   He _____.

4 Write short answers to the questions.

1 Do you like ice cream? ☑
   __Yes, I do.__
2 Does Tom live here? ☒
   _____
3 Do they like English? ☑
   _____
4 Does Mary eat fish? ☑
   _____
5 Do Mark and Peter play football? ☒
   _____

like, love + -ing form

5 Complete the sentences with the correct form of these verbs.

| eat | go | act | wear |
| cook | walk | play | shop |

1 My dad hates __going__ to the shops with Mum. He thinks it's boring.
2 My sister and I love _____ at the weekend. We buy lots of clothes.
3 I love _____ jeans. They're so comfortable.
4 Mum hates _____, so her food is horrible!
5 My brother doesn't like _____ football.
6 My sister really likes _____ vegetables. I can't understand it!
7 I want to be an actor. I love _____.
8 I don't mind running, but I love _____ – it's great exercise.

6 Now write sentences about yourself.

I love going to the shops. I think it's really great.

So do I. / Neither do I.

7 Look at the table and complete the dialogue between Carol and James. Use *So do I, Neither do I, I do* or *I don't* or the correct form of the verbs in brackets.

CAROL 🙂 🙁

vegetarian food / fish / pasta *rock, reggae* *phoning my friends* *swimming* *skateboarding* *hanging out with cool people* *pizza / fast food (not burgers!)*	*football (boring!)* *hanging out with parents* *dogs* *dance music*

JAMES 🙂 🙁

McDonald's, KFC, Burger King (all fast food!) *Oh, and pasta* *reggae* *swimming, windsurfing (anything in water)* *my new mobile* *football, rugby, tennis* *my dog (cats are OK, too)* *hanging out with cool people*	*vegetarian food* *dance music* *doing things with my parents (sorry, Mum)*

Carol So let's see what we have in common. What do you like [1] __eating__ (eat)? I love vegetarian food.
James Oh no, [2] __I don't__. No vegetarian food, please. I like a nice burger.
Carol [3] _____. I hate burgers! I like pasta.
James Yeah, [4] _____. What about music? I love [5] _____ (listen) to reggae.
Carol [6] _____! And I'm a big rock fan. I really don't like dance music.
James No, [7] _____. So, have you got a mobile? I've got a new mobile and I love [8] _____ (phone) my friends.
Carol [9] _____. It's great! How about skateboarding? And swimming – I love [10] _____ (be) in the water.
James [11] _____. I don't like water. I like [12] _____ (play) football.
Carol [13] _____. I hate it – it's so boring! Oh, and I don't like dogs.
James Really? [14] _____. I love [15] _____ (spend) time with my dog. But not with my parents.
Carol No, [16] _____. I just want to hang out with cool people – people like us.

Modal verb *can*

8 Look at the table and write a sentence for each person.

	Jeff	Beth	Helen	Guy
sing	✗	✗	✓	✗
dance	✗	✓	✓	✗
paint	✗	✓	✓	✗
act	✓	✓	✗	✓

1 Jeff _can't sing, dance or paint, but he can act._
_____.
2 Beth _____
_____.
3 Helen _____
_____.
4 Guy _____
_____.

Skills: Reading – Towards PET (Part 3)

1 Read the texts and look at the pictures. Put a tick ☑ by the objects the people mention.

Jim
a ☐   b ☐   c ☐   d ☐

Simone
a ☐   b ☐   c ☐   d ☐

Janet
a ☐   b ☐   c ☐   d ☐

My favourite things

Jim

My skateboards are my best friends. (Don't tell Ben – he thinks *he's* my best friend!) I'm no good at extreme sports – I love them though.

I practise every weekend with Ben. He's a great skater. I can't do a 180° turn yet, but I can go downhill. I know – it's not very good, but one day …

I also have a snowboard, but I can only go when my dad takes us skiing in Italy (and that's never!). I have scuba lessons too. It's really cool, but I can't swim very well.

Simone

Music – I love music! I don't buy a lot of CDs. I've got about fifty, but I've got hundreds of songs on my computer. I use lots of different download sites. You can get music by Lily Allen, Snow Patrol and a lot of other great bands.

My wall is full of posters. I think Chris Brown is fantastic – he's a great singer, a brilliant dancer and he's sooo good-looking. But my favourite thing is my mp3 player. I take it everywhere. I can listen to hundreds of my favourite songs. How cool is that?

Janet

I love reading so much. I read everything I can – mystery, fantasy, newspapers, the Internet (there are some great websites – the newspapers have all got really interesting websites). My mum says I should go out with my friends more, but I really like staying at home with a great book. I also love Clover, my pet dog. We go walking every morning and evening. Clover's my best friend. He sleeps on my bed.

2 Circle T (True) or F (False).

1 Jim is very good at extreme sports. T / F
2 He often goes snowboarding. T / F
3 He enjoys scuba-diving. T / F
4 Simone buys lots of CDs. T / F
5 She hasn't got any posters on her wall. T / F
6 She has always got her mp3 player with her. T / F
7 Janet reads lots of different things. T / F
8 She goes out with her friends a lot. T / F
9 She walks with her dog every day. T / F
10 Janet's dog sleeps outside. T / F

Writing

3 Write an email to an English-speaking friend about some of the things you like doing and some of the things you don't like doing. (70–80 words)

> **► Tips**
> - Use the Reading text above for ideas.
> - Use the Word list for ideas (e.g. *I like playing football. / I don't like listening to guitar music. / I don't like watching thrillers.*).
> - Use some of the verbs from the unit (e.g. *eat / go / be / wear / cook / play*).
> - Connect some of your sentences using *and / but / because*, etc.

Study skills Learning a language

1 Read the tips and tick ☑ the three you like best.

2 Write your own tip in the comment box. Invent an English user name!

---

dreamzone

Question

What are your tips for learning a language?

Answer the question

Answers

| | It's good to find a personal link with the language. It could be music, films, computer games.
rollingstar | ☐ |

| | Reading reading reading. Websites, chatrooms, simplified stories, song words, – even instruction manuals, if that's your sort of thing!
smarty | ☐ |

| | Don't spend too long studying. Little and often is the secret.
silvercar | ☐ |

| | Make a notebook. And write down new words. Then remember to read them again!
fashionista | ☐ |

| | Music! Lots of my favourite bands are American or English. So I learn lots of English! Even the pronunciation.
polarbear | ☐ |

| | I like the CD-ROM that comes with my course. I can use it when I'm on the computer and the exercises are fun! That's a surprise. I enjoy them!
elbow | ☐ |

| | Find a penpal. Write a blog. There are lots of blogs and you can practise your English and make new friends.
wizardwand | ☐ |

| | Don't worry about making mistakes. They are part of learning a language. And you can learn a lot from your mistakes.
mouse2 | ☐ |

Comments

Grammar reference

Present simple: question words

Wh- questions			
Where	do	I/you	live?
	does	he/she/it	
	do	we/you/they	

- Remember that we form present simple questions with:
  do + subject (*I, you, we, they*) + base form
  does + subject (*he, she, it*) + base form
- If the question begins with an interrogative pronoun, adjective or adverb (*Wh-* question), use:
  interrogative + *do/does* + subject + base form
  Where do you live?
  What time do you get up?
- Interrogative pronouns, adjectives and adverbs are called *question words*.

Who?	*Where?*
What?	*When?*
What... like?	*Why?*
What time?	*How often?*
Which?	*How?*

- Form *wh-* questions with:
  question word + *do/does* + subject + base form of verb
- Don't put a preposition in front of question words. If there is a preposition, put it at the end of the sentence.
  How often do you go to the cinema?
  Who do you go with? NOT ~~With who do you go?~~
- **BE CAREFUL!** When the interrogative is the subject of the sentence, form the question with:
  question word + main verb
  Who knows? NOT ~~Who does know?~~
  What makes you happy?
  NOT ~~What does make you happy?~~
  Who plays the piano?
  NOT ~~Who does play the piano?~~

Adverbs of frequency

100%	95%	60%	30%	0%
always	usually	often	sometimes	never

- Put adverbs of frequency before the main verb but after the verb *be*.
  Do you often listen to pop music?
  I'm usually late.

What's she like? v What does she like?

- To ask for an opinion or a description of a person or thing, use:
  What + verb *be* + pronoun / noun + *like*?
  What's Judy like?
- To ask about a person's preferences, use:
  What + *do/does* + pronoun / noun + *like*?
  What does Karl like?
- Note that in the following answer, *like* is a verb.
  He likes sport.

Modal verb would / wouldn't like for preferences

- Use *would like* + noun to offer something.
  Would you like a ticket for The Phantom of the Opera?
- Use *would like* + *to* + base form to invite someone to do something.
  Would you like to see the wax museum?

Object pronouns

Subject pronouns	Object pronouns
I	me
you	you
he	him
she	her
it	it
we	us
you	you
they	them

- Put object pronouns after the verb.
  I can't see her.
  Can you show her the email?
- Put object pronouns after a preposition.
  He likes dancing with her.
- There is only one type of object pronoun, e.g. *her*, *for her* and *to her*.
  Let's ask her.
  I did it for her.
  Give it to her.

Word list

The words in grey appear in the unit, but are not in the vocabulary sections.

Daily activities

do exercise
do my homework
get home
get up
go running
go shopping
go to school (by bike / bus / train)
hang out with friends
have a shower
have breakfast / lunch / dinner
practise the violin / the piano
wake up
walk to school
watch TV / a video / a DVD

Jobs

beautician	**model**
computer programmer	nurse
dancer	office worker
doctor	police officer
electrician	**politician**
engineer	**pop star**
factory worker	sales representative
footballer	secretary
hairdresser	shop assistant
housewife	**sporting personality / sports star**
journalist	**teacher**
judge	**vet**
lawyer	

Vocabulary

Daily activities

1 Match the sentence halves.

MORNING

1 I usually wake ⬚c
2 I go back to sleep, and I don't get ⬚
3 I always have ⬚
4 After breakfast, I have a quick ⬚
5 Then I walk ⬚
6 I sometimes go ⬚

AFTERNOON

7 I usually have ⬚
8 After school, I get ⬚
9 Four days a week I do ⬚
10 On Fridays I always hang ⬚
11 I only watch ⬚

a breakfast – cereal and toast with orange juice.
b TV if I'm bored.
c up early - at 6.00.
d my homework (but not on Fridays).
e by bike if I'm late.
f up before seven thirty.
g shower.
h out with my best friend, Sophie.
i home at about 4.00 or 4.30.
j lunch at about 12.30.
k to school. It takes about half an hour.

2 Circle the correct verbs to complete the text.

I think my brother, Peter, has a very easy day. He usually (wakes up) / sleeps at about ten in the morning. He doesn't ²start / get up then, though. He usually ³starts / gets up at about eleven and ⁴has / practises breakfast. Then he ⁵does / has a cup of coffee and reads the newspaper. After that, he ⁶listens / plays to music. He ⁷does / goes to school by bus. That's at about two o'clock. He ⁸gets / stays home at around six o'clock and ⁹has / is dinner. He ¹⁰makes / does his homework at about eight o'clock. Then he ¹¹hangs out / does with his friends or he stays at home and ¹²watches / listens DVDs. He never ¹³does / goes to the gym and he never walks anywhere! He says he doesn't like ¹⁴being / doing exercise!

Jobs

3 Write the letters in the correct order to make jobs. (Some jobs are in the plural.)

1 A **ociple reffico** works on the streets.
 police officer

2 **croyfat rowreks** make things with machines.
 f_____

3 **suners** work with doctors in hospitals.
 n_____

4 A **ranlijoust** writes for newspapers or magazines.
 u_____

5 A **posh astsantis** helps customers buy things.
 s_____

6 A **aresdsiherr** cuts your hair.
 h_____

7 A **lesas eprenattievers** sells things.
 s_____

8 A **ystecaerr** does things in an office.
 s_____

9 A **weeshoufi** works at home with the children.
 h_____

10 A **cutroemp pregramrom** works with software.
 c_____

11 **steleranicci** work with light and power.
 e_____

Grammar

Present simple: question words

1 Complete the questions with these words.

| who | what | when | how often |
| why | how | which | where |

1 _Where_ do you usually do your homework?
2 _____ good is your English?
3 _____ do you feel tired – morning, afternoon or evening?
4 _____ do you do first in the morning – have a shower or have breakfast?
5 _____ is your favourite singer?
6 _____ do you practise the piano? Only at the weekend?
7 _____ of these books do you prefer?
8 _____'s the weather like today?
9 _____ are the keys? I can't find them.
10 _____ are you always late for school?

2 Match the questions in exercise 1 with these answers.

a Probably Alicia Keys or maybe James Blunt. ☐
b In my bedroom, because that's where my desk is. ☐
c I have a shower and then I have breakfast. ☐
d Oh, it's quite good, I think. ☐
e It's hot and sunny. ☐
f Every day. ☐
g I think they're on the table. ☐
h In the evening because I work hard in the day. ☐
i The science fiction one. It's really scary! ☐
j Because I miss the bus. ☐

3 Complete the dialogues.

1 A _Who_ is your favourite actress?
  B Cameron Diaz.
2 A _____ do you eat for breakfast?
  B Cereal and coffee.
3 A _____ do you go on holiday?
  B We go to the beach.
4 A _____ do you have a part-time job?
  B Because I want some money for clothes.
5 A _____ are your school holidays?
  B They start in July.
6 A _____ do your parents go to the cinema?
  B About once a month.
7 A _____ is better – chocolate or vanilla ice cream?
  B I prefer chocolate.
8 A _____ do you say 'spaghetti' in English?
  B Spaghetti!

4 Circle the correct words.

1 What time *do* / *does* you get up?
2 When *do* / *does* your dad go to work?
3 What sort of car *do* / *does* your parents drive?
4 Why *don't* / *doesn't* we study Arabic at school?
5 Where *do* / *does* your mum do the shopping?
6 Who *do* / *does* you think is the best world leader?
7 Which band *do* / *does* your best friend like?
8 How often *do* / *does* your teachers give you homework?

5 Now answer the questions for you.

1 _I get up at 7 o'clock.._
2 _____
3 _____
4 _____
5 _____
6 _____
7 _____
8 _____

Adverbs of frequency

6 Correct the sentences.

1 Our English teacher sings sometimes in class.
  Our English teacher sometimes sings in class.
2 I go usually to the gym on Fridays.
  _____
3 We go always to school by bike in the summer.
  _____
4 Does your brother play always football at the weekend?
  _____
5 You don't help usually me with my homework.
  _____
6 Do they play often computer games in the evening?
  _____
7 My girlfriend never calls me – I call always her.
  _____
8 Brad often is late for school.
  _____

7 Answer the questions using an adverb of frequency in each sentence.

1 Do you send emails?
   I usually send emails every day.

2 What do you eat for breakfast?
   _____

3 Do you walk to school?
   _____

4 Does your mum help you with your homework?
   _____

5 Where do you do your homework?
   _____

6 What music do you like?
   _____

7 What do you do after school?
   _____

8 What do you do in the summer holidays?
   _____

What's she like? v *What does she like?*

8 Match the questions and answers.

1 [f] What do your parents like doing at the weekend?
2 [ ] What does your sister like?
3 [ ] What's the new teacher, Mr Allen, like?
4 [ ] What does your brother like doing?
5 [ ] What's your girlfriend like?
6 [ ] What are your parents like?

   a He's very nice and he's friendly.
   b He likes playing in his band.
   c She loves old films and books.
   d She's really funny and she's always happy.
   e They're great – they're really kind.
   f They like staying at home and relaxing.

9 Complete the sentences with the correct form of *be* or *do*.

1 Which book _does_ Greg like more – this one or that one?

2 _____ your parents like reading books?

3 What _____ your new shoes like?

4 _____ your friends like doing sport?

5 I don't know what the new history teacher _____ like.

6 This steak is wonderful. _____ you like the food, Chris?

7 What _____ I like? I'm a really nice person!

8 Why _____ your friends like skiing? I think it's great!

Modal verb *would / wouldn't like* for preferences

10 Write sentences or questions with *would / wouldn't like*.

1 you / go to the concert?
   Would you like to go to the concert?

2 he / a journalist
   He'd like to be a journalist.

3 you / go to the café?
   _____

4 I / not work in a factory
   _____

5 you / stay for dinner?
   _____

6 she / learn Chinese
   _____

7 they / have a holiday
   _____

8 we / not live in the city
   _____

Object pronouns

11 Match the sentences with the object pronouns.

1 My mum is easy to talk to. Talk to — a them.
2 My dad's great. You'll love — b her.
3 We're lost. Can you help c you.
4 Listen, I've got something to tell d us?
5 Beata has got five dogs. She really loves e him.
6 Hey, Jack – I need to talk to f it?
7 This is a great CD. What is g you.

12 Complete the sentences with an object pronoun.

1 Your girlfriend is fun. I really like _her_.

2 I think my boyfriend's great, but my parents don't like _____.

3 We don't know where we are. Can you tell _____?

4 These are my new shoes. I bought _____ in New York.

5 It's a fantastic film. I love _____.

6 No, thank you – I don't want fish. I hate _____.

Skills: Reading – towards PET (Part 5)

1 Read what Sonya and Clark say. What jobs do they do?

> singer   office worker   police officer
> writer   DJ   lawyer   sports instructor

Sonya is a _____.   Clark is a _____.

TWO LIVES

Sonya

Well, my day starts at half past three in the morning. I know – can you believe that? I have a hot shower to really wake me up and then a very light [1] <u>breakfast</u> – just cereal and some orange [2]_____. I get to the station at about five o'clock, so that I can talk to my team before I start my show at five [3]_____.

I prepare the music the day before, but I check things one more time to make sure. The show is four hours long, but the time seems to go by really fast. After the show, I get the music ready for the [4]_____ day. I get home after lunch. In the afternoon, I go to the gym or play tennis. I go to bed early – of course! It's the perfect job for me – people pay me to play my favourite music!

Clark

I don't get up early because I don't go out to work. I work at home. I start in the afternoon, after [5]_____. It's not good to work at home. It can be really boring. I don't see other people – I just have my cat to talk to. And it's not a very healthy life, because I sit at my computer all the time.

When I don't know what to write, I sometimes get up and go for a long walk, or make a [6]_____ of tea.

I can listen to music while I work – that's cool – but I think I'd like a different job. I'm quite interested in being a lawyer, or maybe I can work in an office.

2 Complete the two texts. Choose the correct word a, b or c.

1	a dinner	b food	c breakfast
2	a juice	b colour	c fruit
3	a hour	b thirty	c clock
4	a after	b last	c next
5	a noon	b lunch	c work
6	a lunch	b hot	c cup

3 Write S (Sonya), C (Clark) or B (both).

Who…

1 works alone? ☐
2 starts work in the afternoon? ☐
3 gets to work very early? ☐
4 loves their job? ☐
5 doesn't get up very early? ☐
6 has got a cat? ☐
7 listens to music at work? ☐

Writing

4 Write about a typical day in your life. (70–80 words)

> ➤ **Tips**
>
> • Use the Reading text above for ideas.
> • Don't forget to use the daily activities in the Word list for vocabulary.
> • When you write about a typical day, use the present simple.
> • Remember to use adverbs of frequency (e.g. *usually / sometimes / often*).

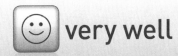 very well   OK   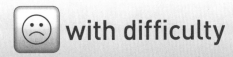 with difficulty

I've finished this module and I can do ☑ these things in English

Module ①

	😊	😐	☹
Listening			
A1 understand numbers, prices and times (p.13)	☐	☐	☐
A1 understand questions addressed carefully and slowly to me (p.15)	☐	☐	☐
A1 understand when someone speaks slowly and clearly about their work (p.23)	☐	☐	☐
Reading			
A1 understand information about people from a magazine article (pp.10, 14, 22) or from a webpage (p.20)	☐	☐	☐
Spoken Interaction			
A1 ask people questions about their favourite sport (p.10), favourite films (p.12), free time activities (pp.8, 20, 22) and answer such questions	☐	☐	☐
A2 discuss with other people what to do and where to go (p.13)	☐	☐	☐
Spoken Production			
A1 describe my daily routine (p.16) and other people's daily routines (p.23)	☐	☐	☐
A1 give personal information about myself, e.g. my hobbies and interests (p.7), what I am good at (p.8), things I own (p.15), the job I'd like to do (p.18)	☐	☐	☐
Writing			
A1 fill in a questionnaire giving an account of my educational background, my job, my interests and my specific skills (p.20)	☐	☐	☐
A1 write simple sentences about myself, e.g. things I own (p.15), my typical day (p.22)	☐	☐	☐

At the end of **Module 1**, I'm a good A1 student.
Now I can start **Module 2**. ➡

Grammar reference

Present continuous: all forms

Positive
full form

I	am	
You	are	
He/She/It	is	walking fast.
We/You/They	are	

short form

I'm	
You're	
He's/She's/It's	walking fast.
We're/You're/They're	

Negative
full form

I	am		
You	are		
He/She/It	is	not	walking fast.
We/You/They	are		

short form

I'm not	
You aren't	
He/She/It isn't	walking fast.
We/You/They aren't	

Questions

Am	I	
Are	you	
Is	he/she/it	walking fast?
Are	we/you/they	

Positive short answers

Yes,	I	am.
Yes,	we/you/they	are.
Yes,	he/she/it	is.

Negative short answers

No,	I	'm not.
No,	we/you/they	aren't.
No,	he/she/it	isn't.

- Form the present continuous with the present of the verb *be* followed by the *-ing* form of the main verb. (See Unit 1 for the formation of the *-ing* form.)
- Form the positive with:
  subject + *am/are/is* (full forms) + *-ing* form
  subject + *'m/'re/'s* (short forms) + *-ing* form
- Form the negative with:
  subject + *am/are/is* + *not* (full forms) + *-ing* form
  subject + *'m not/aren't/isn't* (short forms) + *-ing* form
- Form questions with:
  am/are/is + subject + *-ing* form?
- Form short answers with:
  Yes, + subject pronoun + *am/are/is.*
  No, + subject pronoun + *'m not/aren't/isn't.*
  Note that the short answers are exactly the same as those for the present tense of *be*.
- Remember that we never use short forms in positive short answers.
  Yes, I am. NOT ~~*Yes, I'm.*~~

Usage

- Use the present continuous to talk about:
  - actions happening at the moment of speaking
    Martha can't hear you. She's talking on the phone.
    Are they having lunch? – Yes, they are.
  - temporary situations
    We're revising for the exam this week.
    Are you playing a lot of tennis at the moment?
- We don't usually use the present continuous with these verbs:
  - verbs expressing *likes* and *dislikes*. Use the present simple.
    I love this book!
    NOT ~~*I'm loving this book!*~~
    I hate playing football.
    NOT ~~*I'm hating playing football.*~~
  - verbs of perception, such as *see, hear, feel, sound, smell, taste.*
- Use *can / can't* with *see, hear, feel, smell*:
  I can't see you.
  NOT ~~*I'm not seeing you.*~~
  We can hear a dog.
  NOT ~~*We are hearing a dog.*~~
- Use the present simple with *sound, taste, look.*
  That sounds great!
  NOT ~~*That is sounding great!*~~
  You look nice!
  NOT ~~*You are looking nice!*~~
  The food tastes wonderful.
  NOT ~~*The food is tasting wonderful.*~~

still

- Use *still* with the present continuous to emphasise that a situation is continuing, and that it isn't finished.
- For positive sentences (full forms and short forms) and questions, put *still* before the *-ing* form of the main verb.

  Jim is still waiting for you.
  I'm still reading this book.
  It's still snowing.
  Is he still swimming?
  Are you still looking for John?

- For negative sentences (full forms), put *still* before *not*.

  You are still not listening to me!
  NOT ~~You are not still listening to me!~~
  The dog is still not eating.
  NOT ~~The dog is not still eating.~~

- For negative short forms, put *still* before the verb *be* if this is possible.

  You still aren't listening to me!
  The dog still isn't eating.

- You can also use *still* without the present continuous:

  I'm still here.
  We're still not sure.
  Are you still angry?

Prepositions

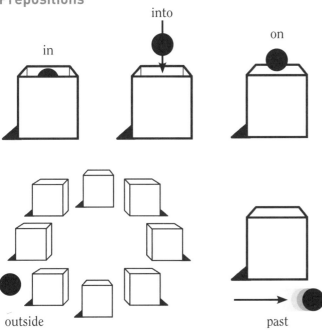

in

into

on

outside

past

I'm **in** the house.
Brian's putting the car **into** the garage.
Put the book **on** the table.
Jack's **outside** the house.
Laura's going **past** the garage.

Word list

The words in grey appear in the unit, but are not in the vocabulary sections.

Clothes

boots	shoes
cap	skirt
coat	suit
dress	tracksuit
jacket	trainers
jeans	trousers
jumper	T-shirt
shirt	

Money

£1 (one pound)	currency
1p (one pence)	debit card
bank account	expensive
cash	pocket money
cashpoint machine	pound sterling
cheap	sale
credit card	

Accessories

belt	necklace
bracelet	ring
chain	scarf
earrings	stud
handbag	sunglasses

Vocabulary

Clothes and accessories

1 Complete the crossword.

Across

Down

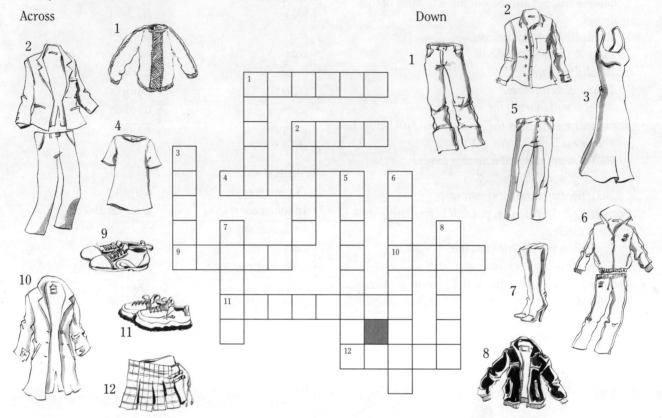

2 Look at the picture. Circle the correct words to complete the description.

Look at her! Where's she going, do you think? She's got a nice grey ¹ *shirt / coat* with a ² *belt / necklace*. It looks good with her ³ *jumper / jacket* and ⁴ *skirt / trousers*. I like her ⁵ *handbag / ring*, too. And look at that ⁶ *scarf / stud* – it's very long and it looks warm. Do you like her ⁷ *boots / trainers*? I like them but I don't think I like the colour.

Money

3 Complete the missing words.

1 A Have you got a bank a_____?
   B No, I haven't. Have you?
2 A Why are we stopping here?
   B Because I want to get some money from the
      c_____ machine.
3 A How much was your new coat?
   B It was sixty p_____.
4 A What c_____ do they have in England? Is it
      the euro?
   B No, it's pounds sterling.
5 A Do you use a c_____ card or a debit card?
   B I don't use cards, I always pay in cash.
6 A Do your parents give you p_____ money?
   B Yes, they give me 10 euros a week.

Grammar

Present continuous: all forms

1 Write positive sentences.

1 Dad / kitchen // cook / dinner.
   Dad's in the kitchen. He's cooking dinner.

2 Ros and George / garden // play with / dog
   _____

3 Greg / bedroom // listen to / music
   _____

4 Sarah / bathroom // have / shower
   _____

5 Grandma / living room // watch / TV
   _____

6 I / bedroom // do / homework
   _____

7 Jake / garage // clean / car
   _____

8 Mum / office // write / a report
   _____

2 Match the questions and answers.

1 ☐ Are you and your friends doing part-time jobs this year?
2 ☐ Are you watching a lot of TV these days?
3 ☐ Are you going out a lot at the moment?
4 ☐ Are you having a good week?
5 ☐ Are your teachers giving you a lot of homework?
6 ☐ Are your parents taking you out much?

a No, they never take me out!
b No, I'm not. I don't like the programmes.
c No, we aren't. We've all got a lot of homework.
d Yes, it's great, thanks.
e Yes, they are! I haven't got time to go out!
f No, I'm not. I haven't got the money!

3 Complete the questions with the correct form of the verbs in brackets. Then write true answers.

1 *Are* you *using* your computer? (use)
   No, I'm not.

2 _____ you _____ lunch? (have)
   _____

3 _____ you _____ to music? (listen)
   _____

4 _____ the teacher _____ a computer? (use)
   _____

5 _____ your friends _____ in class? (work)
   _____

6 _____ your friend _____ an email? (write)
   _____

7 _____ you _____ at your desk? (sit)
   _____

8 _____ you _____ jeans? (wear)
   _____

4 Complete the telephone conversation with the correct form of the words in brackets.

Carla Hi, Chris. [1] *What are you doing*? (what / you / do)

Chris Oh, hi, Carla. Well, right now I'm cooking.

Carla Really? [2]_____? (what / you / cook)

Chris I'm making pizzas. They're really easy.

Carla So, [3]_____ tonight? (why / you / make dinner)

Chris Oh, Mum and Dad are out. So, [4]_____ these days, then? (what / you / do)

Carla Not much. I'm working part-time in a shop in town.

Chris Yes? [5]_____? (which shop / you / work / in)

Carla Greensleeves – it's a clothes shop.

Chris Oh yes, I know the one. [6]_____? (what / you / doing / there)

Carla I'm helping in the shoe department.

Chris It sounds great! Oh, I've got to go – the pizzas are burning!

still

5 Write *still* in the correct place in each sentence.

1 Are you *still* doing your homework?

2 Don't take that magazine. Dominic is reading it.

3 Is he waiting for his dad to come?

4 Shh! Be quiet! The baby's sleeping!

5 Is it snowing outside?

6 We are doing the grammar exercises.

7 He isn't talking to me.

8 I'm not sure I understand the question.

Prepositions

6 Match the prepositions to the pictures.

on   outside   under   in

1 _____   2 _____

3 _____   4 _____

Skills: Reading – Towards PET (Part 3)

1 **Suzy, Yvette and Michaela are looking for boyfriends. Read about the four boys.**
Choose the best boyfriend for each girl.

Suzy doesn't think it's important how people look. She thinks people spend too much money on clothes. She likes cheap clothes and she usually wears jeans and trainers.
Her perfect boyfriend: _____

Yvette likes boys to look 'normal'. She doesn't like people who only wear one colour, or wear expensive designer clothes. She enjoys shopping in big shopping centres.
Her perfect boyfriend: _____

Michaela likes people to dress very well. She thinks it's important to always look good. She likes classic clothes and hairstyles. She loves boots.
Her perfect boyfriend: _____

Ali

My look is important to me. I usually wear blue jumpers and classic white shirts. I don't wear jeans too much. I prefer black trousers. I spend most of the money from my job on my clothes and my hair – and my boots!

Jake

I don't really don't care much what I look like. I wear clothes that are cheap and comfortable – any colour, any style. Some people say I dress badly, but I don't want to spend my money on clothes. I prefer to buy other things like CDs.

Grant

I probably go shopping for clothes about once every two or three months. I'm not a 'fashion junkie' – I just wear what most people wear. I suppose I'm not very cool, but I don't think I'm old-fashioned either.

Stuart

I only wear black. Black jeans, black T-shirt and my old black leather jacket. I buy my clothes from second-hand markets and I like vintage stuff. I hate it when people wear the latest designer clothes. Where do they get the money from?

2 **Circle T (True) or F (False).**

1 Grant is very cool. T / F
2 Jake always wears black. T / F
3 Ali loves spending money on clothes. T / F
4 Stuart doesn't like second-hand clothes. T / F
5 Grant doesn't go shopping for clothes very often. T / F
6 Stuart doesn't like leather jackets. T / F

3 **Choose the correct word to complete the sentences.**

1 My favourite *boots / jacket* are black.
2 It's cold outside. Wear a warm *jumper / shirt*.
3 We have to dress well at work. We can't wear *jeans / jackets*.
4 I like running, so I usually wear *trainers / boots*.
5 I think jeans and a white *shirt / jackets* looks great.

Writing

4 **Write five things you or other people are doing at the moment.**

5 **Write five things you or other people are doing these days.**

> **Tips**

- When you write about things you are doing now or these days, use the present continuous.
- Remember that you can use *still* with the present continuous.
- Look through the unit to find verbs you can use (e.g. *reading / learning / talking / going out with*…).
- Don't forget that there are some verbs that you do not usually use in the present continuous (e.g. *like / love / taste*).

Study skills My workspace

1 **Look at the pictures. What are the advantages and disadvantages of the different study places?**

1

2

3

4

2 **If you have a well-organised place to work, you can study more effectively and more quickly. Think about the things in the list below and put them in order from 1 (the most important) to 12 (the least important). Add any others that you think of.**

- ☐ Sitting comfortably.
- ☐ Having a quiet place to work.
- ☐ Having enough light.
- ☐ Having all the things I need near me.
- ☐ Having plenty of air/not being too cold or too hot.
- ☐ Having a tidy desk, where I can find things quickly.
- ☐ Not being disturbed by the telephone, TV, etc.
- ☐ Listening to my favourite music.
- ☐ Not checking my emails or social networking sites.
- ☐ Having a snack or something to drink by my desk.
- ☐ Knowing that I can ask for help – ask my family, call a friend, etc.
- ☐ Having my favourite things or pictures up on my noticeboard.

3 **When you have finished your list, check it with one of your classmates.**

Grammar reference

there is / there are

Positive

There	is	a computer.	(singular)
	are	two guitars.	(plural)

Negative

There	isn't	a cinema.	(singular)
	aren't	any posters.	(plural)

Questions			Short answers
Is	there	a computer?	Yes, there is.
			No, there isn't.
Are		any CDs?	Yes, there are.
			No, there aren't.

- Use *There is*, *There isn't* and *Is there...?* with a singular countable noun or an uncountable noun.
  There is a new bridge on the Thames.
  Is there any traffic on the bridge? No, there isn't.
- Use *There are*, *There aren't* and *Are there...?* with a plural countable noun.
  There are some old buildings in the city.
  Are there any theatres? No, there aren't.
- Use *There is...* with a list of things, when the first thing is singular.
  There's a table, two chairs and a computer.

Countable and uncountable nouns

- Countable nouns are nouns that have both a singular and plural form. Most nouns belong to this category.
  a computer – two computers
  a mobile phone – many mobile phones
- Uncountable nouns are nouns that only have a singular form.
  water, paper, ink
- Some nouns are countable in some languages and uncountable in English.
  hair, information, money, advice, news, homework
  My hair is blonde.
  Is there any news?
- Some English nouns can be both countable and uncountable.
  Do you like coffee?
  I'd like a coffee. (= a cup of coffee)

- Use the plural of a countable noun with no article to make generalisations.
  I like cats. NOT *I like the cats.*
- Use an uncountable noun with no article to make generalisations.
  I love coffee. NOT *I love the coffee.*
- Note that the word *job* is countable and *work* is uncountable.

a / an, some and any

- Use *a* or *an* with singular countable nouns.
  I haven't got a dog.
  I have got an apple.
- Use *an* before a noun or adjective that begins with a vowel (*a, e, i, o* and *u*).
  an apple
  an idea
  an elephant
  an excellent book
- Use *a* before a noun or adjective that begins with a consonant (all the other letters).
  a boy
  a girl
  a nice teacher
- Use *some* and *any* with both countable and uncountable nouns to talk about indefinite quantities.
  some students, some books
  some tea, some sugar, some water
- Use *some* in positive sentences.
  There's some bread in the kitchen.
  We've got some musical instruments here.
- Use *any* in questions and negative sentences.
  Have you got any CDs?
  We haven't got any money.
- NB Use *some* in questions for offers and requests when you expect the person to answer *yes*.
  Would you like some biscuits?
  Can I have some coffee?

How much? / How many?

- Use *How much...?* with uncountable nouns to ask about quantity.
  How much traffic is there in London today?
- Use *How many...?* with plural countable nouns to ask about quantity.
  How many art galleries are there in London?

Word list

The words in grey appear in the unit, but are not in the vocabulary sections.

Everyday technology

CD	mobile phone
chat online	mp3 player
computer	play video games
email	social networking site
instant messaging	surf the web
Internet	watch TV
listen to music	webcam

Places

art gallery	palace
bridge	park
café	restaurant
cathedral	river
chain store	school
church	sports centre
(multiplex) cinema	stadium
city	theatre
club / nightclub	(music / dance) venue
department store	village
market	zoo
museum	

Verbs

lend	borrow

Vocabulary

Everyday technology

1 Write the letters in the correct order to complete the sentences.

1 Facebook is a good example of a **loscia twinngeork ties**.
   <u>social networking site</u>

2 I like to **thac linnoe** with my friends who live far away.
   c_____

3 I'm writing an **amile** to my friend now. e_____

4 It's fun to **furs** the **bew**! s_____

5 With a **cwbeam** on your **pucotmer** you can see your friends and your friends can see you. w_____

6 I buy a new **lemobi opnhe** every year. m_____

7 My sister spends a lot of time doing **nitasnt sgsinaemg** with her friends. i_____

8 My brother plays a lot of **iedov agsme**. v_____

Places

2 Complete the crossword with place names. What is the mystery word?

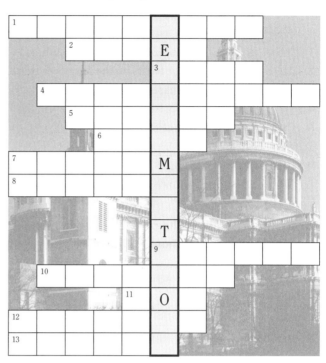

1 St. Paul's is a famous …
2 The Thames is London's …
3 Visit Hyde or Regent's … in London.
4 Eat at a good …
5 San Clemente is a … in Rome.
6 Edinburgh is Scotland's capital …
7 The British … has 7.5 million objects.
8 Buckingham … is the Queen's home.
9 Most children go to …
10 See a play at the …
11 See animals at London …
12 Tate Modern is an art …
13 The Golden Gate is a … in San Francisco.

Mystery word: a place where you can buy everything
_____

Verbs

3 Circle the correct words.

1 I can *lend* / *borrow* you some money if you like.
2 Don't *lend* / *borrow* him your CDs – he always *lends* / *borrows* mine and he never gives them back!
3 Do you want to *lend* / *borrow* any DVDs for the weekend?
4 A bank *lends* / *borrows* money, but it's a bad idea to *lend* / *borrow* a lot from one.
5 Would you like me to *lend* / *borrow* you my bike?
6 Can I *lend* / *borrow* £15 till the weekend? I want to buy a CD.

Grammar

there is / there are

1 Complete the sentences with *is, are, isn't* or *aren't*.

1 There __is__ some ice cream on your jumper!
2 There _____ some books on the desk over there.
3 _____ there any paper in the printer?
4 _____ there any bottles of water in the fridge?
5 There _____ any cake, but there _____ some biscuits.
6 Sorry, there _____ any U2 posters left.
7 There _____ any food in my bag.
8 There _____ some interesting people in my class.

2 Write the words in the correct order to make sentences and questions.

1 children / in / school / your / many / how / there / are ?
   How many children are there in your school?
2 that / a / in / fantastic mp3 player / is / there / shop
   _____
3 are / fifteen / my / badges / there / collection / in
   _____
4 isn't / on / any / there / table / bread / the
   _____
5 that / there / in / milk / any / is / bottle ?
   _____
6 bag / your / money / some / is / in / there
   _____

Countable and uncountable nouns

3 Complete the table with these words.

| jumper cheese money car milk CD |
| information person computer biscuit juice |
| lesson pasta dog job bread shop rice |

Countable	Uncountable
jumper _____	cheese _____
_____ _____	_____ _____
_____ _____	_____ _____
_____ _____	_____ _____

a / an, some and *any*

4 Complete the sentences with *a* or *an*.

1 This is __a__ great CD-ROM!
2 I've got ___ idea! Let's go to the café!
3 Jane is ___ good student.
4 Is there ___ example with this exercise?
5 That's ___ bad idea!
6 This is ___ excellent song!

5 Complete the sentences with *some* or *any*.

1 There isn't __any__ ice cream in the freezer.
2 There's _____ water on the floor.
3 There are _____ good websites for people interested in films.
4 There are _____ nice shops in this town.
5 There aren't _____ good CDs in his house.
6 Would you like _____ bread?
7 Are there _____ quiet beaches near the hotel?
8 Can you give me _____ help, please?
9 Is there _____ milk in that bottle?
10 Are there _____ newspapers on the table?

6 Write sentences about Crichton using the words below.

1 beautiful beaches ☑
   There are some beautiful beaches in Crichton.
2 good hotels ☒
   There aren't any good hotels in Crichton.
3 big park ☑
   _____
4 university ☒
   _____
5 lovely cafes ☑
   _____
6 nightclubs ☒
   _____
7 new multiplex ☑
   _____
8 railway station ☒
   _____

7 **Look at the picture and the words. Write positive and negative sentences.**

~~ink~~ ~~books~~ ~~orange~~ paper water chair
cola pens pencils cup CD-ROMs printer

1 _There's some ink on the desk._
2 _There aren't any books on the desk._
3 _There isn't an orange on the desk._
4 _____
5 _____
6 _____
7 _____
8 _____
9 _____
10 _____
11 _____
12 _____

8 **Answer the questions about yourself.**

1 Are there any schools in your town?
   Yes, of course there are.

2 Is there a computer in your bedroom?
   _____

3 Is there a sandwich in your schoolbag?
   _____

4 Are there any CDs in your classroom?
   _____

5 Is there a cinema in your town?
   _____

6 Are there any interesting places to visit near you?
   _____

7 Are there any nightclubs in your town?
   _____

8 Is there a railway station near your house?
   _____

9 Are there any English people in your class?
   _____

10 Is there a beach near your town?
   _____

How much? / How many?

9 **Complete the questions in the questionnaire.**

MY LIFE IN NUMBERS!

1 How __many__ days a week do you go to school?

2 How _____ pocket money do you get?

3 How _____ teachers are there in your school?

4 How _____ people are there in your family?

5 How _____ money do you spend on music in a month?

6 How _____ ice cream do you eat in a year?

7 How _____ text messages do you send a week?

8 How _____ homework do you get every week?

9 How _____ water do you drink a day?

10 How _____ time do you spend on your computer each day?

10 **Now answer the questions.**

1 _____
2 _____
3 _____
4 _____
5 _____
6 _____
7 _____
8 _____
9 _____
10 _____

Skills: Reading – Towards PET (Part 2)

1 Read the article. Match the questions with the information. There is one extra question.

Which other countries do you travel to?

~~What second language can you speak well?~~

What part-time jobs do you do?

What do you do in your free time?

What language would you like to learn?

Who goes to church?

Euroteen life

Five thousand Europeans aged 15–19 answer questions about their lives.

1 _What second language can you speak well?_

58% say they can have a conversation in English. Almost all young people in Scandinavia and the Netherlands (over 90%) can speak English well. 22% of Europeans can speak French and 12% German. 25% cannot speak a second language. The Danish are the best at foreign languages, but the British, Irish and Spanish aren't good at learning other languages.

2 _____

23% say they want to speak Spanish, and 21% would like to speak French or Italian as a second language. Only 17% say English is the language they want to learn – maybe because they already speak it. 40% of Italians want to learn Spanish. 38% of young Britons don't want to learn a second language!

3 _____

If you think all young people travel to other countries a lot, perhaps you're wrong. 43% don't travel to other countries. 83% of Greeks, 54% of Italians and 50% of Portuguese stay at home. France and Spain are the countries people travel to the most.

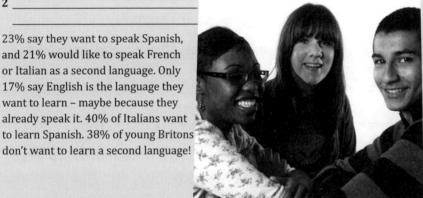

4 _____

Meeting friends (75%), listening to music (67%) and watching TV (63%) are the most popular free-time activities. In Sweden, 88% meet friends regularly. In Belgium, 80% watch TV. In Spain, 70% listen to music. In Greece, 72% read, but only 38% play sport. In Italy, 70% meet friends regularly and 51% listen to music.

5 _____

22% say they go to a place of worship - a church, a mosque, a temple or synagogue. The Irish (49%) the Greeks (42%) and the Italians (41%) go to church most regularly. The Danish (5%), the Swedish and the British (both 8%) don't often go to church.

2 Read the article again and complete the sentences.

1 People are very good at English in _Scandinavia and the Netherlands_ .

2 Spanish, French and _____ are the languages people want to learn.

3 Young people like travelling to _____ .

4 Half of young Portuguese people _____ .

5 The most popular free-time activity in Sweden is _____ .

6 A lot of Greeks don't _____ . They prefer to read.

7 The British don't often _____ .

Writing

3 Answer the questions in the questionnaire.

1 What second languages can you and your classmates speak?

2 What languages would you like to speak?

3 How many hours a week do you study English?

4 What do you like about learning English? What don't you like?

5 What places do you travel to?

6 What do you and your friends do in your free time?

7 What places can visitors see in your town or village?

8 What things are there in your room?

> **Tips**

- Remember to check the Word list for useful vocabulary.
- Always answer using the same tense as the question, e.g. for the question: *What do you like…?* (present simple), answer using the present simple.

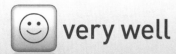 very well   OK   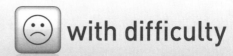 with difficulty

I've finished this module and I can do ☑ these things in English

Module ❷

	☺	☺	☹

Listening

A2 understand phrases, words and expressions related to my immediate surroundings, e.g. shopping (p.33) □ □ □

A2 catch the main point in short, clear, simple messages and announcements, e.g. timetables and prices in tourist attractions (p.40) □ □ □

A2 understand the essential information in short recorded passages dealing with predictable everyday matters, e.g. clothing (p.35), a tourist excursion (p.43) □ □ □

Reading

A2 identify important information in simple newspaper articles or interviews about clothing (p.34), about my town (p.37), about London (p.43) □ □ □

A2 find the most important information in short emails (p.30) or in information leaflets about young people's habits (pp.27, 38), places to visit in London (p.40) □ □ □

Spoken Interaction

A2 make simple purchases by stating what I want and asking the price (p.33) □ □ □

A2 discuss with other people what to do and where to go (p.41) □ □ □

A2 ask people questions about clothing (p.35), about my town (p.36), young people's activities (p.38) and answer such questions □ □ □

Spoken Production

A2 describe the life of adolescents in Britain and in my own country (p.27) □ □ □

A2 describe a famous town or city (p.43) □ □ □

Strategies / Language Quality

A2 make myself understood using memorised phrases and single expressions (pp.33, 41) □ □ □

Writing

A2 write short, simple notes and messages (pp.27, 28) □ □ □

A2 write about aspects of my everyday life in simple phrases and sentences, for example, what a friend is wearing (p.35), what things there are to do in my town (p.36) □ □ □

A2 write simple sentences about my town (p.43) □ □ □

At the end of **Module 2**, I've got some A2 skills. Now I can start **Module 3**.

Grammar reference

Modal verbs: *can, could, may*

Positive		
I/You/He/She/It/We/They	can	dance. (ability)
I/You/He/She/It/We/They	can / could	do it next week. (possibility)

Negative		
I/You/He/She/It/We/They	can't	dance. (ability)
I/You/He/She/It/We/They	can't	come tonight. (possibility)

Questions		
Can	I/you/he/she/it/we/they	dance? (ability)
Can	I/you/he/she/it/we/they	come tonight? (possibility)
May	I/we	leave? (permission)

Positive short answers		
Yes,	I/you/he/she/it/we/they	can / could.
Yes,	you	may.

Negative short answers		
No,	I/you/he/she/it/we/they	can't / couldn't.

Can, could and *may* are modal verbs. Remember, modal verbs:

- don't take *-s* when the subject is *he, she* or *it*
- are followed by the base form of the verb
- form the negative by adding *not* + base form
- go before the subject in questions

Usage

- Use *can* to talk about being able to do something.
  They can sing.
  We can't understand you.
- Use *can, could* and *may* to ask for permission to do something or to make a polite request.
  Can they come to our house?
- Note that *can* is less formal, *could* is more polite and *may* is the most formal of all.
- In questions only use *may* in the first person: *May I...?* and *May we...?*
  May I speak with the teacher? – Yes, you may.
  Can you phone me tonight? – No, I can't.
  Could you let me know soon? – Of course I can.

- Use *can* and *can't* to talk about whether it is possible or not possible to do something.
  You can buy stamps at the post office.
  It's raining. We can't go out without an umbrella.

Can: agreeing and disagreeing

- To agree you can say 'Me, too' or 'Me, neither' after a sentence with *can*. You can also use:
  - *So can I* after a positive sentence.
  - *Neither can I* after a negative sentence.
    I can play the piano. – So can I.
    We can't find the address. – Neither can I.
- To disagree after a sentence with *can* use:
  - *I can't* after a positive sentence.
  - *I can* after a negative sentence.
    I can take a holiday soon. – We can't.
    We can't ride. – I can.

Present simple v present continuous

Revise the forms of the present simple in Units 1 and 2, and the present continuous in Unit 3.

Check you understand the difference in use between the two tenses.

- Use the present simple to talk about actions in our daily routine, about likes and dislikes and about things that are always true.
  I go to school by bus.
  The moon revolves around the earth.
- Use the present simple with adverbs of frequency.
  People usually stand on the right on the escalator.
- Use the present continuous to talk about actions that are happening at the moment.
  Don't interrupt. We're studying.
- Use the present continuous to talk about temporary situations.
  My brother is living in Manchester this year.
- Use the present continuous with *now, at this moment, this week, these days,* etc.
  We're going out every evening this week.

Adjective order

When a noun is preceded by more than one adjective, the order is as follows:

Quantity	Opinion	Size	Age	Shape
Colour	Origin	Material	Noun	

Two lovely small new square grey Italian leather handbags.

Word list

The words in **grey** appear in the unit, but are not in the vocabulary sections.

Transport

Mind the gap	moped
Stand clear of the doors	motorbike
barrier	on foot
belongings	plane
bicycle / bike	platform
boat	railway line
car	return
coach	scooter
destination	single
direction	station
display	ticket
escalator	ticket hall
fare	ticket machine
gap	ticket office
get off	train
get on	travelcard
litter bin	Underground
map	zone

Shapes and materials

cardboard	plastic
cotton	rectangular
glass	round
leather	square
metal	wooden
paper	woolly

Vocabulary

Transport

1 Match the words with the pictures.

a

b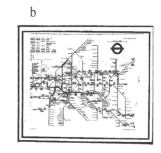

c

d

e

f

g

h

1	☐ railway line		5	☐	ticket
2	☐ escalator		6	☐	ticket machine
3	☐ display		7	☐	litter bin
4	☐ barrier		8	☐	map

2 Complete the dialogues with the words.

> ticket hall ~~Underground~~ ticket office

Paolo   Shall we meet at the ¹<u>Underground</u> station?
Sue   Yes, let's meet in the ²_____, next to the ³_____.

> travelcard   return   singles

Paolo   A ⁴_____ to Marylebone, please.
Clerk   We don't sell them. You can have two ⁵_____ for £8.00, or you can get a one-day ⁶_____ for zones 1 and 2 for £7.20.

> on   train   doors   destination

Paolo   What direction do we need? Southbound?
Sue   No, westbound. There's a ⁷_____ here now. Can you see what the ⁸_____ is?
Paolo   Paddington.
Announcer   Stand clear of the ⁹_____.
Sue   Oh no, it's our train. We can't get ¹⁰_____ now. It's dangerous.

> platform   off   gap

Announcer   Mind the ¹¹_____.
Paolo   What does that mean?
Sue   Oh, it means don't fall between the train and the ¹²_____ when you get ¹³_____.

3 Write the letters in the correct order to make types of transport.

1   I get the **narti** to work every day.
    <u>train</u>
2   I usually ride my **keib** to school.
    b_____
3   Which **sub** goes to Liverpool Street station?
    b_____
4   My brother's got a beautiful new **tkoobrmie**.
    m_____
5   Many people don't like going by **nalpe**.
    p_____
6   It takes a long time to get anywhere when you go by **ohcca**.
    c_____
7   Do you prefer to go to France by plane or **tabo**?
    b_____
8   I never go in a car. I always go **fo oont**.
    o_____

Materials

4 Circle the correct adjective.

1   a *glass / wooden / cotton* chair

2   a *cardboard / glass / leather* jacket

3   a *wooden / metal / woolly* jumper

4   a *plastic / metal / paper* raincoat

5   a *plastic / cotton / cardboard* shirt

6   a *leather / paper / woolly* plane

Grammar

Modal verbs: *can, could, may*

1 Circle the correct word.

1   A   Can you come to the party tonight?
    B   No, I'm sorry. I *can't / couldn't* go out tonight.
2   A   May I close the window?
    B   Of course you *could / may*.
3   A   *Can / May* you play tennis?
    B   Yes, I *can / may* play really well.
4   A   I can't do my homework.
    B   I *could / may* help you if you like.
5   A   *Could / May* you phone me later?
    B   Of course.
6   A   *May / Could* you lend me some money?
    B   I'm sorry, but I haven't got any.

2 Write sentences about yourself. Write three things that you *can't* do and then three things you *can* do.

1 I can't swim.   1 I can play chess.
2 _____   2 _____
3 _____   3 _____
4 _____   4 _____

3 Match the questions and answers.

1 [f] Can I close the window?
2 ☐   Could you speak slowly, please?
3 ☐   May I have another piece of bread, please?
4 ☐   Could you help me with my Maths, please?
5 ☐   Can we watch the football tonight?
6 ☐   Can you speak Portuguese?

a Yes, of course. Help yourself.
b No you can't! It's on very late!
c Yes, I can, but only a little.
d Oh yes, sorry. I often talk fast.
e Sorry, I can't. I'm not very good at it.
f OK. Are you cold?

Can: agreeing and disagreeing

4 Complete the dialogues with *So* or *Neither*.

1 Dan   I can't speak German.
   Mike ¹_____ can I. But I can understand a bit of French.
2 Dan   I can remember our school science teacher.
   Mike ²_____ can I. But I'm still no good at science.
3 Dan   I can draw and paint pictures. But I can't do sculpture.
   Mike ³_____ can I. I haven't got the tools – or the patience!

5 Write answers to agree or disagree with the sentences.

1 I can speak Japanese.
   So can I. / I can't.
2 I can't spell very well.
   Neither can I. / I can.
3 I can't ride a bike.
   _____
4 I can write my name in Arabic.
   _____
5 I can't cook.
   _____
6 I can knit.
   _____
7 I can't drive.
   _____
8 I can make pasta.
   _____

Present simple v present continuous

6 Circle the correct word.

1 *I'm doing* / *do* my homework, so don't interrupt me!
2 My grandma *is going* / *goes* to the gym once a week!
3 We *aren't playing* / *don't play* tennis today. The match is cancelled.
4 How often *do you go* / *are you going* to the dentist?
5 My mum really *is liking* / *likes* rap music.
6 Dad's at home. He *isn't working* / *doesn't work* today.
7 Jenny *is thinking* / *thinks* Johnny Depp is a great actor.
8 My aunt and uncle *are staying* / *stay* for dinner tonight.

7 Complete the sentences with the correct form of the verbs in brackets.

1 I'm staying_____ (stay) with my aunt and uncle at the moment, but I usually live in London.
2 She _____ (sing) at a new club in town this week.
3 They _____ (play) really well today. The new trainer is really good.
4 We always _____ (have) a picnic when it's sunny.
5 We usually _____ (go) to France for our holiday, but this year we _____ (go) to Spain.
6 She _____ (work) in a shop every summer.
7 I _____ (queue) for a ticket – it's a very long queue!
8 He _____ (wear) gloves today because it's so cold.

8 Complete the text with the correct form of the verbs in brackets.

Diane is really happy today because she ¹_____ (not go) to school. It's Friday, and usually she ²_____ (have) five different classes, but today is different. She is free to do what she likes. That's why she ³_____ (lie) on her bed and ⁴_____ (eat) chocolates. Diane usually ⁵_____ (wear) a school uniform, but now she ⁶_____ (wear) a jumper and jeans. Her friends are off school, too. Tania ⁷_____ (work) in her father's shop and Louise ⁸_____ (play) computer games with her little brother.

Skills: Reading – Towards PET (Part 2)

1 Read the article about a lost property auction. Tick ☑ the objects that are not in the auction.

- ☐ watches
- ☐ roller skates
- ☐ bicycles
- ☐ computers
- ☐ toys
- ☐ video players
- ☐ cars
- ☐ perfume
- ☐ shoes
- ☐ mobile phones
- ☐ books
- ☐ footballs

GOING...
GOING...
GONE!

1

It's Tuesday, and I'm walking into Greasby's, a small, dark building in Tooting, south London. People are coming here today to buy cameras, watches, jewellery, perfume and hundreds of other things.

2

But Greasby's is not a department store - in fact, there's only one large room. It's an auction house, and there's an auction every week. This is where the London airports, London Transport and others send thousands of lost or confiscated items.

3

You can imagine what people leave on planes and in airports. There are presents - cigarettes, cameras and mobile phones. But there are also hundreds of suitcases, full of clothes and other possessions. People leave toys, roller skates, musical instruments, trainers, shoes. How can you forget your shoes?

4

From London Transport, we can see footballs and food boxes, bottles of drink and BMX bikes. There are DVD players, mp3 players and even a microwave oven. And there are hundreds of phones and cameras.

5

After three months in the Lost Property Office, all these amazing things go to Greasby's. And that's where I am now. I'm bidding for a camera.
'£10, £12, £14.'
'This is cheap,' I'm thinking.
'£34. £36. Do I hear £40?'
Yes, he does. And now I've got a new camera. I hope it works!

2 Choose a title for each paragraph.

> My new camera   The auction house
> Going to the auction   From the airport
> Things people leave on buses and the Underground

3 Answer the questions.

1 What is Greasby's?

2 Where is it?

3 Where do the items come from?

4 What item is the writer surprised that people can leave at an airport?

5 What do lots of people leave on buses and the Underground?

6 How long do lost items stay at the Lost Property Office?

7 What does the writer buy?

Writing

3 How do people travel around your town or city? (80–100 words)

> ▶ **Tips**
>
> - Remember that you can use *there is / there are*, e.g. *There is a train. / There are lots of buses.*
> - You can use *can* for possibility and ability, e.g. *You can take the bus. / You can't buy tickets at the station.*
> - Don't forget to use words from Transport in the Word list for vocabulary.

Study skills Presentation skills

1a What do you think of the presentation of your work? Is it important to you? Read how these people answered.

A student:

> I haven't got time to think about presentation. If I finish the homework I'm happy.

A teacher:

> I like to be able to read students' work but, of course, it's the content that is important.

A parent:

> I saw my daughter's English book last week. I can't believe how untidy it was! What a mess! How can she learn anything?

A psychologist:

> People are surprised to hear that the 'look' of a piece of work is very important. Results depend on looks as much as content sometimes. All teachers and examiners are influenced by handwriting, layout, etc.

An examiner:

> I don't want to give marks for anything except the correct answers in the correct places, but we're all human, aren't we? If I'm marking 150 exams and I find some work with terrible handwriting, I am probably more critical.

1b What do you think and why?

2 What are the important things to remember about the presentation of written work? Here are the main things:

- Be brief and clear: remember numbers, titles and spaces to help the reader.
- ATQ – Answer the Question! Do what is asked and make your answer clear.
- Keep it tidy.
- Watch your spelling! English spelling isn't easy: check a word if you're not sure. All English people have to!
- Make sure your handwriting is legible or, better still, use a computer!

3 Use this checklist when you write.

CHECKLIST:

I have correctly used...

tenses ☐
pronouns ☐
third person 's ☐
spelling ☐
punctuation ☐
capital letters ☐

4 Look at this student's work and use the checklist to help you correct it.

My town

I live in an very small town in the south of france. The town is very beutiful. There are lots of old buildings. We are living in the centre in a old house. The town is by a rivver and in the summer we going swimming. In the winter we can go skiing because we are near the montains. The my town doesn't very interesting for young people. There aren't a cinema and usually at the evenings we are staying home and watch TV. I'm liking my town, but one day I want to live in a big sity.

Grammar reference

much / many / a lot of / a little / a few

much / many / a lot of

- Use *much*, *many* and *a lot of* for a large quantity.
  There are a lot of people here.
- Use a plural verb form for countable nouns.
  There are a lot of tables.
- Use a singular verb form for uncountable nouns.
  There is a lot of money.
- Use *much* in negative sentences and questions with uncountable nouns.
  There isn't much time.
  Have we got much sugar?
- Use *many* in negative sentences and questions with countable nouns.
  There aren't many people here.
  Are there many people here?

a little / a few

- Use *a little* and *a few* for a small quantity.
  There are a few people here.
  We only have a little money.
- Use *a little* in front of uncountable nouns to express indefinite quantities.
  I only want a little milk in my tea.
- Use *a few* in front of countable nouns to express indefinite quantities.
  There are a few biscuits left.

(not) enough / too much / too many

- Use *(not) enough* in front of countable or uncountable nouns to show that we have (or don't have) what we need.
  I've got enough money – I can buy the DVD.
  I haven't got enough money – I can't buy the DVD.
- To express an excessive amount use:
  - *too much* in front of uncountable nouns.
    Don't put too much sugar in the coffee.
  - *too many* in front of countable nouns.
    She's eating too many sweets these days.

such / so

- Use *such* and *so* to emphasise the adjective in an exclamation.
- How are they different? Use *so* in front of an adjective that is not followed by a noun.
  I'm so sorry!
  This artist is so famous.
- Use *such* in front of an adjective + a singular or plural noun. If the noun is singular, use *such a* or *such an*.
  This is such a famous painting!
  He's sending me such long text messages.

Uses of the *-ing* form

You have already learned how to make the *-ing* form of a verb and have used it to form the present continuous (see Unit 3).

- Use the *-ing* form:
  - after certain verbs like *enjoy*, *love*, *hate*, *like*, *stop*, *suggest*, *can't stand*, *not mind*.
    I enjoy reading magazines.
    I don't mind tidying my desk.
    They love going to the cinema.
    Why don't you stop smoking?
    We can't stand listening to hip hop.
  - after certain prepositions or adjective + prepositions like *instead of*, *good at*, *interested in*, *excited about*, *keen on*.
    He's not interested in listening to the news.
    Instead of reading a book, I like watching TV.
    I'm excited about getting a new car.
    My mum's keen on playing cards.
  - as the subject at the beginning of a sentence.
    Walking is my favourite activity.
    Gardening is hard work.
  - after the expressions *How about...?* and *What about...?*
    How about going for a walk?
    What about watching a film on TV?

Word list

The words in grey appear in the unit, but are not in the vocabulary sections.

Food

apple	lettuce
apricot	milk
aubergine	mushroom
bacon	onion
banana	orange
beef	pasta
butter	peach
cabbage	pear
carrot	pork
cheese	potato
chicken	prawn
chocolate	red pepper
cod	salmon
courgette	sardine
egg	sausage
fruit	**smoothie**
honey	strawberry
ice cream	tomato
lamb	yoghurt

Souvenirs

diary	mug
eraser	pencil
fridge magnet	pencil sharpener
key ring	T-shirt

Linking words

and	or
because	so
but	

Vocabulary

Food

1 Complete the sentences with these words.

> bacon   beef   lettuce   ~~yoghurt~~   pasta
> sausage   salmon   egg   cheese   butter

1 You need a carton of __yoghurt__ to make a smoothie.
2 Don't forget to put _____ on your bread.
3 _____ is meat that comes from cows.
4 A salad often has _____ in it.
5 Some people have a piece of _____ after their meal.
6 The traditional British breakfast includes _____, _____ and _____.
7 Spaghetti is a kind of _____.
8 _____ is a delicious fish – it is usually pink.

2 Match the food and the pictures.

1	milk	f	6	carrots	☐
2	chicken	☐	7	strawberry	☐
3	aubergine	☐	8	mushrooms	☐
4	tomato	☐	9	pear	☐
5	apple	☐	10	prawn	☐

Souvenirs

3 Write the letters in the correct order to make souvenirs.

1 yke ignr _____
2 riyda _____
3 elpcni _____
4 sraere _____
5 epinlc parnsheer _____
6 umg _____
7 gridfe tnagme _____
8 r-shtTi _____

4 What do these sentences describe? Match a word from exercise 3 with each sentence.

1 ☐ It makes my kitchen look fun.
2 ☐ This is useful when I make mistakes.
3 ☐ I use it when I want a big cup of coffee.
4 ☐ I need this when I can't draw with my pencil any more.
5 ☐ I keep my keys on this so they are easy to find.
6 ☐ I use this to write with.
7 ☐ I wear this.
8 ☐ I write about my daily life in here.

Linking words

5 Complete the text with these words.

> and but because or

Christmas ¹_____ New Year are important in the UK ²_____ many people have a long holiday from work. People celebrate with their family ³_____ go to friends for Christmas Day. Christmas Eve does not have many traditions, ⁴_____ Christmas Day is special. The 26th December is called Boxing Day ⁵_____ on that day the Queen traditionally gives 'boxes' of money to the poor.

Grammar

much / many / a lot of / a little / a few; (*not*)
enough / too much / too many

1 Complete the dialogue with these expressions.

> enough   a few   a little   many
> too much   much   ~~too many~~   a lot

Will   There are ¹ _too many_ people on the beach. Let's go to the swimming pool.

Louis OK, that's a good idea. Hang on. I haven't got ²_____ money on me – only about £2. How much does it cost?

Will   £3.50.

Louis No, I haven't got ³_____ money. I can't come.

Will   It's OK. I can lend you some.

Louis Thanks. I hope there isn't ⁴_____ noise. I hate it when it's busy and kids are screaming.

Will   Don't worry. There are only ⁵_____ people at the pool on Thursdays. But let's hurry – there's only ⁶_____ time left before it closes.

Louis I don't think there are ⁷_____ buses at this time.

Will   Come on, Louis! We can walk to the station. There are ⁸_____ of buses from there.

Louis OK. Let's go.

2 Match the questions and answers.

1 [d] Have we got enough bread?
2 [ ] How many people are there in the restaurant?
3 [ ] You eat too many crisps!
4 [ ] How much do those trousers cost?
5 [ ] How many books have you got?
6 [ ] How much milk would you like?
7 [ ] Do you put chocolate on it?
8 [ ] Would you like some orange juice?

a Yes, but only a little.
b I know I eat a lot of them.
c Yes, please. Just half a glass.
d No. We need to get some more.
e Just a little, please.
f Too much! I can't buy them.
g Too many! We can't eat there.
h I've got a few.

3 Write the words in the correct order to make a recipe for a drink.

1 few / need / a / you / apples

_____

2 litre / need / you / then / milk / a / of

_____

3 strawberries / of / add / lot / a / then

_____

4 all / into / ingredients / put / the / blender / a

_____

5 sugar / little / on / sprinkle / top / the / a

_____

6 it / the / keep / fridge / few / for / hours / in / a

_____

7 drink / much / don't / too!

_____

4 Complete the sentences with *enough*, *too much* or *too many*.

1 Oh no! There's _____ sugar in this tea. It's too sweet.

2 Have you got _____ money to get into the museum?

3 There are _____ people here – I can't see the band.

4 We haven't got _____ time to wait for you. Sorry!

5 Do you think our teacher gives us _____ homework? It takes me hours!

6 I've got _____ apples here – do you want one?

7 I can't sleep at night. I think I drink _____ coffee.

8 You can't stay at my house because there isn't _____ space.

such / so

5 Circle the correct word.

1 Our car is *so* / *such* old. It's very slow.
2 It's *so* / *such* a beautiful day. We must go out.
3 I work *so* / *such* hard and still fail my exams!
4 The people next door are making *so* / *such* a noise. Tell them to be quiet!
5 It's *so* / *such* a boring film. Let's go home…
6 Joe is *so* / *such* good-looking. I can't believe it.
7 The Science homework is *so* / *such* hard, I can't do it.
8 This is *so* / *such* good coffee. Where do you buy it?

6 Complete the sentences with *so* or *such*.

1 It's ___such___ a long way!
2 Our cat is _____ old. She sleeps all day.
3 I'm _____ hungry!
4 She's _____ angry – she missed her bus this morning.
5 It's _____ a hot day today. Let's go swimming.
6 This is _____ an important test!
7 This History homework is _____ difficult. I can't do it.
8 They make _____ good music. I can't wait to see them in concert.

Uses of the *-ing* form

7 Complete the sentences with the correct form of the verb in brackets.

1 How about ___staying___ (stay) here tonight?
2 Please finish _____ (talk) now.
3 I really love _____ (swim).
4 _____ (play) football is great!
5 What about _____ (go) to the cinema tonight?
6 Stop _____ (do) that!
7 You've got an hour for the exam. Please start _____ (write) now.
8 _____ (read) magazines is very relaxing.

8 Complete the sentences with *in*, *of*, *at* or nothing (–).

1 I love ___–___ staying up late.
2 We're not very good _____ saying 'sorry'.
3 I hate _____ working at the weekend.
4 I'm not interested _____ seeing him again.
5 I'm quite good _____ swimming.
6 They like _____ playing computer games.
7 I can't stand _____ playing chess. It's so boring!
8 I'm interested _____ working for you.

9 Now complete the sentences about yourself.

All about ME!

1 I like _doing karaoke_____.
2 _____
_____.is my favourite activity.
3 I really love _____
_____.
4 I can't stand _____
_____.
5 I'm interested _____
_____.
6 I hate _____
_____.
7 I'm quite good _____
_____.
8 I'm not very good _____
_____.

Skills: Reading – Towards PET (Part 1)

1 Read the questions and the answers about the Rio carnival. Then read the sentences and circle the correct answer.

1 When does it happen, and what's the weather like?

It's always in February, seven weeks before Easter, so it's never on the same date. It's very hot because it's the end of summer in Brazil. But it always rains at carnival!

2 How many days is the actual carnival?

Officially, it starts on Saturday morning and finishes on Wednesday lunchtime, so everybody has enough time to recover before Thursday, when people go back to work.

3 What happens exactly? Is it one big street party?

There are small street parties in most parts of Rio. A lot of people go to the Saturday Bola Preta (Black Ball) parade in the streets of the city centre. It's the most traditional carnival party, and it's free. But the famous carnival parade is at the Sambódromo.

4 What is the Sambódromo?

It's a stadium near the city centre. They close the streets to traffic. It's a four-day competition. The big samba schools parade on Sunday and Monday night. Each school dances for 50 minutes. It starts at 9 p.m. and finishes at five o'clock in the morning!

5 How do they find the winner?

There are judges – people who give scores for different things. For example, the words of the song, the singing, the costumes, the drumming (it's very loud!) and, of course, the samba dancing.

6 Can I be in the parade?

Yes – buy a costume and learn to samba! It's not so hard in the beginning – just move your arms and feet a lot! But to dance samba very well, you need to be very fit. Remember, you dance for an hour in a heavy costume – and it's 40°!

7 How much is it to watch?

Sunday and Monday is very expensive ($200–$1000). Or, you can see the small schools on Saturday and Tuesday. It costs $1, but it's good – and the atmosphere is still wonderful!

1 Rio carnival is always *before / after* Easter every year.
2 The carnival is in *winter / summer*.
3 The carnival finishes on *Wednesday / Thursday*.
4 The Black Ball parade is *free / expensive*.
5 The Sambódromo parade lasts for *two / four* days.
6 The samba dancing is *one / the only* thing in the competition.
7 Tourists *can / can't* dance in the parade.
8 Saturday night is very *expensive / cheap*.

Writing

2 A friend is coming to see you for the weekend. There is a special event and you hope he / she will like it. Write to him / her explaining what it is. (80–100 words)

> **Tips**
> - Use the Reading text above for ideas.
> - Try to use *much / many / a lot of / a little / a few / so / such*, e.g. *A lot of people go / There aren't many tickets / It's so exciting!*
> - Try to make the event sound interesting. Say what people usually enjoy doing there.
> - Write about food or souvenirs that people can buy there (see the Word list).
> - Remember to use linking words, e.g. *and / but / so / or / when / of course.*

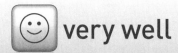 very well   OK   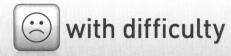 with difficulty

I've finished this module and I can do ☑ these things in English

Module ❸   🙂 😐 🙁

Listening

	🙂	😐	🙁
A2 understand phrases, words and expressions related to my immediate surroundings, e.g. transport (p.53)	☐	☐	☐
A2 catch the main point in short, clear, simple messages and announcements, e.g. at the Underground station (p.53)	☐	☐	☐
A2 identify the main points of a short radio programme about a festival (p.63)	☐	☐	☐

Reading

	🙂	😐	🙁
A2 identify important information in news summaries or simple newspaper articles about lost property (p.54), about a festival (p.62)	☐	☐	☐
A2 find the most important information about young people's activities (p.47), how to travel on the Underground (p.52), recipes (p.56) in information leaflets	☐	☐	☐

Spoken Interaction

	🙂	😐	🙁
A2 use public transport, ask for basic information and buy tickets (p.53)	☐	☐	☐
A2 make simple purchases by stating what I want and asking the price (p.61)	☐	☐	☐
A2 ask for and give directions inside a building (p.60)	☐	☐	☐

Spoken Production

	🙂	😐	🙁
A2 describe activities which are happening now in a brief and simple way (p.50)	☐	☐	☐
A2 describe a festival (p.63)	☐	☐	☐

Strategies / Language quality

	🙂	😐	🙁
A2 indicate when I am following (p.60)	☐	☐	☐
A2 make myself understood using memorised phrases and single expressions (pp.52, 60)	☐	☐	☐

Writing

	🙂	😐	🙁
A2 write about aspects of my everyday life, e.g. some objects (p.55), in simple phrases and sentences	☐	☐	☐
A2 write simple sentences, connecting them with words such as 'and', 'but', 'because' (p.63)	☐	☐	☐

At the end of **Module 3**, I've got more A2 skills. Now I can start **Module 4**.

Grammar reference

Modal verb *must* / *mustn't* and modal verb phrase (*not*) *have to*

Positive		
I/You/He/She/It/We/They	must	go home.

Negative		
I/You/He/She/It/We/They	mustn't	be late.

The verb *must* is a modal verb. Remember:

* it does not take -*s* when the subject is *he*, *she* or *it*
* it is followed by the base form of the verb
* use it in the positive and negative (see above) but not in questions and short answers.

Positive		
I/You/We/They	have to	help.
He/She/It	has to	

Negative		
I/You/We/They	don't have to	help.
He/She/It	doesn't have to	

Questions			
Do	I/you/we/they	have to	help?

Positive short answers		
Yes,	I/you/we/they	do.
Yes,	he/she/it	does.

Negative short answers		
No,	I/you/we/they	don't.
No,	he/she/it	doesn't.

The verb *have to* means 'must'.

* Form the positive with:
  subject + *have to* / *has to* + base form
* Form the negative with:
  subject + *don't* / *doesn't* + *have to* + base form
* Form questions with:
  Do / *Does* + subject + *have to* + base form
* Form short answers with:
  Yes, + personal pronoun + *do* / *does*.
  No, + personal pronoun + *don't* / *doesn't*.

Usage

* Use *I must* and *We must* for personal obligations.
  I must buy a new bag.
  We must help Mum if she's tired.

* Use *must* for giving orders, making recommendations and saying that something is important or urgent.
  You must turn off your mobiles.
  You must start with an easy task.
* *Must not* means 'it is forbidden / it is not allowed to do this'.
  You must not shout in class.
  You mustn't go out now.
* In questions and in short answers it is more usual to use *have to*, not *must*.
  Do I have to sign on this line? NOT ~~Must I sign on this line?~~
  Yes, you do. NOT ~~Yes, you have to.~~
* In the positive, *have to* and *must* can have the same meaning.
  We have to / must buy something for dinner.
* In the negative, *have to* and *must* have completely different meanings. *Don't have to* means 'it is not necessary to do this'.
  You mustn't sit there. (= it is forbidden)
  You don't have to sit there. (= it isn't necessary)
* Use *have to* for obligations, rules or customary routine.
  You have to drive on the left in England.
  He has to cut the grass every weekend.

Agreeing and disagreeing

You have already learned how to express agreement or disagreement after a sentence in the present simple (Unit 1) and after a sentence with *can* (Unit 5).

Remember, to agree:

* after a positive sentence with *must* use *So must I.*
  I must see that film. – So must I.
* after a negative sentence with *don't have to* use *Neither do I.*
  I don't have to be here. – Neither do I.

To disagree:

* after a positive sentence with *must* use *I don't have to.*
  We must leave now. – I don't have to.
* after a negative sentence with *don't have to* use *I do.*
  I don't have to get up early. – I do.

(*not*) *be allowed to*

* Use *be allowed to* to talk about permission and present rules.
  You're allowed to go to the party.
  Are you allowed to wear what clothes you like to school?
* Form the negative with *not.*
  We're not allowed to eat food in class.
  We aren't allowed to eat food in class.

- Use *you* to talk about permission in an impersonal, general way.

  You aren't allowed to use mobile phones in class.
  (This means no one is allowed.)

- Use (*not*) *be allowed to* in the same way as *can / can't* to talk about permission.

  You aren't allowed to listen to mp3 players at school.
  (= *You* can't listen to mp3 players at school.)
  Are we allowed to use our skateboards here?
  (= Can we use our skateboards here?)

Word list

The words in grey appear in the unit, but are not in the vocabulary sections.

School

assistant	**intelligence**
blazer	**languages**
classroom	**Maths**
education	pupil
English	registration
exercise	school rules
extra work	school uniform
Geography	**study**
gym	teacher
homework	

Computers

button	mouse mat
cable	**nickname**
chatroom	**password**
email address	plug
(ISP) Internet Service Provider	printer
keyboard	processor
moderator	screen
monitor	speaker
mouse	USB port

Computer verbs

click on	receive
close down	send
delete	start up
key in	turn off
plug in	turn on
print	unplug

Vocabulary

School

1 Look at the photo and write what the boy and girl are wearing.

1 _____
_____
_____
2 _____
_____
_____

2 Write the letters in the correct order to complete the sentences.

1 My friend thinks **atMsh** is boring, but I think it's really interesting. m_____

2 We have **oewrmohk** every day. h_____

3 I really like **egroaGhyp** because I'm interested in the world. g_____

4 I like modern **aunaglegs** like French, German and English. l_____

5 Another word for a school student is a **lippu**. p_____

6 Are there any weird **loscho lerus** at your school? s_____

7 There's always an **ssitsntaa** and a teacher in our classroom. a_____

8 Do you have to wear a school **founirm**? u_____

Computers

3 Label the parts of the computer.

1	_____	5	_____
2	_____	6	_____
3	_____	7	_____
4	_____	8	_____

Computer verbs

4 Complete the dialogue with these words.

send	turn	~~plug~~	unplug	click
start	key	receive	deletes	close

Gran Can you help me with my new computer, Carl?

Carl First you need to ¹ _plug_ it in, Gran. Then turn it on and wait for it to ² _____ up.

Gran So how do I check my email?

Carl OK, use the mouse to ³ _____ on this icon here.

Gran Why is it called a mouse?

Carl Because it's the same shape as a mouse. Now, you have to ⁴ _____ in your password here.

Gran Right. s-u-p-e-r-g-r-a-n. There we are. How do I ⁵ _____ and ⁶ _____ emails?

Carl Just type your message here, and click on 'send'.

Gran Oh no, what happened?

Carl That button ⁷ _____ everything, Gran! You must be careful. Your email is lost.

Gran Oh, well. I'll do it again later. Let's ⁸ _____ it off. That's enough for today.

Carl OK. First you have to ⁹ _____ it down. Click here. Don't leave it on standbay. Turn it off and you should ¹⁰ _____ it.

Grammar

Modal verb *must* / *mustn't* and modal verb phrase (*not*) *have to*

1 Complete the email with *have to*, *has to*, *don't have to* or *doesn't have to*.

✉

Subject: My brothers!

My twin brothers, Luke and Joel, are so lucky. They ¹ _don't have to_ go to school on Saturdays. But they ² _____ do lots of homework, and Joel ³ _____ do swimming training five days a week. I ⁴ _____ do any homework at the weekends. Luke ⁵ _____ help Dad in his shop, too – he hates it! – but Joel ⁶ _____ help him because of his swimming training. Well, all of us ⁷ _____ help our parents a bit. I help Mum sometimes, but the good thing is that I ⁸ _____ help her every week – I do it when I want to. But I still think Luke and Joel are lucky, because they ⁹ _____ get up early on Saturday mornings!

2 Write questions with *have to*.

1 we / study / for the test
   Do we have to study for the test?

2 they / be quiet / for an hour
   _____

3 I / finish / my homework
   _____

4 they / go / to an interview
   _____

5 she / clean / the house today
   _____

6 she / remember / your name
   _____

7 I / answer / all the questions
   _____

3 Complete the sentences with the correct form of *must* or *have to*.

1 You _must_ work harder.

2 You _____ do that! It's dangerous!

3 We _____ pay for the tickets. They're free.

4 Your sister _____ finish the book today – she can finish it tomorrow.

5 They _____ carry their ID card at all times or they get into trouble.

6 He _____ help his dad every weekend.

7 I _____ finish my homework this evening. I have to hand it in tomorrow!

4 Write sentences explaining to Mark what he must not do.

1 You mustn't cross the road here.

_____ (cross)

2 _____

_____ (go)

3 _____

_____

_____ (drink)

4 _____

_____ (park)

SILENCE

5 _____

_____

_____ (swim)

6 _____

_____ (talk)

5 Now write sentences about yourself.

1 Write five things you have to do at school.
2 Write five things you mustn't do at school.
3 Write five things you can do, but which are not necessary.

1 I have to study Maths.

2 I mustn't talk in the library.

3 I don't have to go to the gym every day.

_____

_____

_____

_____

_____

_____

Agreeing and disagreeing

6 Match the statements with the comments.

1 [c] I don't have to do the essay again.
2 [ ] She has to work on Saturday mornings.
3 [ ] We don't have to do any homework tonight.
4 [ ] I must buy a new blazer.
5 [ ] She doesn't speak English very well.
6 [ ] I must clean the house at the weekend.
7 [ ] I don't have to drive.
8 [ ] I mustn't forget my mobile phone.
9 [ ] They have to practise for the concert next week.

a So do we. There are lots of songs to learn.
b Neither must I. It's in my desk.
c Neither do I.
d Neither do I. But I'm getting better!
e So must I. I hate cleaning!
f Neither do we. Let's go out!
g So do I. I need the money.
h Neither do we. We can go on the bus.
i So must I. My old one is too small!

7 Write answers to agree or disagree with the sentences.

1 I have to get up early for school.
    So do I. / I don't.
2 I don't have to cook at home. ☒

_____

3 I must do more exercise. ☑

_____

4 I have to tidy my room every day. ☒

_____

5 I mustn't eat so many sweets. ☑

_____

(not) be allowed to

8 Complete the sentences so they are true for you. Use the correct form of allowed to or not allowed to. Then add three more positive or negative sentences.

1 Girls at my school _____ wear make-up.
2 You _____ chew gum in class.
3 We _____ wear jewellery to school.
4 We _____ take our mobile phones to lessons.
5 We _____ wear trainers in school.
6 _____
7 _____
8 _____

Skills: Reading – Towards PET (Part 2)

1 Match the pictures with the emails.

Posted by <u>Corey</u>: *Stupid school rules* ☐

Does your school or college have any stupid rules? Our new librarian says you mustn't sit on the tables in the library. Why? The tables in the library never break. Also, you have to be silent, even when there are only two people in the room. Our librarian needs to chill out.

<u>Jellybelly</u> reply: *stupid school rules* ☐

Our uniform rules are stupid. You have to wear a white shirt and tie, and if your top button is undone you get into big trouble. Your top button! They don't pick on girls so much – and they don't have to wear ties. Typical – it's so unfair!

<u>dragon32</u> reply: *stupid school rules* ☐

When we have free periods in the morning, like Lessons 1 and 2, we MUST still turn up at 8:45 and register. It's such a pain. Why can't we come to school at 10:00?

<u>Rizzer</u> reply: *stupid school rules* ☐

We mustn't wear any jewellery – not even an ear stud! And you can't have very long or very short hair, or coloured hair. Oh, and no baseball caps or national football team shirts.

<u>dizzygirl08</u> reply: *stupid school rules* ☐

You can't sing on the school bus. Can you believe that? And you mustn't use your mobile on the bus, or on the STREET outside school! We don't have to wear a uniform, though.

2 Complete the sentences with these words.

mustn't	don't	must	can't	have

1 You _____ be silent in the library.
2 Girls _____ have to wear a tie.
3 You _____ to register at 8.45.
4 You _____ wear any jewellery.
5 You _____ sing on the school bus.

3 Choose the rule you think is most stupid.

Writing

4 Write to a friend telling him / her about your school. (100–120 words)

> ➤ **Tips**
> - Use the Reading text above to help you.
> - Remember to check the Word list for vocabulary.
> - You can write about the subjects you like and don't like (and say why).
> - Write about some of the school rules. Use *must / mustn't / (not) have to / (not) be allowed to.*

Study skills **Learning styles**

1 Look at the pictures. How are these students learning?

VISUAL

AUDITORY

KINAESTHETIC

2 Look at the questionnaire and do the task. Find out your learning style.

What sort of

LEARNER
are you?

Do you learn by seeing things (visual), by hearing things (auditory) or by moving around (kinaesthetic)? Knowing your learning style helps you improve your studies and choose the best approach to your learning. Tick the statements that are true for you.

1 **V** ☐ When I'm reading I see images in my head.
2 **A** ☐ I remember conversations very well.
3 **V** ☐ I learn when I read things.
4 **K** ☐ I learn well when I move around.
5 **K** ☐ I learn phone numbers by the movement of my fingers as I dial.
6 **A** ☐ I repeat things in my head to remember them.
7 **V** ☐ I draw pictures when I listen.
8 **A** ☐ I can remember the words of songs.
9 **V** ☐ I use colour in my notes.
10 **K** ☐ I'm good at sport.
11 **A** ☐ I'm good at music.
12 **K** ☐ I move around a lot and I can't sit still.
13 **A** ☐ I can remember instructions people give me.
14 **K** ☐ I learn by doing things.
15 **A** ☐ I remember phone numbers when I hear them.
16 **V** ☐ I learn from pictures, diagrams and videos.
17 **K** ☐ I'm good at practical things.
18 **A** ☐ I ask a lot of questions in class.

Mostly Vs

You are a **visual learner**. You learn when you can see information. You respond well to pictures, graphs, demonstrations, films etc.

Mostly As

You are an **auditory learner**. You learn when you can hear information. You respond well to explanations, talks, presentations and music.

Mostly Ks

You are a **kinaesthetic learner**. You learn when you can actually do things. You respond well to movement, touch or feeling.

Grammar reference

should / shouldn't

Should is a modal verb. Remember:
- it has the same form for all persons
- it is followed by the base form

Usage

- Use *should* and *shouldn't* to ask for and give advice or to express opinions.
    I'm really tired. – You should go to bed.
    What should we do to help protect the Earth?
- Use *should* to say that something is the right thing to do, or to make suggestions and give advice. Compare:
    This is a dangerous road. You should drive slowly.
    (= It's a good idea.)
    Look at that sign. You must drive slowly.
    (= It's compulsory.)
- Use *shouldn't* to say that something is not the right thing to do.
    You shouldn't eat too much fast food. (= It isn't a good idea.)

ought (to)

The semi-modal verb *ought to* is different from other modal verbs.
- like other semi-modal verbs, it has the same form for all persons
- unlike other semi-modal verbs, it is followed by *to* + base form
- it is usually used in positive sentences
- it is not used much in the negative (*oughtn't to*) and questions (*ought I to…?*)

Usage

- Use *ought to* to say that it is a good idea to do something.
    You ought to buy a new computer.
- You can use *should* and *shouldn't* instead of *ought to* and *oughtn't to.*
    I've got one week to finish this. It ought to / should be enough. You oughtn't to / You shouldn't tell him.

needn't

Needn't is a semi-modal verb. Remember:
- it has the same form for all persons
- it is followed by the base form

However, note the following:
- In the positive, form the verb *need* like a regular verb, so add *-s* to the third person singular.
    She needs to talk to you.
- after *need*, use *to* + base form.
    I need to see you.
- Form the negative with *don't / doesn't* and questions with *do / does.*
    I don't need to come.
    Does she need to see me today?'

Usage

- Use *needn't* to say that it is not necessary to do something.
    You needn't buy a video camera. I can lend you mine.

Articles

Indefinite article *a / an*

Use the indefinite article *a / an* with singular countable nouns:
- the first time something is mentioned
    I saw a boat today.
- to talk about one thing or person among many possible ones
    Has your dad got a car?
- to describe something or someone
    It is a big house with a red door.

Definite article *the*

Use the definite article *the* with singular and plural countable nouns:
- the second time something is mentioned.
    I saw a boat. The boat was green.
- to talk about a single thing or person in a particular context.
    Do you want to visit the new museum in town?
    The teacher wants to see you.
- with the words *morning, afternoon, evening,* but NOT *night.*
    I can study in the afternoon, but not at night.
- with the names of musical instruments.
    Can you play the piano?
- with place names that contain the word *Republic, State* or *Union / United.*
    The United Kingdom
    The Republic of Ireland
    The United States

No article

Don't use an article:

- in front of institutions.

  Mum is at work and the children are at school.
  NOT *at the work, at the school*

- usually in front of place names.

  I want to go to Paris. NOT *to the Paris*

- in front of possessive adjectives.

  your parents NOT *the your parents*

- in front of sports, activities, school subjects, languages and colours.

  He loves football. NOT *He loves the football.*
  I love English!
  Red is my favourite colour.

- in front of days of the week, months, seasons and years.

  See you on Saturday.
  Winter is quite cold in Northern Italy.

- with abstract nouns.

  It is difficult to describe love.

- with plural nouns that denote a whole category.

  I love trees.

Word list

The words in grey appear in the unit, but are not in the vocabulary sections.

Relationships

agony column
ask (someone) out
break up
ex (ex-boyfriend / ex-girlfriend)
get back together
go out (together / with someone)
have strong feelings for someone
shy
well-suited

Places in a town

baker's	newsagent's
bus station	petrol station
butcher's	police station
car park	post office
chemist's	restaurant
fire station	sports centre
florist's	stationer's
greengrocer's	town hall
library	train station

Prepositions of place and movement

across	next to
along	opposite
away from	out of
behind	over
between	past
into	through
in front of	towards
near	

Vocabulary

Relationships

1 Circle the correct words.

1 You should write a letter to an *agony / advisor* column about your problem.

2 How can I *tell / ask* Susan out? I really like her!

3 My brother can't get a girlfriend because he's too *fair / shy*.

4 I still have *big / strong* feelings for my ex-boyfriend.

5 It's always the same – they *go / get* out together for a few weeks, then they break *up / down*. Then they *go / get* back together again!

Places and prepositions

2 Complete the text with these prepositions.

~~near~~	away from	opposite
across	over	next	along

I live in a little village [1] **near** Oxford. My house is [2]_____ to the post office. My best friend, Helen, lives [3]_____ me. I only have to go [4]_____ the road to get to her house. There is a park at the end of our street, and we go there every weekend. It has got a small lake with a bridge [5]_____ it. Sometimes we walk [6]_____ the path by the lake and just talk and make plans to get [7]_____ this place! It's a really boring place to live!

3 Match the names of the shops with the things they sell.

1	newsagent's	a	fruit and vegetables
2	stationer's	b	bread and cakes
3	greengrocer's	c	beef and chicken
4	chemist's	d	flowers and plants
5	florist's	e	magazines and newspapers
6	butcher's	f	pens and paper
7	baker's	g	medicine and cosmetics

4 Complete the sentences with these words.

petrol station   in front of   ~~town hall~~   towards   out of
train station   through   ~~past~~   opposite   post office

1 To get to the
   __town hall__ , go
   __past__ the cinema.

2 They're standing
   _____ the
   _____ .

3 The _____
   is _____ the
   sports centre.

4 They're walking
   _____ the theatre.

5 They're coming
   _____ the
   _____ .

6 They're walking
   _____ the park.

Grammar

should / ought to / needn't

1 Match the sentences with the advice.

1 ☐ Our dog is getting very fat.
2 ☐ The teacher always shouts at me.
3 ☐ My mum isn't happy at work.
4 ☐ I'm very tired.
5 ☐ Mum and Dad aren't enjoying their holiday.
6 ☐ My phone bill is enormous.
7 ☐ Jane's mp3 player doesn't work.
8 ☐ My boyfriend never has any money.

a She should get a new job.
b You shouldn't go out tonight.
c They ought to come home early.
d You should put it on a diet.
e You shouldn't talk on it so much.
f He should get a job.
g She ought to get a new one.
h You ought to do your homework on time.

2 Give advice using *should* or *shouldn't*.

1 She __shouldn't__ smoke
   so much.

2 She _____ get a
   cleaner!

3 He _____ spend so
   much money.

4 They _____ fight.

5 She _____ do more exercise.

6 They _____ listen in class.

3 Complete Zoe's reply to a letter. Circle the correct words.

Ask Zoe

Dear Zoe,

I need your help! My boyfriend doesn't understand why I'm angry with him. He always goes out with his mates and doesn't phone me. Now my friends tell me he says he doesn't really love me. What should I do?

LUCY

Dear Lucy,

I'm sorry you've got a problem with your boyfriend. I think you ¹*need / needn't* to speak to him. You ²*needn't / need* to make him understand your feelings. He is probably very sorry too. You ³*should / oughtn't to* find out how he is feeling. When you talk, you ⁴*oughtn't / needn't* to be angry with him: try to explain that he ⁵*needn't / oughtn't to* be perfect, but he ⁶*ought / need* to really love you!

ZOE

Articles

4 Circle the correct word.

1 I always feel tired in *the / a / -* evening.
2 It should be *the / a / -* fantastic weather tomorrow.
3 We're moving soon to *the / a / -* Republic of Ireland.
4 My favourite meal of the day is *the / a / -* dinner.
5 My aunt's *the / a / -* journalist and she speaks *the / a / -* Chinese!
6 Do you play *the / a / -* piano?
7 *The / A / -* cricket is a great game.
8 How many countries are in *the / a / -* European Union?
9 I'm not very good in *the / a / -* morning.
10 Joe's training to be *the / a / -* plumber.

5 Complete the text with *the, a, an,* or – (for no article).

In ¹*the* morning I jump quickly out of ²___ my bed and go to ³___ bathroom. Then I get dressed. I have ⁴___ fruit and yoghurt for ⁵___ breakfast because I want to run ⁶___ marathon soon. I usually have ⁷___ glass of orange juice too. I leave ⁸___ home at eight. ⁹___ traffic in ¹⁰___ city centre is terrible, so it usually takes about ¹¹___ hour to get to ¹²___ school. I get to ¹³___ class at about half past eight. Today, I'm going to take ¹⁴___ my bike. I've got ¹⁵___ new bike – it's really fast, so I may arrive early!

6 Complete the questions with the correct article. Then answer them for you.

1 Do you like *the / a / -* swimming?
_____

2 Would you like to be *the / a / -* doctor?
_____

3 Do you prefer *the / a / -* dogs or *the / a / -* cats?
_____

4 Are you learning to play *the / an / -* instrument?
_____

5 Do you study best in *the / a / -* morning or *the / an / -* evening?
_____

6 Is your birthday in *the / a / -* summer or *the / a / -* winter?
_____

7 Does *the / a / -* your family live in *the / a / -* country?
_____

8 Would you like to learn *the / a / -* Chinese?
_____

Skills: Reading – towards PET (Part 2)

1 Read opinions 1–6 and the reactions of the people in an Internet chatroom. Match each opinion with the person who made the comment.

1 You should be allowed to get married at 16 without your parents' consent. _Angelina_

2 You shouldn't be allowed to get a tattoo until you are 16. _____

3 You shouldn't be allowed to buy alcohol at 16. _____

4 You should be allowed to buy cigarettes before the age of 16. _____

5 You should be allowed to drive at 16. _____

6 You should be allowed to change your name at the age of 16. _____

There should be a law...

• I don't see why not. I think that most kids who want to smoke already smoke by the age of 13 or 14. You can't really stop them smoking, so the law is a bit of a waste of time. **Daniel Robbins, 17**

• I don't know. I think it's OK to drink at that age with your parents, but maybe it isn't a good idea to be allowed to go into pubs and buy beer. **Parvinder Singh, 18**

• I think it's a stupid thing to do anyway. You think it's a good idea at the time, but then you have to keep it for the rest of your life. You might have the name of an old girlfriend or boyfriend on your arm for ever! I think the law's a good idea. **Nina Lukic, 15**

• I think that's a bad idea. Lots of young people have car crashes, so it isn't a good idea to change the age from 17 to 16. **Joss van Helder, 17**

• Some parents call their children really stupid things like Tree or Star. It sounds OK when they're young, but not when they grow up. So, yeah, I think you ought to be allowed to do something about it when you're 16. **Ken Mutawa, 19**

• This is a difficult question. I think that 16 is too young to get married, but I don't think the law ought to stop you if you want to. It's a personal thing. **Angelina Scott, 17**

2 Answer the questions.

1 What does Daniel think about children who already smoke?

2 Is there an occasion when Parvinder thinks it's OK to drink at 16? When?

3 Why does Nina think getting a tattoo when you're young is a bad idea?

4 Why doesn't Joss think it's a good idea to change the age for driving?

5 Why does Ken think teenagers should be allowed to change their name?

6 What does Angelina say about getting married?

Writing

3 Imagine you are writing on your favourite Internet site. Write what you think about two of the opinions in _There should be a law..._ (100–120 words)

> ▶ **Tips**

• Remember to use _should / ought to / needn't / must / have to_.

• Write about other people's opinions, e.g. _Some people think... but I...._

• Use phrases from the Reading text, e.g. _It's a waste of time. / This is a difficult question... / Maybe it isn't a good idea to... / I think it's OK to... / I think that's a bad idea..._

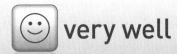 very well   OK   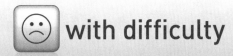 with difficulty

I've finished this module and I can do ☑ these things in English

Module ④

	☺	☺	☹

Listening

	☺	☺	☹
A2 understand what is being said during a simple conversation about age limits and young people's activities (p.82)	☐	☐	☐
A2 catch the main point in short, clear, simple messages, e.g. how to use a computer (p.74)	☐	☐	☐
A2 understand the essential information in short recorded passages about school rules (p.70), road directions (p.81)	☐	☐	☐

Reading

	☺	☺	☹
A2 identify important information in simple newspaper articles about different subjects (multiple intelligences) (p.72), Internet safety (p.75), Internet addiction (p.78), young people's rights (pp. 82, 83)	☐	☐	☐
A2 skim messages and identify the most important pieces of information (p.70)	☐	☐	☐
A2 understand feedback messages or simple help indications in computer programmes (p.74)	☐	☐	☐

Spoken Interaction

	☺	☺	☹
A2 ask for and give directions referring to a map or plan (pp.80, 81)	☐	☐	☐
A2 ask people questions about schools rules (p.70), Internet safety (p.75), Internet addiction (p.78) and answer such questions	☐	☐	☐
A2 discuss what the age limits are for young people's activities (p.83)	☐	☐	☐

Spoken Production

	☺	☺	☹
A2 give a short, basic description of a project developed by my group (p.73)	☐	☐	☐

Strategies / Language Quality

	☺	☺	☹
A2 make myself understood using memorised phrases and single expressions (pp.72, 80)	☐	☐	☐

Writing

	☺	☺	☹
A2 write about aspects of my everyday life in simple phrases and sentences e.g. the multiple intelligences used when learning (p.72), how to use a computer (p.74), the age limits for young people's activities (p.83)	☐	☐	☐
A2 briefly introduce myself in a letter with simple phrases and sentences (p.76)	☐	☐	☐

At the end of **Module 4**, I've got a lot of A2 skills.
Now I can start **Module 5**.

Grammar reference

Past simple of *be*

Positive

I	was
You	were
He/She/It	was
We/You/They	were

Negative

full form

I	was not
You	were not
He/She/It	was not
We/You/They	were not

short form

I/He/She/It	wasn't
We/You/They	weren't

Questions

Was	I/he/she/it...?
Were	we/you/they...?

Short answers

positive	negative
Yes, I/he/she/it was.	No, I/he/she/it wasn't.
Yes, we/you/they were.	No, we/you/they weren't.

- Form the positive past simple of *be* with:
  subject + *was / were* (full forms)
- Form the negative with:
  subject + *was / were* + *not* (full forms)
  subject + *wasn't / weren't* (short forms)
- Form questions with:
  was / were + subject
- Form short answers with:
  Yes, + subject pronoun + *was / were*.
  No, + subject pronoun + *wasn't / weren't*.

Usage

- Use the past simple of *be* to talk about the past.
  We were in the restaurant. It was my birthday.
  Were they really happy? – Yes, they were.

Past simple regular verbs

Positive

I/You/He/She/It/We/You/They	walked.

Negative

I/You/He/She/It/We/You/They	did not / didn't	walk.

Questions

Did	I/you/he/she/it/we/you/they	walk?

Positive short answers

Yes,	I/you/he/she/it/we/you/they	did.

Negative short answers

No,	I/you/he/she/it/we/you/they	didn't.

The past simple of regular verbs is the same for all persons.

- Form the past simple positive with:
  subject + base form + *-ed*
- Form the past simple negative with:
  subject + *did not* (full form) + base form
  subject + *didn't* (short form) + base form
- Form past simple questions with:
  did + subject + base form
- Form positive short answers with:
  Yes, + subject + *did*.
- Form negative short answers with:
  No, + subject + *didn't*.
- If the question begins with an interrogative pronoun, adjective or adverb (*Wh-* question), use:
  interrogative + *did* + subject + base form
  Who did you help?
  Why did she lie?

Usage

- Use the past simple to talk about actions that began and ended in the past. You often use it with past time expressions.
  We visited the museum but we didn't enjoy it.
  Hiram Bingham discovered the ruins of Machu Picchu in 1911.
  I tried to phone you yesterday because I wanted some help.

Spelling and pronunciation of past simple verb endings

Spelling rules

- If the base form of the verb ends in -e, add -d.
    notice —→ *noticed*
- If the verb ends in a consonant + -y, change the -y to -i and add -ed.
    study —→ *studied*
- If the verb ends in a vowel + -y, add -ed as usual.
    play —→ *played*
- If the verb ends in a single consonant after a single stressed vowel, double the final consonant and add -ed.
    stop —→ *stopped*
- If the verb ends in 'l' after a single vowel, always double the 'l', even if the vowel is not stressed.
    travel —→ *travelled*

Pronunciation rules

- Pronounce the final -ed as /t/ after the sounds /k/, /f/, /p/, /s/, /ʃ/, /tʃ/.
    liked, laughed, helped, missed, finished, watched
- Pronounce the final -ed as /ɪd/ after the sounds /d/ or /t/.
    avoided, decided, wanted, waited, visited
- Pronounce the final -ed as /d/ after all other sounds.
    listened, studied, played

Past time expressions

Here are some past time expressions. Notice that you can use *ago, last, yesterday* in many expressions.

last night/week/Monday/month/year/Christmas
an hour/five days/a week/a month/20 years ago
the day before yesterday
yesterday
yesterday morning/afternoon/evening
this morning
at the weekend
in 2000

Put these past time expressions at the beginning or at the end of the sentence.

At the weekend I played golf.
Did you study last night?

Word list

The words in grey appear in the unit, but are not in the vocabulary sections.

Jobs

actor / actress	flight attendant
artist	lorry driver
businessman / woman	mechanic
butcher	pharmacist
cashier	psychologist
dentist	singer
farmer	surveyor
film director	waiter / waitress

Physical appearance

Height

short	tall

Build

average build	thin
plump	well built
slim	

Face

chubby face	small nose
long face	thin face
round face	

Hair colour

black	brown
blond	red

Hair length & shape

bald	medium-length
curly	short
long	wavy

Hair style

beard	hair loose
clean-shaven	hair tied back
dreadlocks	moustache

Eyes

blue eyes	green eyes
brown eyes	greeny-blue eyes

Ornaments & other

eyebrow piercing	stud in her lip
glasses	tattoo
pierced ears	

Personality

decisive – indecisive	outgoing – shy
friendly – unfriendly	patient – impatient
funny – serious	reliable – unreliable
generous – mean	sensitive – insensitive
hard-working – lazy	sincere – insincere
imaginative – unimaginative	thoughtful – thoughtless
loyal – disloyal	unselfish – selfish

Mood

angry	nervous
bored	sad
depressed	scared
happy	upset

Vocabulary

Jobs

1 Write the jobs.

1 This person takes money in a shop. _cashier_
2 This person looks after your teeth. _____
3 This person paints pictures. _____
4 This person fixes cars. _____
5 This person acts in plays. _____
6 This person sells meat. _____
7 This person makes films. _____
8 This person works in a restaurant. _____

Physical appearance

2 Look at the pictures and answer the questions.

Which person…

1 is quite short and slim, and has got a beard and curly hair? ☐
2 is average build, wears glasses, and has got short wavy hair? ☐
3 has got a round face, a small nose and long hair tied back? ☐
4 is very well-built, clean-shaven, and has got dreadlocks and a pierced ear? ☐
5 is tall and bald with a long face, a moustache and an eyebrow piercing? ☐

Personality and mood

3 Find eight adjectives to describe somebody's mood.

V	N	T	Y	B	O	R	E	D
I	E	U	A	H	I	S	A	L
K	R	P	N	J	S	A	D	K
P	V	S	G	R	U	P	S	E
T	O	E	R	A	N	G	U	H
R	U	T	Y	S	E	W	J	G
N	S	S	S	C	A	R	E	D
D	E	P	R	E	S	S	E	D
M	K	H	A	P	P	Y	V	S

4 Complete the sentences with these words.

> lazy   reliable   indecisive   ~~insincere~~
> mean   shy   friendly   selfish

1 I don't mean what I say. I'm _insincere_ .
2 I like people and have lots of friends. I'm _____.
3 I lie on my bed all day and watch TV. I'm _____.
4 I don't like spending money. I'm _____.
5 I'm only interested in me, me, me! I'm _____.
6 I can't make decisions about things. I'm _____.
7 People can depend on me. I'm _____.
8 I'm quiet around other people. I'm _____.

Grammar

Past simple of *be*

1 Complete the sentences with the correct form of the verb *be*.

1 He _was_ hungry yesterday.
2 I _____ bored last weekend.
3 You _____ sad last Saturday.
4 She _____ tired yesterday.
5 We _____ busy yesterday.
6 They _____ angry last night.

2 Write the words in the correct order.

1 was / nervous / very / match / before / I / the
   I was very nervous before the match.
2 yesterday / open / wasn't / shop / the / evening
   _____
3 he / the / at / was / theatre / night / last ?
   _____
4 weren't / we / school / yesterday / at /
   _____
5 the / in / you / book / were / interested ?
   _____
6 night / she / tired / was / last
   _____

3 Correct the statements.

1 John F. Kennedy was Italian. (American)
   No, he wasn't! He was American!

2 Lord Nelson was Italian. (British)
   _____

3 Julius Caesar was English. (Italian)
   _____

4 The Beatles were from Greece. (England)
   _____

5 Einstein was French. (German)
   _____

6 Michael Jackson was Scottish. (American)
   _____

7 Picasso and Dali were Mexican. (Spanish)
   _____

8 Darwin was from Ireland. (England)
   _____

Past simple regular

4 Complete the sentences with the past simple of the verbs in brackets.

1 They _watched_ TV last night. (watch)
2 Clive _____ very hard for his exams last year. (study)
3 Tess _____ to finish her homework last night. (try)
4 Rick _____ to play football yesterday. (decide)
5 My parents _____ to arrive early. (hope)
6 She _____ all last weekend. (work)
7 I _____ a drink. (want)
8 Glen _____ playing tennis at five o'clock. (stop)

5 Write these sentences in the negative.

1 I helped my parents last weekend.
   I didn't help my parents last weekend.

2 They opened a new shop in London yesterday.
   _____

3 I watched the new film last night.
   _____

4 We started our homework at five o'clock.
   _____

5 He discovered it 20 years ago.
   _____

6 The new teacher talked to the class this morning.
   _____

7 He worked for McDonald's last summer.
   _____

8 They played at Wimbledon last year.
   _____

6 Complete the text with the correct form of the verbs in brackets.

My Gap Year

Last summer I [1]_____ (finish) school and [2]_____ (decide) to have a gap year. I [3]_____ (not know) what to do, but first I [4]_____ (need) some money so I got a job in a restaurant. It [5]_____ (be) really hard work and I [6]_____ (not enjoy) it much, but I [7]_____ (want) to make enough money for a ticket to Thailand. In the end I [8]_____ (manage) to persuade my friend David to come with me too. We [9]_____ (start) our trip in February and [10]_____ (stop) first in Bangkok. We [11]_____ (stay) in a really cheap hostel in the city. There [12]_____ (be) lots of other travellers and we [13]_____ (talk) to everyone and [14]_____ (listen) to all their adventures. After Bangkok we [15]_____ (plan) to go to Cambodia, but because of a problem with the visas, we [16]_____ (end) up going to Laos instead. We [17]_____ (love) it! We [18]_____ (not want) to leave and when we [19]_____ (arrive) back home we [20]_____ (organise) another trip. We're going back next year!

7 Answer the questions with true short answers.

1 Did you talk to your teacher yesterday?
   _____

2 Did you do any sports last week?
   _____

3 Was your best friend at primary school with you?
   _____

4 Did you watch TV last night?
   _____

5 Did you send a text message this morning?
   _____

6 Was it cold yesterday?
   _____

7 Were you on holiday in August last year?
   _____

Skills: Reading – Towards PET (Part 4)

1 Read the article and answer the questions.

1 What did Alexandra Burke win?

2 How old was she when she started singing?

3 What records does she hold?

Have you got the X Factor?

At the end of 2008 there were three people left in the British singing talent competition, *The X Factor*. On the final night, over eight million people called to vote for their favourite singer. 58% of those votes went to Alexandra Burke, a young girl from London. She won the competition and a recording contract worth £1 million.

Alexandra always wanted to be a singer. She was born in August 1988 in Islington in London, where she lived with her mother, four brothers and one sister. She started singing when she was five but, before *The X Factor*, had no professional training. When she was twelve, she entered the TV talent show *Star for a Night*, where she was the youngest person in the competition. Joss Stone won the competition and Alexandra came second.

Alexandra went to school in Islington, but left after taking her GCSE exams to follow a career in music. Before her *X Factor* success, she worked as a singer at weekends in clubs.

When Alexandra won *The X Factor*, she recorded an old song called 'Hallelujah'. The song sold 105,000 copies in one day and in December 2008 she became the European record holder for the most singles sold in a period of twenty-four hours. Later 'Hallelujah' became the top-selling song of the year. It is the first time that an *X Factor* winner has topped the end of year chart in the UK with their winner's single. On 9th January 2009 Alexandra Burke became the first British female solo artist to sell a million copies of a single in the UK.

2 Circle the correct answers.

1 What is the writer's main purpose in writing the text?
   A to describe the *X Factor* competition
   B to explain who Alexandra Burke is
   C to say what sort of music he likes

2 What do you learn about Alexandra from the text?
   A she's a talented singer
   B she doesn't get on with her family
   C she is very rich

3 What do you learn about Alexandra's childhood?
   A she wasn't very good at school
   B she started singing when she was very young
   C she was friends with the singer, Joss Stone

4 What do you learn about the song 'Hallelujah'?
   A it's a good song
   B Alexandra wrote it
   C it sold a lot of copies

Writing

3 Write a passage about a famous person. Describe him / her and explain how he / she became famous. It can be a real or an imaginary person. (about 120 words)

> ► **Tips**

- Use the Reading text above for ideas.
- Write some things about the person's physical appearance and personality (see the Word list).
- Write some things about his / her childhood and schooldays. Remember to use the past simple.
- What did he / she do to become famous?

Study skills Time circles

1 Read the article on time. Does Jenna spend more time 'working' or 'playing'?

>>Time circles

We are often not sure where our time goes. We forget our plans for homework or reading a book because we are chatting on the Internet or watching a good film! How do we get a good balance between work and play? It's useful to make a time circle to see where time goes. Jenna has divided her day up in a time circle.

Jenna's typical day

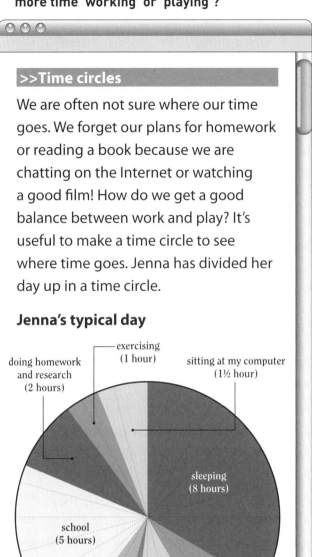

2 Draw two pie charts for you.

A

How I spend my time now

On this circle use different colours or shading to identify what you do. Be honest about a normal day. Where does your time go?

B

How I want to use my time

On this circle create an ideal day. What can you change from the previous circle? This second circle can become your new plan to help you balance your life. Remember young people need lots of sleep, so don't cut back your sleeping time too much!

Grammar reference

Past simple irregular

Positive	
I/You/He/She/It/We/You/They	went.

Negative		
I/You/He/She/It/We/They	did not / didn't	go.

Questions		
Did	I/you/he/she/it/we/they	go?

Positive short answers		
Yes,	I/you/he/she/it/we/they	did.

Negative short answers		
No,	I/you/he/she/it/we/they	didn't.

- Form the past simple of regular verbs by adding -ed to the base form, but irregular verbs have a special form for the past simple positive.
- Each person in the past simple has the same form.
- There are no specific rules for the way you form the past simple positive of irregular verbs. Although some sound similar eg
    break, broke
    wake, woke
    buy, bought
    catch, caught
    think, thought
- You have to learn them by heart. You will find a list of irregular verbs at the end of the Student's Book. Or you can look the verb up in a dictionary.

> **take** /teɪk/ vt (past **took** /tʊk/ pp **taken** /teɪkən/)
> **1** use as a means of transport
> *I took the bus to go to school.*
> **2** cause to go with one
> *Did you take the dog for a walk?*

- Form the negative with:
  subject + *did not / didn't* + base form
- Form questions with:
  did + subject + base form
- Form positive short answers with:
  Yes, + subject + *did.*
- Form negative short answers with:
  No, + subject + *didn't.*

Usage
- Remember that you use the past simple to talk about actions that began and ended in the past. It is often used with past time expressions.
    The expedition spent two months at the North Pole.
    The American swimmer Michael Phelps won eight gold medals at the Beijing Olympics.
    We didn't understand their language but they drew a map to show us the route.

Modal verb *could*
Could is the past of *can* (*to be able*). It is a modal verb. Remember:
- it has the same form for all persons
- it is followed by the base form
- add only *not* to form the negative
- put it before the subject in questions

Usage
- Use *could*
  - to talk about ability and sensations in the past.
  - for a description in the past.
      I couldn't understand him.
      They could see he was ill.
  - to talk about a general possibility in the past.
      You could walk away.

was / were able to
- Use *was / were able to* instead of *could* to talk about ability in the past. Use it to say that somebody succeeded or didn't succeed in doing something difficult.
    He was able to finish the race.
    We weren't able to find him.
    Were you able to do exercise 5? I wasn't.

had to, didn't have / need to
- Use *had to* and *didn't have to* for the past of *must*. The forms *must* and *mustn't* are only used in the present.
- Use *had to* for an obligation or necessity in the past.
    They had to have a ticket to get in.
    He wasn't at home. I had to call him on the mobile.
- Use *didn't have to* for the absence of an obligation or necessity in the past.
    We didn't have to show our passports.
    (= it wasn't compulsory)
    It was late. Luckily I didn't have to stop for petrol. (= it wasn't necessary)
- You can use *didn't need to* instead of *didn't have to*, when there is no obligation or necessity in the past. In this case use *need* like a main verb, not a modal.
    She didn't need to shout. We knew we were wrong.

Word list

The words in grey appear in the unit, but are not in the vocabulary sections.

Adventures

adventurer	**life jacket**
attack	**machinery**
careful	polar bear
challenge	pull
conditions	put up (a tent)
danger / dangerous	return
drown	risk
environment	ski
equipment	**skills**
expedition	sledge
experience	**storm**
explorer	**sub-zero**
fall overboard	survive
fall through (the ice)	team
freezing	temperature
give up	travel
hurt	trek
ice	trip
journey	**wave**
life-changing (experience)	

Vocabulary

Adventures

1 Circle the correct words.

1 It's really difficult to *give / put* up a tent when it's raining.
2 Did you take a lot of *equipment / experience* with you when you went exploring?
3 I like the *challenge / environment* of new experiences.
4 I'm very glad that I *survived / returned* the journey – it was very dangerous.
5 We often experienced *subzero / dangerous* temperatures.
6 Did you hear that *sledge / storm* last night? There was a lot of rain.
7 The dogs *fell / pulled* the sledge that carried all our food.
8 I like it when we go on school *teams / trips* to interesting places.

2 Complete the email with these words.

journey   freezing   dangerous   waves
risk   drown   ice   environment

✉

Hi Jake

I'm back! I went to the Arctic with the university to study climate change. We wanted to find out more about the melting ¹_____ and the effect this has on our ²_____. We went by ship. It was a terrible ³_____! It was SO cold.
We had temperatures below ⁴_____ and huge ⁵_____ around the ship. There was a real ⁶_____ that someone would fall overboard and ⁷_____. It was very very ⁸_____, but I survived and I'm glad to be home.

Love Annie

Grammar

Past simple irregular

1 Complete the table with the irregular forms.

Base form	Past simple
buy	*bought*
drink	_____
fall	_____
get	_____
have	_____
hear	_____
meet	_____
run	_____
say	_____
see	_____
take	_____

2 Complete the text with the past simple form of these verbs.

take	be	come	have	build
drive	say	be	read	pay

Our trip to Stonehenge ¹_____ really interesting.
We got up at six o'clock and we ²_____ a big
breakfast. We travelled to Stonehenge by car. My mum
³_____ because my dad doesn't like driving. We
arrived at nine thirty, and the site ⁴_____ very busy
already. We ⁵_____ quite a lot for our tickets, but
the place was fantastic and we ⁶_____ lots of photos.
My dad ⁷_____ the guidebook
as we went around and explained everything to us.
He ⁸_____ that the ancient people of Britain
⁹_____ Stonehenge thousands of years ago,
and the stones ¹⁰_____ all the way from Wales!
It's impossible to imagine how they did it.

3 Write the negative form of these sentences.

1 I went to bed early last night.
   I didn't go to bed early last night.

2 I found a wallet in the road yesterday.
   _____

3 My mum bought some new shoes in the market.
   _____
   _____

4 We saw a rhino at the zoo.
   _____

5 Jack lost his mobile phone last week.
   _____

6 Sally and Sue got good marks for the Maths test.
   _____
   _____

7 The teachers spoke to us about the exams.
   _____

8 Dad had a meeting this morning.
   _____

9 We ate a big dinner last night.
   _____

10 I knew all the answers to the quiz.
   _____

4 React to these comments, explaining what you did. Use the words in brackets.

1 You didn't do your homework yesterday. (last week)
   No, I did it last week.

2 You didn't have any ice cream. (fruit)
   No, I had some fruit.

3 You didn't practise the guitar today. (piano)
   _____

4 You didn't speak to Tim in the lesson. (Glen)
   _____

5 You didn't buy a new mobile phone last week.
   (last month)
   _____

6 You didn't meet Sue in town. (Jill)
   _____

7 You didn't go shopping yesterday. (on Saturday)
   _____

8 You didn't find your bag. (jacket)
   _____

9 You didn't lose your mp3 player. (mobile phone)
   _____

10 You didn't send me an email today. (yesterday)
   _____

Modal verb *could*

5 Look at the picture. Write sentences with *could*.

When Mr Green was young
1 _he could run really fast._
2 _____
3 _____
4 _____
5 _____
6 _____

6 Answer the questions.

1 When you were two, could you talk?
   Yes, I could. / No, I couldn't.
   _____

2 When you were five, could you ride a bike?
   _____

3 When you were five, could you write?
   _____

4 When you were six, could you swim?
   _____

5 When you were eight, could you play an
   instrument?
   _____

6 When you were nine, could you speak
   English?
   _____

7 When you were ten, could you cross the
   road on your own?
   _____

8 When you were twelve, could you make
   a cake?
   _____

had to, didn't have to / need to

7 Match the sentence halves.

1	b	I'm really tired this morning
2	☐	Dad needed the car today
3	☐	We didn't have to go to training
4	☐	Baz couldn't go out last night
5	☐	They didn't have to wait long
6	☐	Jen didn't have to cook dinner
7	☐	I couldn't go to the picnic
8	☐	They wore helmets

a   because the match was cancelled.
b   because I had to stay out late last night.
c   because he had to finish his homework.
d   because they had to go by motorbike.
e   because Dad got a takeaway.
f   because the bus was on time.
g   because I had to visit my gran.
h   because he had to take Mum to the airport.

8 Complete the sentences with *had to* or *didn't have to* and the information in brackets.

1 Because the party was out of town, we
   had to go by car. (go / car)

2 I _____ to London because
   we went by train. (drive)

3 We were late so _____ to
   get there quickly. (take / taxi)

4 We _____ on the clothes
   because there was a sale. (spend / a lot)

5 Sarah _____ her brother
   to the station. (take)

6 I _____ far to school. We
   only lived five minutes from school. (walk)

7 Mum was sick today so I _____
   _____ Dad cook the dinner. (help)

8 We were very late home last night. We _____
   _____ why we were so late. (explain)

9 Complete the dialogue with the correct form of the verbs in brackets.

Joe   ¹ _Did you hear_ _____ (you/hear) about our
       holiday?

Bill   No, what ² _____ (happen)?

Joe   It was a disaster. We ³ _____
       (leave) home on time, but we ⁴ _____
       _____ (forget) our passports!

Bill   Oh no! What ⁵ _____ (you/do)?

Joe   We ⁶ _____ (have to) go back
       home and get the next flight.

Bill   ⁷ _____ (you/have to) pay for it?

Joe   Of course! And then we ⁸ _____
       (realise) we had to have a visa.

Bill   Why ⁹ _____ (you/need to) have
       a visa?

Joe   It's a new regulation! Luckily, we ¹⁰ _____
       _____ (can) buy them at the airport.
       But then….

Skills: Reading – Towards PET (Part 3)

1 Read the article and complete the sentences.

1 Ewart Grogan was _____.
2 He wanted to walk _____.
3 He didn't need to use _____.
4 He found his way by _____.
5 The Dinka people can be _____.

Just going out for a walk!

Ewart Grogan, a 24-year-old Cambridge University student, took a break from his studies early in 1898 and left England on a walking holiday. But this was no ordinary holiday. He didn't return until almost two years later. Grogan wanted to do something really amazing to impress the father of his fiancée, Gertrude. He planned to walk all the way through Africa, from south to north, with his friend, Arthur Sharp.

Other famous explorers in Africa used guns and violence on local people. Grogan carried his white umbrella and a charming smile. He and his small group paid for the food they ate with gifts, and they only had real trouble on one or two occasions.

At the Dinka swampland in south Sudan, his friend Sharp turned back. He thought it was impossible to get through 650 km of thick vegetation and unknown danger. But Grogan continued.

Sharp was almost correct. There were no maps - all Grogan had was a compass to tell him which way was north. He became very ill from mosquito bites and some of his men died from fever. Finally, with the help of the Dinka people (who are often two metres tall), and twenty months and eleven thousand kilometres after leaving Cape Town in South Africa, Grogan walked on into Cairo, Egypt.

Back in England, Grogan married Gertrude and returned to Africa to do many more remarkable things. He even became the first person to fly from Cairo to Cape Town - his return trip.

2 Circle T (True) or F (False). Correct the false statements.

1 Ewart Grogan finished his studies in 1898. T / (F)
   He took a break from his studies in 1898.

2 He walked through Africa to impress his fiancée. T / F
   _____

3 He walked from south to north. T / F
   _____

4 Grogan's group didn't kill people. T / F
   _____

5 Grogan stopped in Sudan because it was too dangerous. T / F
   _____

6 The Dinka were very helpful people. T / F
   _____

7 Grogan walked over 10,000 km. T / F.
   _____

8 Grogan never returned to Africa. T / F
   _____

Writing

3 Write a letter to a magazine describing an embarrassing experience. It can be real or imaginary. (about 120 words)

> **Tips**

- Try to answer the questions *Where? / When? / What? / Who? / How? / Why?*
- Remember to use the past simple. Check the unit for irregular past tense verbs you can use.
- Include *could(n't) / was(n't) able to / had to / didn't have to / didn't need to*.
- Try to give your story a surprise ending.
- Remember to say how you felt.

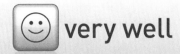 very well   OK   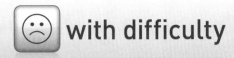 with difficulty

I've finished this module and I can do ☑ these things in English

Module 5

	☺	☺	☹
Listening			
A2 understand phrases, words and expressions related to my immediate surroundings, e.g. physical appearance of a person (pp.92, 93)	☐	☐	☐
A2 identify the main point of TV news items or quiz shows (pp.95, 102)	☐	☐	☐
Reading			
A2 identify important information in news summaries or simple newspaper articles, e.g. on flash mobbing (p.94), on exploration and adventures (pp.96, 98)	☐	☐	☐
A2 understand short narratives about everyday things dealing with topics which are familiar to me if the text is written in simple language (pp.100, 101)	☐	☐	☐
Spoken Interaction			
A2 ask people questions about past events (pp.88, 90), the physical appearance of a person (p.93) and answer such questions	☐	☐	☐
A2 ask general culture questions (p.102) and answer such questions	☐	☐	☐
Spoken Production			
A2 give short, basic descriptions of events (p.95)	☐	☐	☐
A2 describe past activities and personal experiences, e.g. an embarrassing experience (p.101)	☐	☐	☐
Strategies / Language Quality			
A2 make myself understood using memorised phrases and single expressions (pp.93, 100)	☐	☐	☐
Writing			
A2 describe an event in simple sentences and report what happened when and where, e.g. a flash mobbing event (p.95)	☐	☐	☐
A2 write about aspects of my everyday life in simple phrases and sentences, e.g. physical appearance, personality, temperament (pp.92, 93), work activities (p.98), embarrassing experiences (p.100)	☐	☐	☐

At the end of **Module 5**, I've got a lot more A2 skills. Now I can start **Module 6**. ➡

Grammar reference

Comparative adjectives

One-syllable adjectives

- To form the comparative of adjectives, add -er to most one-syllable adjectives.

    tall – taller   old – older   young – younger

- If the adjective ends in -e, add only -r.

    wide – wider   safe – safer   nice – nicer

- If the adjective ends in a single vowel + a single consonant (except 'r', 'w' or 'x'), double the consonant and add -er.

    big – bigger   slim – slimmer   hot – hotter

Two-syllable adjectives

- To form the comparative of most two-syllable adjectives add *more* before the adjective.

    polite – more polite
    famous – more famous

- If the adjective ends in -ow, -er, -le, -et, we add -er or -r.

    narrow – narrower   clever – cleverer
    simple – simpler   quiet – quieter

- If the adjective ends in -y, change the -y to -ier.

    easy – easier   happy – happier   tidy – tidier

Adjectives with more than two syllables

- To form the comparative of all adjectives with more than two syllables, add *more* before the adjective.

    beautiful – more beautiful
    important – more important

Irregular adjectives

- These adjectives and comparatives are irregular:

    good – better   bad – worse
    far – further / farther

- Remember to always use *than* after a comparative to compare two things, animals or people.

    Tim is taller than Josie.
    I think Maths is more difficult than French.

- Sometimes you understand the second thing, animal or person and don't use *than*.

    I think this house is nicer. (you understand 'than the last house / than the other houses')
    I want this book. It looks more interesting. (you understand 'than the other books')

Making comparisons

- To say that two things, animals or people are the same, use:
  - *as* + adjective + *as* (NEVER with a comparative)
    This CD is as expensive as that one.
    (= equal comparison)

- To say that two things are not the same, use:
  - the comparative of the adjective + *than* (= a greater comparison)
    Linda is more beautiful than Maya.
    Maya is nicer than Linda.
  - *less* + adjective + *than* (NEVER with a comparative) (= a lesser comparison)
    Maya is less beautiful than Linda.
  - *not as* + adjective + *as* (NEVER with a comparative) (= equal comparison in the negative)
    This is not as interesting as the lesson we had yesterday.
    Linda is not as nice as Maya.

Qualifiers: *a lot, a bit, a little, enough, really, fairly, too*

- Use qualifiers (adverbs or adverbial phrases) to strengthen or weaken the meaning of an adjective or a comparative.

- The following qualifiers always go before the adjective or the comparative:

    a bit, a little, fairly, a lot, much, really, too, very

- Use *a bit* in spoken English and *a little* in written English. They both weaken a comparative or an adjective.

    I think she is a bit embarrassed.
    They are a little younger than me.

- Use *much* and *a lot* to strengthen a comparative.

    The new PC is a lot faster than the old one.
    I'm much happier now.

- Use *fairly, really, too* and *very* to strengthen an adjective (NEVER with a comparative).

    You can't complain. It's fairly cheap.
    It was a really nice party.
    It's too expensive. NOT ~~It's too more expensive.~~

- Always put the adverb *enough* after the adjective.

    She's clever enough to work out the solution.
    NOT ~~She's enough clever …~~
    This room isn't warm enough. I can't work in it.
    NOT ~~This room isn't enough warm.~~

very and *much*

- Use *very* + adjective and *much* + comparative.
    Marta is very quiet today.
    Today Marta is much quieter than yesterday.

too and *enough*

- Always put *too* before the adjective and *enough* after it.
    This coffee is too strong. It will keep me awake.
    This coffee is not strong enough. I don't like it.

too and *very*

- *Too* means 'excessively'. *Very* means 'extremely'.
    This suitcase is too heavy for me.
    This suitcase is very heavy.

Comparative adverbs

- Use comparative adverbs to compare verbs.
    John works more quickly than Bob.
- Form the comparative of adverbs that end in *-ly* by putting *more* in front of the adverb.
    Can you do this task more carefully?
- Some adverbs are identical to the adjective. For these, form the comparative by adding *–er*.
    fast – faster
    high – higher
    hard – harder
    I can't run faster than this.
- Some adverbs are irregular.
    well – better
    badly – worse
    He understands better than you think.

Word list

The words in grey appear in the unit, but are not in the vocabulary sections.

Weather

below freezing	storm / stormy
cloud / cloudy	sunshine / sunny
fog / foggy	thunder and lightning
frost / frosty	very cold
hail	warm
rain / rainy	wind / windy
snow / snowy	

Parts of the body

arm	heel
back	hip
chest	knee
chin	leg
ear	neck
elbow	shoulder
finger	**stomach**
foot, feet	**throat**
forehead	toe
hand	**tooth, teeth**
head	wrist

Illnesses

cough	prescription
earache	problem
feel sick	sore throat
headache	stay in bed
hurt	stomach ache
medicine	temperature
pain	toothache

Vocabulary

Weather

1 Write the weather forecast.

On the west coast today it is _____
_____
_____

In the centre of the island today it is
_____
_____
_____

On the east coast today it is _____
_____
_____
_____

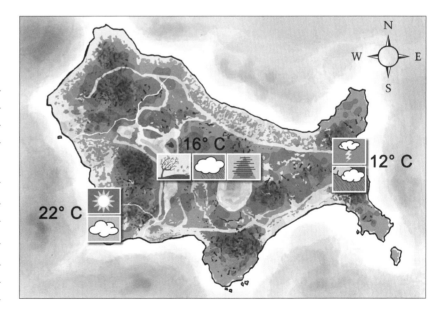

2 Write the letters in the correct order to make weather words.

1 It's really **nsynu** today – a lovely summer day.
   sunny

2 You couldn't see the mountains yesterday. It was really **gfoyg**. f_____

3 It's very cold this morning – there was a hard **rsfot** last night. f_____

4 It is so cold – it's **ewolb erziefgn**. b_____

5 There was a terrible storm last night – with **euhndtr** and **higgntiln**. t_____ _____

6 It's a very grey day – very **lyuodc**. c_____

Parts of the body

3 Match the pictures and the words.

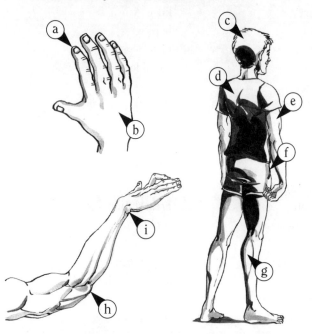

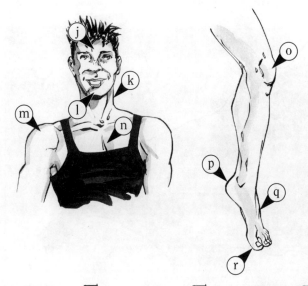

1	foot	q	7	arm	☐	13	finger	☐
2	elbow	☐	8	forehead	☐	14	knee	☐
3	wrist	☐	9	chest	☐	15	heel	☐
4	back	☐	10	toe	☐	16	hip	☐
5	leg	☐	11	chin	☐	17	hand	☐
6	shoulder	☐	12	neck	☐	18	head	☐

Illnesses

4 Circle the correct words.

1 I feel very hot – I think I've got a *cough / temperature*.

2 I went to the doctor and he gave me a *medicine / prescription*.

3 My brother isn't at school today. He's at the dentist's because he's got *toothache / a stomach ache*.

4 I've got a really bad *headache / sore throat* – I can't eat anything because it hurts.

5 Julia wants to *feel sick / stay in bed* today because she's got flu.

6 She's got a *pain / problem* in her leg – it really hurts.

Grammar

Comparative adjectives

1 Complete the sentences with the comparative form of one of these adjectives.

| happy | friendly | ~~old~~ | big | clever | nice |

1 Liam is 16. He's _older_ than his brother Jake.

2 Madeleine is really friendly – she's _____ than my other friends.

3 We're _____ living here than in our old house. It's a great place to live.

4 This bag is much _____ than that bag – you can get a lot of things in it.

5 Our new teacher is great – she's much _____ than our old one!

6 Simon is _____ than his friends – he got the best marks in all his exams.

2 Complete the text with the comparative of *good*, *bad* and *far*.

- - UK Travel Advice - - - - -

It's a long journey to Glasgow. It's much
¹_____ from London than Manchester is. Travelling by car is ²_____ than going by train as the train is very expensive. And, of course, there's nothing ³_____ than missing your train because you can often wait a long time for the next one. Because of the mountains, the roads in Scotland are a bit ⁴_____ than in England – they can be dangerous. But it's still
⁵_____ in the car because you can listen to the radio and stop for a rest. Also if you take the train when you arrive at the railway station you have ⁶_____ to walk to your hotel!

Making comparisons

3 Complete the sentences with *more* or *less*.

1 The film was not very good. It was __more__ boring than the news.

2 Riding a bike is _____ dangerous than skiing.

3 The English exam is _____ difficult than the last one. I don't think I can pass.

4 I'll do it for you. I'm _____ nervous than you.

5 She's _____ ambitious than me – she wants to be the head of the company.

6 This dress is _____ expensive than you think. You should buy it!

4 Complete the text with *as* or *than*.

I'm not as tall [1]__as__ my brother Chris, but I'm stronger [2]_____ him. He's taller [3]_____ me, but I'm more muscular [4]_____ him. We're as clever [5]_____ each other, and my marks at school are [6]_____ good as his. But I hate skiing with him. He's faster [7]_____ me and goes as fast [8]_____ our dad. He's better [9]_____ me, but luckily I'm as good [10]_____ most of the people in my class.

5 Write sentences comparing the two things. Give your opinion.

1 cola / nice / water
  I think cola is nicer than water.

2 cinema / good / TV
  _____

3 Maths / hard / English
  _____

4 football / interesting / rugby
  _____

5 George Clooney / good-looking / Brad Pitt
  _____

6 Skiing / enjoyable / walking
  _____

Qualifiers: *a lot*, *a bit*, *a little*, *enough*, *really*, *fairly*, *too*

6 Match the statements with the comments.

1 ☐ It's really cold in here!
2 ☐ I'm very upset.
3 ☐ She's too impatient for this job.
4 ☐ I think she's a bit rude.
5 ☐ She's really beautiful.
6 ☐ It's quite warm today.
7 ☐ They're fairly friendly.

a Yes, they're nice, but they can be a bit shy.
b No, I think she's a bit shy, that's all.
c Sorry, I'll close the window.
d I agree – she isn't calm enough.
e I know – and she's really rich, too.
f I know, but he didn't mean to say that.
g Yeah, it's a really nice day.

7 Rewrite the sentences to include the word in brackets.

1 Mia sings better than me. (a lot)
  Mia sings a lot better than me.

2 My brother is taller than our dad. (a bit)
  _____

3 It's too hot in this office. (a little)
  _____

4 The news is shocking. (really)
  _____

5 I'm certain we'll win the competition. (fairly)
  _____

6 She was slow and lost the race. (too)
  _____

Comparative adverbs

8 Add a comment using a comparative adverb.

1 I can sing quite well.
  Yes, but _I can sing better._

2 He's working really hard.
  Yes, but _____.

3 She walked really far yesterday.
  Yes, but _____.

4 I always check my work carefully.
  Yes, but _____.

5 I speak English quite fluently.
  Yes, but _____.

6 She paints beautifully.
  Yes, but _____.

7 I play football really well.
  Yes, but _____.

8 He talks very loudly.
  Yes, but _____.

Skills: Reading – Towards PET (Part 5)

1 Match the titles and the paragraphs.

Who can take part?   How do I pay for the challenge trip?

What challenges can I do?   Why do a charity challenge?

CHALLENGE YOURSELF

1 _____

Why go on a regular holiday when you can have the [1]_____ of a lifetime? On a charity challenge trip you will experience different cultures, meet new [2]_____, get fit, raise money for charity, and make a real difference to somebody's life.

2 _____

If you want to help [3]_____ money for charity these days there are hundreds of events you can take part in. You can sell cakes at a coffee morning, go on a sponsored walk or sell your old clothes. But maybe you're looking for something a little more challenging? How about cycling around Cuba or [4]_____ Mount Kilimanjaro? Maybe you'd like to run a marathon? Go trekking in Borneo?

3 _____

Most charity challenges are [5]_____ to anyone over 18. Younger people can go if they're with their parents. There's no age limit – a 72-year-old man successfully climbed Kilimanjaro recently! You need to be quite fit though and you should have a good sense of adventure, an ability to get on with people and a [6]_____ attitude.

4 _____

Most people promise to raise a minimum [7]_____ of money for the charity – usually at least £2500. The charity pays for the trip and keeps the rest of the sponsorship money. It is [8]_____ to pay for your own trip and just make a donation to the charity, but you should still raise as much money as you can for the charity.

So, what are you waiting for?

2 Circle the correct word for each space.

1 A meeting	B adventure	C difference
2 A people	B places	C limits
3 A have	B find	C raise
4 A running	B climbing	C making
5 A good	B ready	C open
6 A positive	B minimum	C charity
7 A pounds	B amount	C number
8 A possible	B available	C clear

Writing

3 Write a report for your school magazine. Compare your town with another town that you know. (about 120 words)

> **Tips**

- Use adjectives and adverbs in the comparative, e.g. *My town is prettier but people drive more dangerously here.*
- Use qualifiers, e.g. *a lot, a bit, a little, enough, really, fairly, too.*
- Remember to use *than* for comparing two things.
- You can also use (*not*) *as* + adjective + *as* and *less* + adjective + *than.*

Study skills Taking notes

Taking notes is a useful study skill. We take notes when our teacher tells us things, when we are reading or when we are listening. Good note-taking helps you get good school results, so it is important to improve your strategies.

1 Read what the four students say. Which ones are useful for you? Number them in order.

○ ○ ○

Question
What are your tips for taking notes?

Answer the question

Answers

I always use clear headings so I can find the information I need quickly.
Sue
☐

I use different colours so my book doesn't look so grey and depressing.
Colours can really help you remember, too.
Dave
☐

Keep notes as short as possible. If you write too much, you can't learn anything
before a test. I write down what's really important and nothing else.
Kelly
☐

I always look at what other people put in their notes: it reminds me of things
I've forgotten. But, of course, I always ask them first!
John
☐

**2 Here is a checklist to help you write better notes.
Look at some notes in your notebook and
answer the questions.**

1 Are they easy to understand?
2 Are they brief and to the point?
3 Are they well-organised?
4 Do you use numbering and labelling?
5 Can you study easily from your notes?
6 Do you use effective abbreviations?
7 Do the important ideas stand out with
   colours or underlining?

Grammar reference

Superlative adjectives

One-syllable adjectives

- To form the superlative of adjectives, add *the* before the adjective and *-est* to most one-syllable adjectives.
  tall – the tallest
  old – the oldest
  young – the youngest
- If the adjective ends in *-e*, add *-st*.
  wide – the widest
  safe – the safest
  nice – the nicest
- If the adjective ends in a vowel and a consonant, double the consonant and add *-est*.
  big – the biggest
  slim – the slimmest
  hot – the hottest

Two-syllable adjectives

- To form the superlative of most two-syllable adjectives add *the most* before the adjective.
  polite – the most polite
  famous – the most famous
  common – the most common
- If the adjective ends in *-y*, the *-y* becomes *-iest*.
  easy – the easiest
  happy – the happiest
  tidy – the tidiest
- If the adjective ends in *-ow*, *-er*, *-le*, *-et*, add *-est* or *-st*.
  narrow – the narrowest
  clever – the cleverest
  simple – the simplest
  quiet – the quietest

Adjectives with more than two syllables

- To form the superlative of all adjectives with more than two syllables add *the most* before the adjective.
  beautiful – the most beautiful
  important – the most important
  attractive – the most attractive

Irregular adjectives

- These adjectives and superlatives are irregular:
  good – the best
  bad – the worst
  far – the furthest / the farthest
  much / many – the most
  little – the least

Usage

- To say that a person or thing has a particular quality to the greatest degree in comparison to other people or things in the same category, use the superlative.
  This is the most interesting DVD.
- To say that a person or thing has a particular quality to the least degree in comparison to other people or things in the same category, use
  the least + base form of the adjective
  This is the least interesting DVD.
- Use phrases after the relative superlative to be more specific, e.g.
  in + a place
  of + a group of things, animals, people, etc.
  She is the most beautiful girl in the school.
  She is the most beautiful girl of all.
- Always put the superlative of the adjective before the noun.
  They're looking for the cheapest hotel in town.

Question tags

- Use a question tag at the end of a sentence to ask for confirmation.
- If the sentence is positive, the question tag is negative.
- If the sentence is negative, the question tag is positive.
- Match the verb tense and type of verb or auxiliary in the question tag with those in the main clause.

Main clause Positive	Question tag Negative
We are near the station,	aren't we?
They know this game,	don't they?
She's got a guitar,	hasn't she?
You're singing today,	aren't you?
You were late this morning,	weren't you?
She went to the party,	didn't she?
I can try to do the same,	can't I?

Main clause Negative	Question tag Positive
You aren't Italian,	are you?
I don't know him,	do I?
He hasn't got a dog,	has he?
He isn't playing today,	is he?
He wasn't at school,	was he?
She didn't buy this PC herself,	did she?
They shouldn't work so hard,	should they?

Word list

The words in grey appear in the unit, but are not in the vocabulary sections.

Houses

Types of houses

apartment	detached house
cottage	terraced town house

Parts of the house

bathroom	hall
bedroom	kitchen
dining room	living room
downstairs	spare room
en-suite bathroom	study
garage	upstairs
garden	

Furniture and objects

armchair	cupboard
barbecue	dishwasher
basin	fireplace
bath	kitchen sink
bed	sofa
bedside table	table
bookcase	toilet
chair	TV
chest of drawers	wardrobe
coffee table	washing machine
cooker	

Landscape

beach	island
city centre	lake
country / countryside	mountain
docks	river
forest	seaside
hill	wood

Vocabulary

Houses

1 Match the furniture and objects with the parts of the house.

1	coats and hats	a	dining room
2	desk and bookcase	b	bathroom
3	cooker and dishwasher	c	hall
4	wardrobe and chest of drawers	d	living room
5	towels and shower	e	study
6	table and chairs	f	kitchen
7	TV and armchair	g	bedroom

2 Find 10 pieces of furniture or objects. The words can be horizontal, diagonal or vertical.

D	K	H	W	C	T	T	I	Z	I	E	T	R
V	I	E	T	E	Z	E	K	S	O	F	A	B
W	T	S	T	N	R	Z	M	U	P	D	O	E
A	C	T	H	J	D	S	A	G	C	B	E	D
E	H	O	D	W	E	S	R	T	U	K	H	S
K	E	F	O	I	A	D	M	O	P	Y	K	I
R	N	D	T	K	E	S	C	I	B	J	S	D
O	S	R	R	S	E	B	H	L	O	R	T	E
P	I	A	I	A	U	R	A	E	A	E	A	T
Q	N	W	W	R	T	J	I	T	R	S	B	A
U	K	E	C	H	A	I	R	Y	D	E	L	B
E	E	R	C	G	P	P	N	U	C	X	E	L
T	A	S	H	C	N	G	Z	A	C	I	N	E

3 Write down the words that you found in exercise 2.

3 letters: _b e d_

4 letters: _ _ _ _, _ _ _ _

5 letters: _ _ _ _ _, _ _ _ _ _

6 letters: _ _ _ _ _ _, _ _ _ _ _ _

8 letters: _ _ _ _ _ _ _ _, _ _ _ _ _ _ _ _

10 letters: _ _ _ _ _ _ _ _ _ _

2 words: _ _ _ _ _ _ _ _ _ _ _ (7, 4),

_ _ _ _ _ _ _ _ _ _ (7, 5)

4 Answer the questions.

1 Do you live in the country or a city?

_____

2 What sort of house do you live in?

_____

3 How many rooms has your house got?

_____

4 How many people live in your house?

_____

5 Do you live near the seaside?

_____

6 Which room do you do your homework in?

_____

7 Have you got a large garden?

_____

8 What furniture have you got in your bedroom?

_____

Landscape

5 Match the words and the pictures.

1	mountains ☐	5	river ☐
2	island ☐	6	beach ☐
3	hills ☐	7	lake ☐
4	wood ☐	8	docks ☐

a

b

c

d

e

f

g

h

Grammar

Superlative adjectives

1 Complete the table with comparatives and superlatives.

Adjective	Comparative	Superlative
cold	colder	the coldest
nice	_____	_____
dry	_____	_____
careful	_____	_____
difficult	_____	_____
pretty	_____	_____
good	_____	_____
bad	_____	_____
far	_____	_____
much / many	_____	_____
little	_____	_____

2 Complete the sentences with irregular superlatives.

1 Venus Williams is one of the __best__ tennis players in the world.
2 He is one of the _____ singers I know – he's terrible!
3 South Africa won the 2008 Rugby World Cup. They are the _____ in the world.
4 I usually drive long distances at night when there is the _____ traffic.
5 Who spent the _____? – My sister – she bought three dresses and a jacket!
6 Pluto is the _____ planet from the sun.

3 Write true sentences about people you know. Use the adjectives in brackets.

1 (kind) _Marsha is the kindest person I know._
2 (short) _____
_____
3 (hard-working) _____
_____
4 (shy) _____
_____
5 (thin) _____
_____
6 (lazy) _____
_____
7 (friendly) _____
_____
8 (sensitive) _____
_____

4a Write questions with the superlative.

1 Who / good / guitarist / in the world
   Who is the best guitarist in the world?

2 Who / good-looking / actor or actress
   _____

3 What / famous / building in your country
   _____

4 Where / good / place to shop in your town
   _____

5 Which / little / interesting / newspaper or magazine
   _____

6 Which / bad / colour for a jumper
   _____

7 Which / difficult / subject
   _____

8 When / bad / time to have an exam
   _____

9 When / good / time to get up
   _____

10 What / sad / story you know
   _____

4b Now answer the questions.

1 _I think The Edge from U2 is the best guitarist in the world._

Question tags

5 Complete the sentences with the correct question tags.

1 He's from Scotland, _isn't he?_
2 They've got a really big house, _____?
3 I can't sing very well, _____?
4 We don't want a drink, _____?
5 She wasn't very happy, _____?
6 You must practise more every day, _____?
7 I saw you there, _____?
8 They're sitting here, _____?
9 He isn't frightened, _____?
10 He hasn't got much money, _____?

6 Check the statements using question tags.

1 A New York is the biggest city in the world.
   B New York? _The biggest city is Mexico City, isn't it?_
2 A Martin Luther King was Australian.
   B Australian? _____
3 A Enrique Iglesias is from France.
   B France? _____
4 A You should drive on the left in Italy.
   B On the left? _____
5 A The 2008 Olympics were in Japan.
   B Japan? _____
6 A A man walked on the moon in 1970.
   B 1970? _____

7 Complete the dialogue with the correct question tags.

Policeman   So, you're Mr Tom Sheen, [1] _aren't you_ ?
Mr Sheen   Yes, that's right.
Policeman   And you live at 6 York Road, [2] _____?
Mr Sheen   Yes.
Policeman   And you were in the Cartier jewellery shop at 9.30 am yesterday, [3] _____?
Mr Sheen   Yes, I think I was.
Policeman   And you took the diamonds, [4] _____?
Mr Sheen   Ah, no, no, I didn't!
Policeman   You're lying, [5] _____?
Mr Sheen   No, I'm not lying. I never lie.
Policeman   Ah, so you didn't lie a few minutes ago, [6] _____, when you said your name was Stevens?
Mr Sheen   No! You can't prove my name's different, [7] _____?
Policeman   No, but you'd like me to believe you, [8] _____? So tell me the truth!

Skills: Reading - Towards PET (Part 2)

1 Read the article and complete the table with examples.

Type of site		World Heritage Site
mountain	1	Mount Kenya
wall	2	_____
ancient stone circle	3	_____
ecological sites	4	_____
city	5	_____
volcanic island	6	_____
statue	7	_____

2 Answer the questions.

1 Which committee decides on World Heritage Sites?
2 How often does it meet?
3 How many World Heritage Sites are there?
4 Are there more cultural or natural sites?
5 Which continents have the most sites? Which country?
6 How and when did the island of Surtsey appear?
7 Can all World Heritage Sites get money from UNESCO?
8 What are the advantages of having a World Heritage Site?

●WORLD HERITAGE SITES

How does a place become a World Heritage Site?

World Heritage Sites must have 'outstanding universal value' which can be either cultural or natural, or both. Countries nominate sites and the UNESCO* World Heritage Committee meets every year to decide which nominations to accept.

What kind of places are World Heritage Sites?

A World Heritage Site can be many things including a work of art, a city, an individual building, or a monument, forest, mountain or other natural phenomenon. At the moment there are 890 World Heritage Sites which include 689 cultural sites and 176 natural sites (with 25 mixed sites). However, this balance may change as people become more and more interested in the environment.

Are there the same number of World Heritage Sites in most countries?

No, there aren't. For political, historical and economic reasons, 50% of World Heritage Sites are in Europe and North America. Only 9% are in Africa and 7% in Arab countries. The country with the most sites is Italy, which has 44.

What are some examples of World Heritage Sites?

The following are all World Heritage Sites: the Great Wall of China, Mount Kenya, the Serengeti, the Pyramids of Giza, Edinburgh's Old and New Town, Stonehenge, the Statue of Liberty, the Great Barrier Reef. In 2008, the committee added the Monarch Butterfly Reserve in Mexico, where one billion butterflies spend the winter each year, and the Icelandic island of Surtsey, which appeared in the 1960s as a result of volcanic eruptions.

What are the advantages and disadvantages?

A World Heritage Site can bring status and extra tourists. Developing countries can get money for their sites from UNESCO's preservation fund. However, sometimes large numbers of tourists can damage the site or the area or unbalance the ecosystem, particularly in poor countries.

*The United Nations Educational, Scientific and Cultural Organisation

Writing

3 You are staying with a family in England. Write an email to an English-speaking friend. Describe the house and your room. (about 120 words)

> **Tips**

- Use your imagination when you describe the house and the room. Try to make it sound interesting.
- Use the different sections in *Houses* in the Word list for ideas.
- Remember to use superlatives.

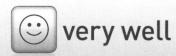 very well   OK   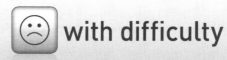 with difficulty

I've finished this module and I can do ☑ these things in English

Module ❻

	😊	😐	☹
Listening			
A2 understand what is said clearly, slowly and directly to me in a simple everyday conversation, e.g. at the doctor's (p.113)	☐	☐	☐
A2 understand the essential information in short recorded passages dealing with predictable everyday matters, e.g. activities for Peace Day (p.115), description of a flat (p. 120), problems of a country in South-East Asia (p. 123)	☐	☐	☐
Reading			
A2 identify important information in news summaries or simple newspaper articles, e.g. about Peace Day (p.115), extreme places (p.117), World Heritage Sites (p.123)	☐	☐	☐
A2 skim property advertisements in newspapers and identify the most important pieces of information (p.121)	☐	☐	☐
Spoken Interaction			
A2 ask how people are and react to news (p.113)	☐	☐	☐
A2 ask questions about the weather and answer (p.107)	☐	☐	☐
Spoken Production			
A2 describe a project for Peace Day (p.115), my house (p.121), a place to visit with my school (p.123)	☐	☐	☐
Strategies / Language Quality			
A2 indicate when I am following and express hesitation (p.120)	☐	☐	☐
Writing			
A2 write simple sentences describing an event and reporting what happened, e.g. the founding of Peace Day (p.115), the description of a World Heritage Site (p.123)	☐	☐	☐

At the end of **Module 6**, I've got most A2 skills.
Now I can start **Module 7**. ➔

Grammar reference

Present continuous for future

- Use the present continuous to talk about plans and arrangements already made for the future.
  We're leaving on the midday train tomorrow.
- Use time expressions to specify the future moment, e.g.
  this evening, tonight, next week, next Monday, in an hour, in five days, tomorrow, tomorrow morning, the day after tomorrow
- Put future time expressions at the beginning or end of the sentence.
  At the weekend I'm playing tennis.
  Are you going on holiday next month?

be going to

Positive

full form

I	am	
You	are	
He/She/It	is	going to tidy up.
We/You/They	are	

short form

I	'm	
You	're	
He/She/It	's	going to tidy up.
We/You/They	're	

Negative

full form

I	am not	
You	are not	
He / She / It	is not	going to tidy up.
We/You/They	are	

short form

I	'm not	
You	aren't	
He / She / It	isn't	going to tidy up.
We/You/They	aren't	

Questions

Am	I	
Are	you	
Is	he/she/it	going to tidy up?
Are	we/you/they	

Short answers

	positive				negative	
Yes,	I	am.	No,	I	'm not.
	we/you/they	are.		we/you/they	aren't.
	he/she/it	is.		he/she/it	isn't.

- Form *be going to* with the present tense of the verb *be* + *going to* + base form of the main verb.
- Form the positive with:
  subject + *am / are / is* (full forms) + *going to* + base form
  subject + *'m / 're / 's* (short forms) + *going to* + base form
- Form the negative with:
  subject + *am / are / is* + not (full forms) + *going to* + base form
  subject + *'m not / aren't / isn't* (short forms) + *going to* + base form
- Form questions with:
  am / are / is + subject + *going to* + base form
- Form short answers with:
  Yes, + subject + *am / are / is*.
  No, + subject + *'m not / aren't / isn't*.
- Short answers are the same as those for the present tense of *be*. Never use short forms in positive short answers.
  Yes, she is. NOT ~~Yes, she's.~~

Usage

- Use *be going to* to talk about intentions for the future.
  This room is a mess. I'm going to tidy it up.
  They've gone to Canada. I'm going to visit them next year.
- Use *be going to* to make predictions for the future when you know (or can see) now that something is going to happen.
  She's going to have a baby in January.
  Look at that car! It's going to crash into the lorry.

Present continuous v *be going to*

- The present continuous and *be going to* are often interchangable. However, we usually use the present continuous to talk about plans already set for the future and *be going to* to talk about future intentions or about what is about to happen.
  They're getting married at the end of May.
  They're going to get married at some time or other.
  Did you see the lightning? Now we're going to hear the thunder.

Word list

The words in grey appear in the unit, but are not in the vocabulary sections.

Holidays

activity holiday
adventure holiday
book your accommodation
buy a guidebook
city break
flight
get currency
go on a boat trip
go to galleries
go walking / fishing / cycling, etc.
guided tour
international driving licence
outdoor activities
pack your suitcase
passport
relax
ski suit
sunbathe
sun cream
swimming costume
ticket
travel by train / plane, etc.
vaccination documents
view
villa
visit

Vocabulary

Holidays

1 Circle the correct word.

1 First you have to buy a plane *pass / ticket / flight*.
2 Then you have to *buy / take / book* your accommodation.
3 It's a good idea to get some *tours / currency / passport* before you leave.
4 If you want to hire a car abroad you mustn't forget your international driving *licence / permit / vaccination*.
5 When you *make / take / pack* your suitcase, don't forget the baggage allowance!
6 If you go somewhere hot, you must take *sun cream / sunbathe / swimming costume*.

2 Complete the email with holiday words.

Hi David!

We had a fab holiday! Our hotel was lovely with a great v_____ from the bedroom window. The only bad thing was the f_____ which was really long – over nine hours on the plane! Luckily I remembered my p_____ when I packed my s_____ this time, so we were allowed on the plane!!!! But I did forget the g_____ so I got lost all the time! We didn't s_____ on the beach much because it was too hot. Dad and I went on a b_____ trip out to sea and saw some wonderful islands while Mum was having a g_____ tour of the city.

See you soon.

Xxx Tamsin

3 Match the comments to make dialogues.

1 Why do you need to go to the doctor's?
2 Hello. I want to take the next train to London, please.
3 How was the beach?
4 Did you enjoy your city break?
5 I'm thinking of taking the car across Europe next year.
6 Hey, this sounds great. You can go fishing, diving or cycling – and you can do lots of other sports.

a Awful! I forgot my swimming costume so I had to watch while the others enjoyed themselves in the sea.
b How much is it? These activity holidays can be very expensive.
c Well, don't forget to get an international driving licence.
d Yes sir. It's leaving in fifteen minutes. You can buy a ticket over there.
e Yes – we went on a guided tour and saw all the famous buildings in one day.
f I'm going to have a vaccination. I'm travelling to India next week.

Grammar

Present continuous for future

1 Complete the sentences with the correct form of the verbs in brackets.

In May

1 Chris and Sue _____ to Australia in May for a holiday. (fly)

Next Monday

2 Helen _____ the Queen next Monday. (meet)

Tonight

3 Clive _____ the football tonight. (watch)

Next week

4 Robert _____ in a play all next week. (act)

On Friday

5 They _____ a party on Friday. (have)

On 25th December

6 He _____ on the 25th. (come)

2 Write questions.

1 Tim / have / an exam / tomorrow ?
  <u>Is Tim having an exam tomorrow?</u>

2 Lisa / work / in the shop / this weekend ?
  _____

3 your brothers / play / golf / on Saturday ?
  _____

4 you / go / swimming / tonight ?
  _____

5 the lesson / finish / six / today ?
  _____

3 Write short answers.

1 Are you going to town tomorrow?
  No, <u>I'm not</u>_____.

2 Are they coming here next weekend?
  Yes, _____.

3 Is he leaving tomorrow?
  No, _____.

4 Am I acting in the play next term?
  Yes, _____.

5 Are you singing at the party next weekend?
  Yes, _____.

6 Is she working on Saturday?
  Yes, _____.

7 Are we visiting Granddad next week?
  No, _____.

be going to

4 Complete the sentences with the correct form of *be going to*.

1 He<u>'s going to</u> go to the beach next summer.
2 My brother _____ buy a new computer.
3 She _____ play volleyball next week.
4 He _____ see the World Cup final.
5 They _____ do karate at evening class.
6 We _____ watch American idol on the TV.
7 I _____ visit my cousin in New York next summer.
8 My parents _____ buy a new car at the weekend.

5 Answer the questions for you.

1 What are you going to do tonight?
  _____

2 Where are you going to go on holiday this year?
  _____

3 How old are you going to be next birthday?
  _____

4 Are you going to play any sport this week?
  _____

5 What are you going to eat for dinner tonight?
  _____

6 Where are you going to go to school next year?
  _____

222

6 What is going to happen? Write a sentence for each picture.

1 Clare / hit / computer
Clare is going to hit her computer.
_____

2 the ship / hit / the rocks
_____
_____

3 Penny / fall / off her bike
_____
_____

4 Len / lose / his wallet
_____
_____

5 he / fall / in the river
_____
_____

7 Write negative sentences.

1 help / you
I'm not going to help you.

2 go / the cinema today
_____

3 play / football tomorrow
_____

4 do / my homework today
_____

5 change / my plans
_____

6 dance / in the competition
_____

7 watch / TV tonight
_____

8 listen / to her any more
_____

8 Write the words in the correct order to make questions and sentences.

1 you / clothes / going / your / change / to / are ?
Are you going to change your clothes?

2 is / going / her / do / to / she / homework ?
_____

3 for / going / are / you / where / to / us / the / school trip / take ?
_____

4 lose / he / is / to / going ?
_____

5 going / miss / they / to / train / are / their
_____

6 we / long / are / wait / how / going / to ?
_____

7 you / going / she / to / to / again / listen / never / is
_____

8 Alex / book / next / a / going / write / to / is / year
_____

9 not / anyone / going / I / tell / to / am
_____

10 not / see / going / you / to / she / be / to / happy / is /
_____

Present continuous v *be going to*

9 Write I (Intention), P (Prediction) or PA (Plan or Arrangement).

1 I'm going to change my life! ☐
2 I'm going to learn Spanish next year. ☐
3 It's going to snow – look at the clouds. ☐
4 I'm going swimming tomorrow night. ☐
5 They're going to win! It's 5–0! ☐
6 She's watching the tennis tomorrow. ☐
7 We're going to paint this room yellow. ☐

10 Complete the sentences with the correct form of the verb in brackets.

1 I forgot to phone my mum. She _____ (be) so angry!

2 We _____ (meet) our friends at the pool tomorrow.

3 The sky is really clear. The sun _____ (shine) in the morning.

4 The train's leaving now. It _____ (arrive) in London on time today!

5 Next summer we _____ (visit) our relatives in Canada.

6 I _____ (get) tickets for Wimbledon to watch the tennis in June.

7 The cat doesn't look well. I think it _____ (be) ill.

Skills: Reading – Towards PET (Part 5)

1 Choose the correct word to complete the texts.

1	a	house	b	computer	c	office
2	a	best	b	teacher	c	student
3	a	get	b	go	c	start
4	a	driving	b	car	c	test
5	a	group	b	tent	c	car

THE SUMMER BEFORE **UNIVERSITY**

"I'm going to work next summer to save some money before I start university. A friend of my mum's has got me a job in her ¹_____, just filing and putting information into their computer system. Nothing too hard, but the money's all right."

Aidan

"My best friend had the idea of going to Africa with the Oxfam charity to help teach English to young kids. I'm not actually going to be the ²_____, but I'll be the teacher's help. It's really exciting, but I'm a bit nervous about it, too."

Kari

"My dad wants me to get a job, but I don't really know what I want to do. I don't want to work in a supermarket or anything like that. I'll probably just stay at home and get bored. I can't wait to get away from home and ³_____ university."

Stewart

"Well, the main thing I'm going to do is take driving lessons. My mum's going to give me her old car to take with me to university, so I have to pass my ⁴_____! Oh, and of course I'm going to watch the World Cup Finals on TV. Come on, England!"

Melissa

"I'm going to do a course in the summer. I'm going to do a computer science degree at university, but before I start that I want to learn how to design webpages. It's a four-week course, and after that I'm going to go camping in Italy with a ⁵_____ of friends."

Kelly

2 Read and answer the questions.

Who…

1 hasn't got any plans for the summer?
2 is going to do a course to learn a new skill?
3 is going to work in an office?
4 is going to work with children?
5 wants to learn how to drive?

Writing

3 Write about some of the things you plan to do in the next week. (about 120 words)

> **Tips**

- Use the Reading text above for ideas.
- Don't forget to use the present continuous for future plans and *be going to*.
- Use time expressions, e.g. *tomorrow afternoon / the day after tomorrow / next Monday*.

Study skills

Effective speaking

1 Read the article and think about the questions you find in it.

Accuracy (and) *fluency*

Scary speaking

Speaking is an important skill, but it can be quite scary! Learners worry about their pronunciation, vocabulary and grammar. They worry about what people are going to say to them and they worry about understanding.

Accuracy v fluency

There are two main aspects to your spoken English – accuracy and fluency. It is necessary to be accurate enough for people to understand your message, but it is also important to speak naturally in real time and not to worry about mistakes or hesitations.

The right balance

Eve worries about accuracy, she is often scared of making mistakes and she often avoids speaking. Joe, on the other hand, is never worried, he makes a lot of mistakes – he can be difficult to understand. Both these students need to get the balance right between fluency and accuracy.

Your learning style

Are you similar to Eve or to Joe? What kind of learner are you? Is being correct the most important thing? Or do you always take risks? You need to recognise where you should focus your attention.

How to improve

How do you develop both accuracy and fluency? If you worry about mistakes, try not to worry – focus instead on making sure your friend understands you. Try to speed up a bit and think less about the impression you are making. If you are fluent but you make a lot of mistakes, say with tenses, just focus on tenses and work on that area. Also try and slow down a bit.

Getting varied practice

Make sure you get practice in both fluency and accuracy. Discussions are good fluency activities and activities with an exchange of factual information are good for accuracy.

In the end, communication is the most important thing and you need to be both accurate and fluent to be a good communicator.

How can you sound more confident?
- ⌁ Practise often
- ⌁ Relax and think about the message
- ⌁ Rehearse what you are going to say

2 Think about your own profile as a language learner. Think of a time recently you used English. Did you focus on fluency or accuracy?

3 Imagine you are joining a new club. How would you introduce yourself? What would you tell the other people about you and your life? Practise doing this on your own. Preparing like this will help both your fluency and accuracy.

Grammar reference

Present perfect

Positive

full form		
I/You/We/They	have	worked.
He/She/It	has	

short form		
I/You/We/They	've	worked.
He/She/It	's	

Negative

full form		
I/You/We/They	have not	worked.
He/She/It	has not	

short form		
I/You/We/They	haven't	worked.
He/She/It	hasn't	

Questions

Have	I/you/we/they	worked?
Has	he/she/it	

Short answers

positive				negative		
Yes,	I/you/we/they	have.	No,	I/you/we/they	haven't.
	he/she/it	has.		he/she/it	hasn't.

- Form the present perfect with:
  the present tense of the verb *have* + past participle
- Form the present perfect positive with:
  subject + *have / has* (full forms) + past participle
  subject + *'ve / 's* (short forms) + past participle
  I have finished.
  She has done her homework.
- Form the negative with:
  subject + *have / has* + *not* (full forms) + past participle
  subject + *haven't / hasn't* (short forms) + past participle
  I have not finished.
  She hasn't done her homework.
- Form questions with:
  have / has + subject + past participle
  Have you finished?
  Has she done her homework?

- Form short answers with:
  Yes, + subject + *have / has.*
  No, + subject + *haven't / hasn't.*
  Have you finished? – Yes, I have.
  Has she done her homework? – No, she hasn't.
- Note that short answers are the same as those for the present tense of *have* (*got*). Remember never to use short forms in positive short answers.

Usage

- Use the present perfect to talk about a past action when you're more interested in its relation to the present than when it happened. The exact moment is not important.
  She's broken her ankle (and now she can't walk).
  Have you heard the news? (Do you know now?).
  – No, I've been away for a few days. (So I don't know now.)
- Use the present perfect to talk about all your experiences up to now.
  I've been to London several times.
- Use *never* in sentences with the present perfect to say that you have not had a particular experience at any time in the past.
  We've never travelled to Australia.
- Use *ever* in questions with the present perfect to find out if something has happened at any time in the past.
  Have you ever seen Ayers Rock? – No, I've never been to Australia.
- Note that you do not say when something happened with the present perfect. To give more details about an experience, use the past simple.
  We have been to Amsterdam. We went there last year. We had a great time.
  NOT *We have been there last year. We have had a great time.*

Past participles

- Form the past participle of regular verbs in the same way as the past simple, by adding *-ed* to the base form. The rules regarding spelling and pronunciation are the same as for the past simple (see Unit 9).
- The past participle of irregular verbs has a special form, sometimes the same as the past simple form (e.g. *hear, heard, heard*), sometimes different (e.g. *write, wrote, written*). You will find them in the list of irregular verbs at the end of the Student's Book. Or you can look the verb up in a dictionary; the past participle is the third form in the principal parts given (see the dictionary entry in Unit 11).

Present perfect with *for* / *since*

- Use the present perfect with *for* or *since* to say how long something has lasted or when it started.

  I have lived here for three years.
  I have known John since 2007.

- Make these sentences negative by adding *not* before the past participle.

  I have not (haven't) watched TV for a long time.
  I have not (haven't) seen John since 2007.

Usage

- Use *for* to talk about a period of time.

  I have been at this school for a week / two days / three years / six months, etc.

- Use *since* to talk about a point in time in the past.

  I have been at this school since last week /
  I was five / July / 2008 / Tuesday, etc.

Prepositions of place and movement

Prepositions of place

- Use the preposition *in* to say where someone or something is, e.g. in a room, in a shop, in a street, in a square, in a town / country / continent.

  in the garden   in Edinburgh
  in Oxford Street   in Europe

- Use the preposition *at* to refer to a specific point, e.g. *at the bus stop, at the traffic lights,* and to refer to a building's function.

  at + the hospital / the cinema / the dentist

Comparison between *in* and *at*

- The preposition *in* indicates the space in the building; the preposition *at* indicates the function of the building.

  The visitors were in the school. (= the building)
  We were at school. (= for lessons)
  Everybody was quiet in the library.
  (= the room or the building)
  I was at the library doing some research.
  (= as a place to do research)

- Note these fixed phrases.

  at + home / work / school / the seaside /
  the back of the queue / the bottom of the road
  in + the book / the open air / the sun / the rain /
  the cold / the middle of / the back of the car /
  a queue / line / row

Prepositions of movement

- Use the preposition *to* after a verb of motion to talk about direction.

  I went to London.
  She drove to the airport.

- The preposition changes according to the verb it follows.

  Sam and Joanna went to London a year ago.
  Sam and Joanna are in London.

Word list

The words in grey appear in the unit, but are not in the vocabulary sections.

Food

artichoke	mushrooms
aubergines	mustard
avocado	nuts
bacon	octopus
banana	olives
basil	omelette
beans	onions
bread (white / brown)	orange juice
cabbage	pasta
carrots	peppers
cheese	pine nuts
chicken	pizza
chips	potatoes
chocolate cake	prawn
courgettes	rice
eggs	salad
filter coffee	sandwich
fish	sauce
ham	seafood
hamburgers	snails
herb	soup
hot chocolate	spinach
houmous	steak
ice cream	sun-dried tomato
lamb	tomatoes
lettuce	tripe
liquorice	tuna
liver	vegetable
mayonnaise	yoghurt
mineral water	

Ways of cooking

fried	roast
grilled	toasted

Vocabulary

Food

1 Complete the crossword.

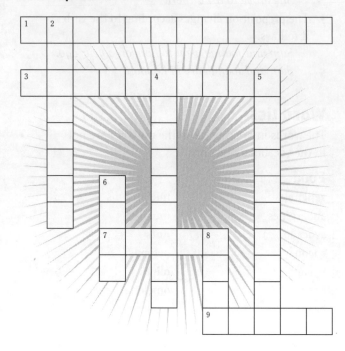

Across

1 This is a hot sweet drink. (2 words)
3 This is the name for things like onions, potatoes, carrots, etc.
7 These are made from potatoes and deep fried.
9 Italians eat a lot of this, usually with a sauce.

Down

2 You make this with eggs and milk or water.
4 This is a purple vegetable – people use it a lot in the Mediterranean.
5 Lots of people eat these for lunch – they are two pieces of bread with a filling.
6 People in China and Japan eat a lot of this with other food.
8 This is often a starter, and you eat it with a spoon.

2 Write the letters in the correct order to complete the dialogues.

1

Mark Do you want me to get you some fruit from the market?
Julie Yes, please, but we only need ¹ _bananas_ (aanansb).
Mark How about vegetables?
Julie We need ²p_____ (tptaoeso), ³c_____ (rcrtaos), ⁴c_____ (babgace), ⁵m_____ (usrhoomms) and ⁶o_____ (oonins).

2

Waiter Do you like seafood?
Carol I like ⁷t_____ (utan), but I don't like ⁸p_____ (rapnws).
Waiter Well, how about meat?
Carol No, I'm vegetarian. Can I have a three-⁹e_____ (geg) omelette with ¹⁰c_____ (ehcees) and ¹¹h_____ (rhbes), please? Oh, and a ¹²l_____ (teutcle) and ¹³t_____ (amotto) salad, please.
Waiter Certainly madam. And what would you like on your pizza, sir?
Tim I'll have ¹⁴h_____ (ahm), ¹⁵a_____ (tricoahke) and red ¹⁶p_____ (eerppps), please.

Grammar

Present perfect

1 Match the sentences with the pictures.

a
b

c
d

e
f

1 She's won the marathon. ☐
2 He's eaten his lunch. ☐
3 She's broken her leg. ☐
4 We've had an accident. ☐
5 They've all seen the film. ☐
6 They've finished a game of tennis. ☐

2 Look at the table and answer the questions.

	see a whale	meet a famous person	eat octopus	lose some money
Lucy	once	twice	never	never
Mark	never	never	never	never
Petra	twice	once	once	once
Sonia	once	never	twice	never

1 Has Lucy ever seen a whale?
   Yes, she's seen a whale once.

2 Has Mark ever met a famous person?
   _____

3 Has Sonia ever eaten octopus?
   _____

4 Have Lucy and Mark ever lost any money?
   _____

5 Has Petra ever lost any money?
   _____

3 Now write another three questions based on the table and answer them.

1 _____
   _____
2 _____
   _____
3 _____
   _____

4 Answer these questions for you. If the answer is *Yes*, explain where and when it happened.

Have you ever seen…

1 an elephant in real life?   4 a play?
2 a James Bond film?   5 a Formula 1 race?
3 a double-decker bus?   6 a tiger?

1 _____
2 _____
3 _____
4 _____
5 _____
6 _____

Present perfect with *for / since*

5 Complete the sentences with *for* or *since*.

1 She has been friends with Tina _since_ last April.

2 I haven't seen Michael _____ we went to Donna-Marie's party together.

3 Have you known Judith _____ a long time?

4 What have you done _____ last week?

5 They have lived in the same house _____ 2003.

6 We've had the same car _____ ten years.

6 Write sentences in the present perfect. Include *for* or *since*.

1 I / not / see / a good film / six months
   I haven't seen a good film for six months.

2 They / not / speak / to me / a month
   _____

3 He / have / that dog / he was four years old
   _____

4 She / not / eat / pizza / her birthday party
   _____

5 We / be / here / hours
   _____

6 I / study / English / three years
   _____

7 He / not / ride / a horse / last year
   _____

8 They / live / in that house / their wedding
   _____

Past participles

7 Write the base form for these past participles.

1 collected   _collect_
2 come   _____
3 eaten   _____
4 had   _____
5 listened   _____
6 read   _____
7 seen   _____
8 sent   _____
9 slept   _____
10 stopped   _____
11 talked   _____
12 watched   _____
13 written   _____

Prepositions of place and movement

8 Complete the passage with *in*, *to* or *at*.

UK Travel Advice

Greenacre is a great town to spend a few days in. It doesn't take very long to walk [1]___ the centre of town from our hotel and there are lots of cafés and bars [2]___ the centre. You can get a really good meal [3]___ a restaurant, or have a drink [4]___ a bar. There are three cinemas – that's more than [5]___ home. There are always at least five films on [6]___ the cinema near our hotel – so we're never bored! When it's sunny, you can sit [7]___ the sun and read [8]___ one of the lovely parks. Or you can spend your time [9]___ the open air, climbing or sailing. You can also cycle [10]___ the sports centre – it's only about ten minutes from the centre.

Skills: Reading – Towards PET (Part 3)

1 Write the name of the most suitable restaurant for each person.

1 Karen likes meat and hot, spicy food – especially Asian. She doesn't like big, noisy places, but would like to go somewhere romantic with her boyfriend. _____

2 Harriet loves pasta and most Mediterranean food – salads, olives, cheese and vegetables. She doesn't eat much meat. She likes a fun atmosphere and places that have live music. _____

3 Ken doesn't like sophisticated restaurants. He prefers simple places with a good, fun atmosphere. He likes pizza and pasta, and also Indian, Thai and other spicy food. He hasn't got a lot of money, so the place must be cheap. _____

4 Mike is happy when he's eating a nice juicy steak. He likes going out with big groups of friends, and likes places that are really lively. _____

Where to eat

Mario's

22 Small Street, WC2
In the centre of London's trendy West End, Mario's is the best place in town for lovers of simple but classic Italian food. All the pasta dishes are made with lots of fresh tomatoes and herbs and the beautiful thin crust real Italian pizzas are like the ones Grandma made. You can take your own bottle of wine for no extra charge. Don't expect sophisticated surroundings – Mario's just offers good home cooking at sensible prices.

Mezze

239 West Street, N10
This is a great Greek place to come with your family. Excellent aubergine and bean side dishes. Mezze serves the best Greek salad in London, washed down with the best Ouzo this side of Athens. On Fridays and Saturday enjoy live bouzouki music from 8 pm.

Galangal

1 Mede House, SE3
South London's premier Asian restaurant serves excellent food in a quiet, romantic setting. Thai is the main influence, but you'll also find beautifully-spiced dishes from Cambodia, Laos and Burma on the menu.

Rio

45 Greys Road, W10
This is a place for meat lovers. This new Brazilian barbecue house offers meat paradise for you and your friends – all-you-can-eat steaks, pork fillet, leg of lamb, pork and chicken sausages, and for the non-meat eaters, grilled salmon and prawns with a full salad buffet. This isn't the place for a romantic dinner though – Friday and Saturday nights are very noisy.

2 Circle T (True) or F (False). Correct the false statements.

1 You can eat a lot of meat at Mezze. T / F
2 Mario's is a simple restaurant with typical Italian food. T / F
3 Mezze serves great vegetable dishes but there isn't any music. T / F
4 Rio serves only meat dishes. T / F
5 Galangal is a good place for large groups of teenagers to have a lot of fun. T / F
6 Rio is a quiet place to eat. T / F
7 You don't have to buy wine at Mario's. T / F
8 Galangal serves fantastic Italian pasta dishes. T / F

Writing

3 Write a review for a website about your local food. Mention some of the foods you have and haven't tried, as well as some restaurants you have and haven't visited. (about 120 words)

► Tips

- Use the Reading text above for ideas.
- Use the Word list for food vocabulary.
- Don't forget to use the present perfect to talk about your experiences but continue in the past simple, e.g. *I have been to the most expensive restaurant in town. I went there in… and I ate… .*
- You can use prepositions of place and movement to say where a restaurant is or to describe a visit, e.g. *The Eagles Restaurant is in the main square. To get there by bus, go to the Town Hall…*

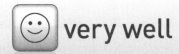 very well　　 OK　　 with difficulty

I've finished this module and I can do ☑ these things in English

Module 7 　　　☺　☺　☹

Listening

	☺	☺	☹
A2 understand what is said clearly, slowly and directly to me in a simple everyday conversation, e.g. at a restaurant (pp.140, 141)	☐	☐	☐
A2 understand the essential information in short recorded passages dealing with predictable everyday matters, e.g. plans for the future (p.130), holiday choices (p.134)	☐	☐	☐
B1 understand the main points of a radio programme on food and diet (p.143)	☐	☐	☐

Reading

A2 find the most important information in leaflets, e.g. a menu (p.141)	☐	☐	☐
A2 skim holiday advertisements in newspapers and identify the most important pieces of information (p.134)	☐	☐	☐
B1 understand the main points in short newspaper articles about current and familiar topics, e.g. food (p.143)	☐	☐	☐

Spoken Interaction

A2 ask people questions about what they do in their free time, and answer such questions (p.130)	☐	☐	☐
A2 discuss with other people what to do, where to go and make arrangements to meet (p.133)	☐	☐	☐

Spoken Production

A2 describe my plan for a trip to Europe and explain the choices I have made (p.134)	☐	☐	☐
A2 describe past activities and personal experiences (p.136)	☐	☐	☐

Strategies / Language Quality

A2 use some simple structures correctly (p.136)	☐	☐	☐

Writing

A2 write a holiday plan (p.134)	☐	☐	☐
A2 write about aspects of my everyday life in simple phrases and sentences, e.g. a plan for the weekend (p.133)	☐	☐	☐
B1 write simple connected texts on a range of topics within my field of interest and express personal views and opinions, e.g. about diet (p.143)	☐	☐	☐

At the end of **Module 7**, I'm a good A2 student. Now I can start *For Real Pre-Intermediate* and go on to the B1 level.

PLAN AND PREPARE

Notes and Messages

- Notes and Messages should be short, simple and factual.
- Think about who you are writing to and why you are writing.
- Don't include unnecessary information.

1 Read the two tasks below. Then use the words in the box to complete the notes.

can't | let's | don't | tonight | playing | want

1 You want to see a film with your sister. Write a message to her.
- Tell her about the film.
- Arrange to meet her at the cinema.
- Suggest another activity to do after the film.

> Hi Sarah
> There's a good Johnny Depp film on at the cinema ¹_____. It starts at 7.30, so ²_____ meet at 7.00 outside the cinema. Do you ³_____ to go out for dinner after the film? Palms Café is good and it's cheap!
> Love
> Jill

2 You can't meet your friend for lunch because you are looking after your little sister. Write a message to him.
- Explain why you can't meet him.
- Tell him what you are doing.
- Suggest another time to meet.

> Hi Jake
> I'm sorry, I ⁴_____ meet you for lunch today. I'm looking after my little sister. We're ⁵_____ card games. She's having great fun, but I'm really bored! Why ⁶_____ we meet up tomorrow afternoon at about 3 o'clock?
> Cheers
> Frida

2 Read the task below and write a message.

You want to meet your friend for lunch.
- Suggest a place and a time.
- Think of another activity to do after lunch.
- Ask your friend to call you.

LINKING WORDS: *AND* AND *BUT*

We use linking words to join two ideas in one sentence.

- *and* joins two similar ideas

  This department store is noisy and expensive.

- *but* joins two different ideas

  I don't like opera, but my brother loves it.

PLAN AND PREPARE

Explain why you are writing ↓	*I'm writing to thank you for the lovely present.* *I'm so sorry that I can't come to your party.*
Give some more details ↓	*It's perfect because … I'm afraid it's my brother's birthday on the same day.*
Add a personal comment ↓	*I hope we can meet up again soon. I hope you have a fantastic day.*
Repeat the thanks / apology	*Thank you again. Once again, I'm so sorry.*

1 Use these sentences to complete the two cards below. One is a thank you card and one is an apology card.

a I hope you have a great time.

b Maybe you can visit soon and see the picture on my wall.

c I love the colours and it looks really great in my bedroom.

d I'm so sorry that I can't meet you this weekend.

e Thank you so much for the wonderful picture.

f I've got an exam next week and I'm studying hard every day.

> Dear Sam
> 1 _____
> 2 _____
> 3 _____
> Once again, very many thanks.
> With lots of love
> Pete

> Dear Jade
> 1 _____
> 2 _____
> 3 _____
> With apologies again.
> Best wishes
> Tracey

LINKING WORDS: *BECAUSE* AND *SO*

- **because joins an idea with a reason**
  I really like the scarf because it's the same colour as my coat.

- **so joins an idea with a result**
  The scarf is the same colour as my coat, so I really like it.

2 Read the task below and write your answer.

Your friend, Sharon, gave you a CD for your birthday. Write a card to Sharon. In the card you should:
- thank Sharon for the CD
- say why you like it
- suggest that you meet up soon

Write 35-45 words.

CONFIRM AND CHECK

Postcards
We use informal, simple language in postcards, but it's still important that spelling, grammar and punctuation are correct.

CAPITAL LETTERS
• at the beginning of a new sentence
• for names (Peter) and places (Paris, Mexico)
• for nationalities (Brazilian), languages (Portuguese), months (January) and days (Tuesday)

PUNCTUATION
• Question mark (?) at the end of a question
• Full point (.) at the end of a sentence
• Exclamation mark (!) at the end of a funny or unusual remark

1 Look at the task and the two postcards below. Match the teacher's comments to the correct postcard.

Write a postcard to a friend. Tell him or her where you are, what the weather is like and what you are doing. Write 40-60 words.

1

> Hi Tim
> I'm on the beach in corfu
> It's very hot and I'm
> reading a magazine and
> drinking a milkshake
> Are you OK
> Gemma

A
You have some interesting points, but check your grammar. Look again at the use of Present simple and Present continuous. Please read the task carefully – you should write something about the weather.

2

> Hello Rachel
> We're have a lot of fun
> in Paris. We meet much
> interesting people and
> eat delicious food at the
> cafés. I loving the amazing
> shops and there is lots of
> galleries and museums. At
> the moment, I sit in a café
> by the River Seine and
> watch the people on the
> street.
> Tilly

B
Your grammar and spelling are excellent, but remember to use proper punctuation. This postcard is too short – you should write between 40 and 60 words.

2 Now write out correct versions of the postcards from activity 1.

TIME EXPRESSIONS

• We use *now, at the moment, right now, today* with the **present continuous.**
  At the moment I'm watching a DVD.
  Today we're visiting an art gallery.

• We use *every day/month/week, usually, always, often* with the **present simple.**
  I usually get up at six o'clock in the morning.
  We go to the beach every day after breakfast.

Trinity ISE 0 Controlled Written section – Task 2 (75 words)
PET Paper 1 Writing Part 3 (100 words)

PLAN AND PREPARE

- Make a rough plan before you begin writing. Use headings or bullet points to list all the information you will need.
- Think of things that will make your writing more interesting for the reader. Include funny or unusual information if possible, but keep to the topic.

1 Read the task and then look at the plan and the letter below. Use the notes in the plan to complete the letter.

1 This is part of a letter you receive from your English friend, Penny.

> I love hanging out with my friends and listening to music.
> How do you like to spend your free time?

2 Now write a letter to Penny, telling her about how you spend your free time. Write between 75-100 words.
- like listening to music
- evening: do homework / listen to music on radio
- weekends: go to concerts with Kurt
- watch football on TV – favourite club Manchester City
- play guitar – go to Bill's house on Thursday evenings

Hi Penny
Thanks for your letter.
I like ¹_____ as well. In the evenings I either
²_____ or I listen to music on the radio.
Sometimes I ³_____ at the weekend with
my older brother, Kurt. I don't like playing football, but I love
⁴_____!
    My favourite football club is Manchester City. I can
⁵_____ quite well, and on Thursday evenings
I usually go to my friend Bill's house and we play our guitars
and sing together. We want to form a band, but we need to
find a drummer first.
Best wishes
Keith

2 Now read the task below and write your answer.

Your English friend, Henry, is staying with you and wants to know what places he can visit in your town. Write a letter to him. Tell him:
- what places you like in your town
- why you like them.
Write between 75-100 words.

EITHER ... OR

- **We use *either ... or* to talk about two different options.**
  I have ham and cheese in my fridge. I can have either a ham sandwich or a cheese sandwich.
- ***Either* comes after the verb when the verb is the same, but the nouns are different:**
  I can play either tennis or football.
- ***Either* comes before the verb when the actions are different.**
  I can either read a book or watch a movie.

Trinity ISE 0 Portfolio Section 1 - Correspondence (40-60 words)
PET Paper 1 Writing Part 2 (35-45 words)

CONFIRM AND CHECK

When you complete your writing, read through it again:
• Check that the grammar, spelling and punctuation are correct.
• Check that your writing has a good range of vocabulary.
• Check that all the important information is included.
• Check that your writing is clear and easy to understand.
• Count the words and make sure that you don't have too many words or too few.

---

1 Read the task and the email below. The email is too long. There are two unnecessary sentences. Cross them out.

1 Your friend wants to have a healthier lifestyle. Write an email to her. Suggest ways that she can become fitter and healthier. Tell her about the ways that you keep fit.
Write 40-60 words.

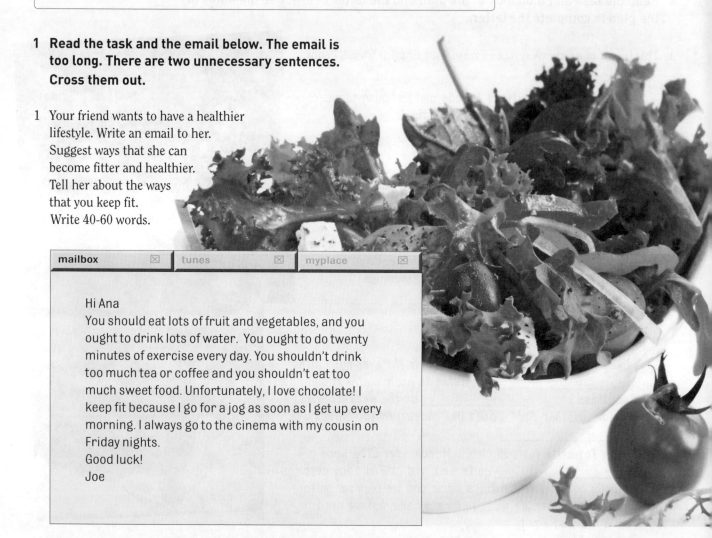

| mailbox ☒ | tunes ☒ | myplace ☒ |

Hi Ana
You should eat lots of fruit and vegetables, and you ought to drink lots of water. You ought to do twenty minutes of exercise every day. You shouldn't drink too much tea or coffee and you shouldn't eat too much sweet food. Unfortunately, I love chocolate! I keep fit because I go for a jog as soon as I get up every morning. I always go to the cinema with my cousin on Friday nights.
Good luck!
Joe

2 Your friend is learning English but she is finding it very difficult. Write an email to her. Suggest ways that she can improve her English. Tell her about how you study and practise English.
Write 40-60 words.

AS SOON AS

• *As soon as* means *immediately after*. It comes at the beginning of the clause it describes:
  As soon as I get home from school, I have a cup of tea.
  ➜ *I get home from school and then I have a cup of tea.*
  I have a shower as soon as I finish breakfast.
  ➜ *I finish breakfast and then I have a shower.*

Trinity ISE 0 Portfolio Section 3 – Creative and Descriptive writing (80-100 words)
PET Paper 1 Writing Part 3 (100 words)

PLAN AND PREPARE

You can make a mind map to plan your description of someone.

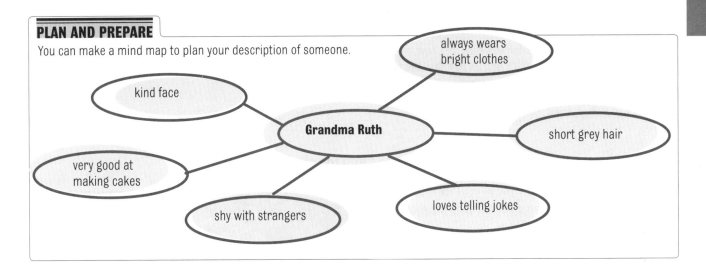

- kind face
- always wears bright clothes
- **Grandma Ruth**
- short grey hair
- very good at making cakes
- shy with strangers
- loves telling jokes

1a Read the task and the description on the right.

Find adjectives in the description to match these definitions.

a) caring and helpful

   k _____

b) nervous and embarrassed with other people

   s _____

c) happy to be with other people

   o _____

d) wonderful

   f _____

e) different or strange

   u _____

1b Write a description of someone in your family. Describe how they look and their personality. Say why you like this person. Write 80-100 words.

My Grandma Ruth is my mother's mother. She's seventy years old, but she looks younger. She's got short grey hair and a very kind face. She always wears bright clothes and unusual scarves and jewellery. She makes fantastic cakes – her Dutch Apple Cake is famous in our family. She's sometimes shy and sometimes outgoing. On the one hand, she's a very lively person at home and she loves telling jokes. But on the other hand, she's very quiet with strangers. I like my Grandma because she always tries to make people feel happy.

---

2 Now read the task below and write your answer.

1 This is part of a letter you receive from your English penfriend, Jim.

> In your next letter, please tell me about your family. Who is in your family and what are they like?

2 Now write a letter to Jim, telling him about your family. Write between 75-100 words.

ON THE ONE HAND … ON THE OTHER HAND

- **We use *on the one hand … on the other hand* to contrast two different facts, or two different ways of thinking about something.**

On the one hand she is very excited about moving to the USA, but on the other hand she is worried about being so far from home.

On the one hand George is very clever, but on the other hand he is also quite arrogant.

CONFIRM AND CHECK

When you write instructions for someone to follow, they must be very clear and well-organised. Read your instructions carefully and try to follow them yourself. Ask yourself these questions.
• Are the instructions in the correct order?
• Are they clear?
• Have I included all the necessary steps?

---

1 Read the task below and put these instructions into the correct order.

You are going to have a picnic in your local park next weekend. Write some instructions for your friends, telling them when the picnic is, how to get there, and what food and drink to bring.
Write 80-100 words.

a ☐ Don't forget to bring some plates, knives and forks, cups and a picnic rug too!

b ☐ Hanover Park is just opposite the railway station, or you can take a no. 7 bus from the shopping centre and get off by the post office.

c ☐1☐ I hope you can come to the picnic next Saturday.

d ☐ See you there!

e ☐ Please could you bring some bread and cheese and also some fruit juice to drink?

f ☐ It's at Hanover Park at midday.

g ☐ Turn left into Quarry Street and the park is at the end of this road.

2 Now read this task. Choose the correct verbs to complete the recipe.

Your friend wants to know how to cook your favourite dish. Write the recipe for her, saying what to use and how to make it. Write 80-100 words.

You need four eggs, a little milk, some olive oil, an onion, some garlic, a pepper and some chorizo. First, [1] chop/add the onion, the garlic, the pepper and the chorizo into small pieces. Next, [2] slice/heat up the olive oil in a frying pan. [3] Fry/Boil the onion for one minute, then [4] add/complete the garlic, pepper and chorizo. In a bowl, [5] join/mix together the four eggs and the milk. Then add the egg and milk mixture to the frying pan. [6] Bake/Cook the omelette gently for a few minutes, until the egg is set.

3 Now read the task below and write your answer.

A new neighbour wants to know where the local sports centre is. Write directions to the sports centre from your street. Tell your neighbour how to join the centre and what activities he can do there.

SEQUENCING WORDS

• We use *first*, *next*, *then* and *finally* to show the order of events.

First you put a teabag into your cup.
Next you boil some water.
Then you pour the hot water into the cup.
Finally you add milk and take out the teabag.

PLAN AND PREPARE

Summarising
• Make sure that you understand the text before you start writing.
• Read the text carefully and underline the important information.
• Try to think of synonyms and other ways to phrase the information in the text.

1 Read the task and look at the student's letter on the right. The letter has lots of mistakes. Find and underline:
   • **three grammatical mistakes**
   • **three spelling mistakes**
   • **two punctuation mistakes**

You are going to Fun Parks Holiday Camp in Devon for a week in July. Read the text below and then, in your own words, write a letter (approximately 75 words) to your English penfriend:
i) saying what you are going to see and do at the Holiday Camp and
ii) inviting your friend to come with you.

Fun Parks Holiday Camp

A place to have fun, relax and enjoy yourself!

Sports
You can try out lots of different sports at Fun Parks, including:
• tennis
• sailing
• windsurfing
• horseriding
• golf

Food
There are two excellent restaurants and three cafés at Fun Parks. Or you can buy some delicious food at our Fun Parks Supermarket and prepare your own meals.

Nightlife
We have a great choice of evening entertainment, including:
• disco
• live music
• quiz games

Have a wonderful time at Fun Parks!

Dear Nicky

I'm going to go to Fun Parks Holiday Camp in the last week of july. ?Would you like to come too. I'm loving sports, so I'm going to go sailing and windsurfing. Maybe I'll take some golf lesons as well! Although there is restaurants at the camp, I'm going to cook my own meals to save some monay. And in the evening I'm going listen to some live music.

I'm sure you will really enjoi this kind of holiday, so please come with me!

Best wishes

Jon

---

2 Now use your own ideas and write your answer to the task in activity 1.

ALTHOUGH

• **We use *although* to contrast two ideas. It can go at the beginning or in the middle of the sentence.**

Although the weather is hot, he's wearing a jacket.

He's wearing a jacket, although the weather is hot.

across (prep) /əˈkrɒs/

act in plays (v) /ˈæktɪŋ ɪn ˈpleɪz/

action film (n) /ˈækʃən/

activity holiday (n) /ækˈtɪvɪti ˌhɒlɪdeɪ/

actor / actress (n) /ˈæktə/ /ˈæktrəs/

adventure holiday (n) /ədˈventʃə ˌhɒlɪdeɪ/

adventurer (n) /ədˈventʃərə/

advice (n) /ədˈvaɪs/

advisor (n) /ədˈvaɪzə/

agony column (n) /ˈægəni kɒləm/

along (prep) /əˈlɒŋ/

angry (adj) /ˈæŋgri/

apartment (n) /əˈpɑːtmənt/

apple (n) /ˈæpl/

apricot (n) /ˈeɪprɪkɒt/

arm (n) /ɑːm/

armchair (n) /ˈɑːmtʃeə/

art gallery (n) /ˈɑːt gæləri/

artichoke (n) /ˈɑːtɪtʃəʊk/

artist (n) /ˈɑːtɪst/

ask (someone) out (v) /ˌɑːsk sʌmwʌn ˈaʊt/

assistant (n) /əˈsɪstənt/

athletics (n) /æθˈletɪks/

attack (v) /əˈtæk/

aubergine (n) /ˈəʊbəʒiːn/

average build (adj) /ˌævərɪdʒ ˈbɪld/

avocado (n) /ævəˈkɑːdəʊ/

away from prep) /əˈweɪ frɒm/

baby buggy (n) /ˈbeɪbi bʌgi/

back (n) /bæk/

bacon (n) /ˈbeɪkən/

baker's (n) /ˈbeɪkəz/

bald (adj) /bɔːld/

bank account (n) /ˈbæŋk əkaʊnt/

barbecue (n) /ˈbɑːbəkjuː/

barrier (n) /ˈbæriə/

basil (n) /ˈbæzl/

basin (n) /ˈbeɪsn/

basketball (n) /ˈbɑːskɪtbɔːl/

bath (n) /bɑːθ/

bathroom (n) /ˈbɑːθruːm/

beach (n) /biːtʃ/

beans (n) /biːnz/

beard (n) /bɪəd/

beautician (n) /bjuːˈtɪʃn/

because (conj) /bɪˈkɒz/

bed (n) /bed/

bedroom (n) /ˈbedruːm/

bedside table (n) /ˌbedsaɪd ˈteɪbl/

beef (n) /biːf/

behind (prep) /bɪˈhaɪnd/

belongings (n) /bɪˈlɒŋɪŋz/

below (prep) /bɪˈləʊ/

belt (n) /belt/

between (prep) /bɪˈtwiːn/

bicycle / bike (n) /ˈbaɪsɪkl/ /baɪk/

black (adj) /blæk/

blazer (n) /ˈbleɪzə/

blockbuster (n) /ˈblɒkbʌstə/

blonde (adj) /blɒnd/

blue (adj) /bluː/

boat (n) /bəʊt/

book your accommodation (v) /ˌbʊk yɔːr əkɒməˈdeɪʃn/

bookcase (n) /ˈbʊkkeɪs/

boots (n) /buːts/

bored (adj) /bɔːd/

borrow (v) /ˈbɒrəʊ/

bracelet (n) /ˈbreɪslət/

bread (white / brown) (n) /bred (waɪt / braʊn)/

break up (v) /breɪk ˈʌp/

bridge (n) /brɪdʒ/

brown (adj) /braʊn/

bully (v) /ˈbʊli/

bus station (n) /ˈbʌs steɪʃn/

businessman / woman (n) /ˈbɪznɪsmæn/ /ˈbɪznɪswʊmən/

busy (adj) /ˈbɪzi/

but (conj) /bʌt/

butcher (n) /ˈbʊtʃə/

butcher's (n) /ˈbʊtʃəz/

butter (n) /ˈbʌtə/

button (n) /ˈbʌtn/

buy a guidebook (v) /ˌbaɪ ə ˈgaɪdbʊk/

cabbage (n) /ˈkæbɪdʒ/

cable (n) /ˈkeɪbl/

café (n) /ˈkæfeɪ/

campaign (v) /kæmˈpeɪn/

canoeing (n) /kəˈnuːɪŋ/

cap (n) /kæp/

car park (n) /ˈkɑː pɑːk/

car (n) /kɑː/

cardboard (n, adj) /ˈkɑːdbɔːd/

careful (adj) /ˈkeəfl/

carrot (n) /ˈkærət/

cartoon (n) /kɑːˈtuːn/

cash (n) /kæʃ/

cashier (n) /kəˈʃɪə/

cashpoint machine (n) /ˈkæʃpɔɪnt məʃiːn/

cathedral (n) /kəˈθiːdrəl/

CD (n) /siːˈdiː/

ceasefire (n) /ˈsiːsfaɪə/

celebrity (n) /səˈlebrəti/

chain store (n) /ˈtʃeɪn stɔː/

chain (n) /tʃeɪn/

chair (n) /tʃeə/

challenge (n) /ˈtʃæləndʒ/

chat online (v) /tʃæt ɒnˈlaɪn/

chatroom (n) /ˈtʃætruːm/

cheap (adj) /tʃiːp/

cheese (n) /tʃiːz/

chemist's (n) /ˈkemɪsts/

chest (n) /tʃest/

chest of drawers (n) /ˌtʃest əv ˈdrɔːz/

chicken (n) /ˈtʃɪkɪn/
chin (n) /tʃɪn/
chips (n) /tʃɪps/
chocolate cake (n) /ˈtʃɒklət keɪk/
choice (n) /tʃɔɪs/
chubby (adj) /ˈtʃʌbi/
church (n) /tʃɜːtʃ/
city (n) /ˈsɪti/
city break (n) /ˈsɪti breɪk/
city centre (n) /ˌsɪti ˈsentə/
clarinet (n) /klærɪˈnet/
classmate (n) /ˈklɑːsmeɪt/
classroom (n) /ˈklɑːsruːm/
clean-shaven (adj) /kliːn ˈʃeɪvn/
click on (v) /ˈklɪk ɒn/
close down (v) /kləʊz ˈdaʊn/
cloud / cloudy (adj) /klaʊd/ /ˈklaʊdi/
club / nightclub (n) /klʌb/ /ˈnaɪtklʌb/
coach (n) /kəʊtʃ/
coat (n) /kəʊt/
cockpit (n) /ˈkɒkpɪt/
cod (n) /kɒd/
coffee table (n) /ˈkɒfi teɪbl/
collecting things (v) /kəˈlektɪŋ θɪŋz/
comedy (n,adj) /ˈkɒmədi/
competition (n) /kɒmpəˈtɪʃn/
compulsory (adj) /kəmˈpʌlsəri/
computer (n) /kɒmˈpjuːtə/
computer programmer (n) /kəmˌpjuːtə ˈprəʊgræmə/
cooker (n) /ˈkʊkə/
cookery (n) /ˈkʊkəri/
cottage (n) /ˈkɒtɪdʒ/
cotton (adj) /ˈkɒtn/
cough (n) /kɒf/
country / countryside (n) /ˈkʌntri/ /ˈkʌntrisaɪd/
courgette (n) /kʊəˈʒet/
credit card (n) /ˈkredɪt kɑːd/
cupboard (n) /ˈkʌbəd/
curly (adj) /ˈkɜːli/
currency (n) /ˈkʌrənsi/
cycling (n) /ˈsaɪklɪŋ/

dancer (n) /ˈdɑːnsə/

danger / dangerous (n/v) /ˈdeɪndʒə/ /ˈdeɪndʒərəs/
debit card (n) /ˈdebɪt kɑːd/
decisive – /dɪˈsaɪsɪv/
delete (v) /dɪˈliːt/
deliver (v) /dɪˈlɪvə/
dentist (n) /ˈdentɪst/
department store (n) /dɪˈpɑːtmənt stɔː/
depressed (adj) /dɪˈprest/
destination (n) /destɪˈneɪʃn/
detached house (n) /dɪˌtætʃt ˈhaʊs/
diary (n) /ˈdaɪəri/
dining room (n) /ˈdaɪnɪŋ ruːm/
direction (n) /dəˈrekʃən/
disease (n) /dɪˈziːz/

dishwasher (n) /ˈdɪʃwɒʃə/
disloyal (adj) /dɪsˈlɔɪəl/
display (n) /dɪsˈpleɪ/
diving (n) /ˈdaɪvɪŋ/
do exercise (v) /duː ˈeksəsaɪz/
do instant messaging (v) /ˌduː ɪnstənt ˈmesɪdʒɪŋ/
do my homework (v) /ˌduː maɪ ˈhəʊmwɜːk/
docks (n) /dɒks/
doctor (n) /ˈdɒktə/
downstairs (n) /daʊnˈsteəz/
draw (v) /ˈdrɔːɪŋ/
dreadlocks (n) /ˈdredlɒks/
dream (n) /driːm/
dress (n) /dres/
drown (v) /draʊn/
drums (n) /drʌmz/

ear (n) /ɪə/

earache (n) /ˈɪəreɪk/
earrings (n) /ˈɪerɪŋz/
education (n) /ˌedʒuˈkeɪʃn/
egg (n) /eg/
elbow (n) /ˈelbəʊ/
electrician (n) /ɪlekˈtrɪʃən/
email address (n) /ˈiːmeɪl ədres/
engineer (n) /endʒəˈnɪə/
en-suite bathroom (n) /ˌɒnswiːt ˈbɑːθruːm/
environment (n) /enˈvaɪrənmənt/
equipment (n) /ɪˈkwɪpmənt/
eraser (n) /ɪˈreɪzə/
escalator (n) /ˈeskəleɪtə/
ex (ex-boyfriend / ex-girlfriend) (n) /eks/ /eks ˈbɔɪfrend/ /
      eks ˈgɜːlfrend/
exercise (n) /ˈeksəsaɪz/
expedition (n) /ekspəˈdɪʃn/
expensive (adj) /eksˈpensɪv/
experience (n) /eksˈpɪəriəns/
explorer (n) /eksˈplɔːrə/
extra work (n) /ˌekstrə ˈwɜːk/
eyebrow piercing (n) /ˈaɪbraʊ pɪəsɪŋ/

factory worker (n) /ˈfæktri wɜːkə/

fair (adj) /feə/
fall overboard (v) /fɔːl ˈəʊvəbɔːd/
fall through (the ice) (v) /ˌfɔːl θruː ði ˈaɪs/
fare (n) /feə/
farmer (n) /ˈfɑːmə/
feel sick (v) /fiːl ˈsɪk/
film director (n) /ˈfɪlm dɪrektə/
filter coffee (n) /ˌfɪltə ˈkɒfi/
finger (n) /ˈfɪŋgə/
fire station (n) /ˈfaɪə steɪʃn/
fireplace (n) /ˈfaɪəpleɪs/
fish (n) /fɪʃ/
flight attendant (n) /ˈflaɪt ətendənt/
flight (n) /flaɪt/
florist's (n) /ˈflɒrɪsts/

fog / foggy (n/adj) /fɒg/ /ˈfɒgi/
foot, feet (n) /fʊt/ /fiːt/
footballer /ˈfʊtbɔːlə/
forehead (n) /ˈfɔːhed/
forest (n) /ˈfɒrəst/
freezing (adj) /ˈfriːzɪŋ/
fridge magnet (n) /ˈfrɪdʒ mægnət/
fried (adj) /fraɪd/
friendly (adj) /ˈfrendli/
frost / frosty (n/adj) /frɒst/ /ˈfrɒsti/
fruit (n) /fruːt/
full (adj) /fʊl/
funny (adj) /ˈfʌni/
fur (n) /fɜː/

gap (n) /gæp/

garage (n) /ˈgærɑːʒ/
garden (n) /ˈgɑːdn/
gathering (n) /ˈgæðərɪŋ/
generous (adj) /ˈdʒenərəs/
Geography (n) /dʒiˈɒgrəfi/
get back together (v) /get bæk təˈgeðə/
get currency (v) /get ˈkʌrənsi/
get home (v) /get ˈhəʊm/
get off (v) /get ˈɒf/
get on (v) /get ˈɒn/
get up (v) /get ˈʌp/
give up (v) /gɪv ˈʌp/
glass (n,adj) /glɑːs/
glasses (npl) /ˈglɑːsəs/
go on a boat trip (v) /ˌgəʊ ɒn ə ˈbəʊt trɪp/
go out (together / with someone) (v) /gəʊ ˈaʊt (təgeðə / wɪð ˌsʌmwʌn)/
go running (v) /gəʊ ˈrʌnɪŋ/
go shopping (v) /gəʊ ˈʃɒpɪŋ/
go to galleries (v) /ˌgəʊ tə ˈgæləriz/
go to school (by bike / bus / train) (v) /gəʊ tə ˈskuːl (baɪ ˈbaɪk / ˈbʌs / ˈtreɪn)/
go walking / fishing / cycling, etc. (v) /gəʊ ˈwɔːkɪŋ/ /ˈfɪʃɪŋ/ /ˈsaɪklɪŋ/
golf (n) /gɒlf/
green (adj) /griːn/
greengrocer's (n) /ˈgriːngrəʊsəz/
greeny-blue /ˌgriːni ˈbluː/
grilled (adj) /grɪld/
guided tour (n) /ˌgaɪdəd ˈtʊə/
guitar (n) /gɪˈtɑː/
gym (n) /dʒɪm/
gymnastics (n) /dʒɪmˈnæstɪks/

hail (n) /heɪl/

hairdresser (n) /ˈheədresə/
hall (n) /hɔːl/
ham (n) /hæm/
hand (n) /hænd/
handbag (n) /ˈhændbæg/
hang out with friends (v) /hæŋ ˌaʊt wɪð ˈfrendz/

happy (adj) /ˈhæpi/
hard-working (adj) /hɑːdˈwɜːkɪŋ/
have a shower (v) /hæv ə ˈʃaʊə/
have breakfast / lunch / dinner (v) /hæv ˈbrekfəst / ˈlʌnʃ / ˈdɪnə/
have strong feelings for someone (v) /hæv ˌstrɒŋ ˈfiːlɪŋz fə ˌsʌmwʌn/
head (n) /hed/
headache (n) /ˈhedeɪk/
headphones (npl) /ˈhedfəʊnz/
heel (n) /hiːl/
herb (n) /hɜːb/
hill (n) /hɪl/
hip (n) /hɪp/
hockey (n) /ˈhɒki/
homeless (adj) /ˈhəʊmləs/
homework (n) /ˈhəʊmwɜːk/
honey (n) /ˈhʌni/
horrible (adj) /ˈhɒrɪbl/
horror film (n) /ˈhɒrə fɪlm/
hot chocolate (n) /hɒt ˈtʃɒklət/
houmous (n) /ˈhuməs/
housewife (n) /ˈhaʊswaɪf/
hurt (v) /hɜːt/ far /

ice cream (n) /aɪs ˈkriːm/

ice (n) /aɪs/
imaginative (adj) /ɪˈmædʒənɪtɪv/
impatient /ɪmˈpeɪʃnt/
in front of (prep) /ɪn ˈfrʌnt ɒv/
increase (v) /ɪnˈkriːs/
indecisive (adj) /ˌɪndɪˈsaɪsɪv/
insensitive /ɪnˈsensɪtɪv/
insincere /ˌɪnsɪnˈsɪə/
intelligence (n) /ɪnˈtelɪdʒəns/
international driving licence (n) /ˌɪntəˌnæʃnəl ˈdraɪvɪŋ laɪsəns/
Internet Service Provider (n) /ˌɪntənet ˈsɜːvɪs prəvaɪdə/
into (prep) /ˈɪntuː/
island (n) /ˈaɪlənd/

jacket (n) /ˈdʒækɪt/

jeans (npl) /dʒiːnz/
journalist (n) /ˈdʒɜːnəlɪst/
journey (n) /ˈdʒɜːni/
judge (n) /dʒʌdʒ/
jumper (n) /ˈdʒʌmpə/

key in (v) /kiː ˈɪn/

key ring (n) /ˈkiː rɪŋ/
keyboard (n) /ˈkiːbɔːd/
kitchen (n) /ˈkɪtʃn/
kitchen sink (n) /ˌkɪtʃən ˈsɪŋk/
knee (n) /niː/

lake (n) /leɪk/

lamb (n) /læm/
languages (npl) /ˈlæŋgwɪdʒəz/
lawyer (n) /ˈlɔːjə/
lazy (adj) /ˈleɪzi/
leather (n,adj) /ˈleðə/
leg (n) /leg/
lend (v) /lend/
lettuce (n) /ˈletɪs/
library (n) /ˈlaɪbrəri/
life jacket (n) /ˈlaɪf dʒækɪt/
life-changing (experience) (n) /ˌlaɪf tʃeɪndʒɪŋ eksˈpɪəriəns/
liquorice (n) /ˈlɪkərɪʃ/
listen to music (v) /ˌlɪsən tə ˈmjuːzɪk/
litter bin (n) /ˈlɪtə bɪn/
liver (n) /ˈlɪvə/
living room (n) /ˈlɪvɪŋ ruːm/
lock (n) /lɒk/
long (adj) /lɒŋ/
look forward to (v) /lʊk ˈfɔːwəd tuː/
loose (adj) /luːs/
lorry driver (n) /ˈlɒri draɪvə/
loyal (adj) /ˈlɔɪəl/

machinery (n) /məˈʃiːnəri/

map (n) /mæp/
market (n) /ˈmɑːkɪt/
Maths (n) /mæθs/
mayonnaise (n) /ˌmeɪəˈneɪz/
mean (adj) /miːn/
mechanic (n) /məˈkænɪk/
medicine (n) /ˈmedsn/
medium-length (adj) /ˌmiːdiəm ˈleŋθ/
metal (n,adj) /ˈmetl/
milk (n) /mɪlk/
mind the gap (v) /ˌmaɪnd ðə ˈgæp/
mineral water (n) /ˈmɪnərəl wɔːtə/
mobile phone (n) /ˌməʊbaɪl ˈfəʊn/
model (n) /ˈmɒdl/
moderator (n) /ˈmɒdəreɪtə/
moped (n) /ˈməʊped/
motorbike (n) /ˈməʊtəbaɪk/
mountain (n) /ˈmaʊntən/
mouse mat (n) /ˈmaʊs mæt/
moustache (n) /məˈstæʃ/
mp3 player (n) /ˌempiːˈθriː pleɪə/
mug (n) /mʌg/
(multiplex) cinema (n) /ˌmʌltɪpleks ˈsɪnəmə/
(music / dance) venue (n) /(ˈmjuːzɪk / ˈdɑːns) ˌvenjuː/
museum (n) /mjuːˈziːəm/
mushroom (n) /ˈmʌʃrʊm/
musical (n) /ˈmjuːzɪkl/
mustard (n) /ˈmʌstəd/

near (prep) /nɪə/

neck (n) /nek/
necklace (n) /ˈnekləs/
nervous (adj) /ˈnɜːvəs/

newsagent's (n) /ˈnjuːzeɪdʒənts/
next to (prep) /ˈneks tuː/
nickname (n) /ˈnɪkneɪm/
no point (n) /nəʊ ˈpɔɪnt/
noise (n) /nɔɪz/
nurse (n) /nɜːs/
nuts (npl) /nʌts/

octopus (n) /ˈɒktəpəs/

office worker (n) /ˈɒfɪs wɜːkə/
olives (n) /ˈɒlɪvz/
£1 (one pound) (n) /wʌn ˈpaʊnd/
1p (one pence) (n) /wʌn ˈpens/
on foot (adv) /ɒn ˈfʊt/
onion (n) /ˈʌnjən/
opposite (prep) /ˈɒpəzɪt/
or (conj) /ɔː/
orange (n) /ˈɒrɪndʒ/
orange juice (n) /ˈɒrɪndʒ dʒuːs/
out of (prep) /ˈaʊt əv/
outdoor activities (npl) /ˌaʊtdɔːr ækˈtɪvətiz/
out-going /aʊtˈgəʊɪŋ/
over (prep) /ˈəʊvə/

pack your suitcase (v) /ˌpæk jɔː ˈsuːtkeɪs/

pain (n) /peɪn/
painting pictures (v) /peɪntɪŋ ˈpɪktʃəz/
palace (n) /ˈpæləs/
paper (n) /ˈpeɪpə/
park (n) /pɑːk/
passport (n) /ˈpɑːspɔːt/
password (n) /ˈpɑːswɜːd/
past (n) /pɑːst/
patient (adj) /ˈpeɪʃnt/
pavement (n) /ˈpeɪvmənt/
peach (n) /piːtʃ/
pear (n) /peə/
pencil sharpener (n) /ˈpensl ʃɑːpnə/
pencil (n) /ˈpensl/
peppers (npl) /ˈpepəz/
petrol station (n) /ˈpetrəl steɪʃn/
pharmacist (n) /ˈfɑːməsɪst/
pierced ears (n) /pɪəst ˈɪəz/
pillowfight (n) /ˈpɪləʊfaɪt/
pine nuts (npl) /ˈpaɪn nʌts/
plane (n) /pleɪn/
plastic (n,adj) /ˈplæstɪk/
platform (n) /ˈplætfɔːm/
play video games (v) /pleɪ ˈvɪdiəʊ geɪmz/
play an instrument (v) /ˌpleɪ ən ˈɪnstrəmənt/
play computer games (v) /ˌpleɪ kəmˈpjuːtə geɪmz/
plug (n) /plʌg/
plug in (v) /plʌg ˈɪn/
plump (adj) /plʌmp/
pocket money (n) /ˈpɒkɪt mʌni/
polar bear (n) /ˈpəʊlə beə/
police officer (n) /pəˈliːs ɒfɪsə/

police station (n) /pə'liːs steɪʃn/
politician (n) /ˌpɒlɪ'tɪʃn/
pop star (n) /'pɒp stɑː/
pork (n) /pɔːk/
post office (n) /'pəʊst ɒfɪs/
potato (n) /pə'teɪtəʊ/
pound sterling (n) /paʊnd 'stɜːlɪŋ/
practise the violin / the piano (v) /ˌpræktɪs ðə vaɪə'lɪn/ /
    ðə pi'ænəʊ/
prawn (n) /prɔːn/
prescription (n) /prɪ'skrɪpʃn/
print (v) /prɪnt/
printer (n) /'prɪntə/
problem (n) /'prɒbləm/
processor (n) /'prəʊsesə/
psychologist (n) /saɪ'kɒlədʒɪst/
pull (v) /pʊl/
pupil (n) /'pjuːpl/
put up (a tent) (v) /pʊt ˌʌp ə 'tent/

queue (n) /kjuː/

railway line (n) /'reɪlweɪ laɪn/
rain / rainy (n/adj) /reɪn/ /'reɪni/
read (v) /riːd/
receive (v) /rɪ'siːv/
rectangular (adj) /rek'tæŋgjələ/
red pepper (n) /red 'pepə/
red (adj) /red/
refugee (n) /refju'dʒiː/
registration (n) /redʒɪ'streɪʃn/
relax (v) /rɪ'læks/
reliable (adj) /rɪ'laɪəbl/
restaurant (n) /'restrənt/
return (n) /rɪ'tɜːn/
return (v) /rɪ'tɜːn/
revolting (adj) /rɪ'vəʊltɪŋ/
rice (n) /raɪs/
riding (n) /'raɪdɪŋ/
ring (n) /rɪŋ/
risk (n) /rɪsk/
river (n) /'rɪvə/
roast (n,adj) /rəʊst/
round (adj) /raʊnd/
running (n) /'rʌnɪŋ/

sad (adj) /sæd/
safe (adj) /seɪf/
sailing (n) /'seɪlɪŋ/
salad (n) /'sæləd/
sale (n) /seɪl/
sales representative (n) /'seɪlz reprɪzentətɪv/
salmon (n) /'sæmən/
sandwich (n) /'sændwɪtʃ/
sardine (n) /sɑː'diːn/
sauce (n) /sɔːs/
sausage (n) /'sɒsɪdʒ/

scared (adj) /skeəd/
scarf (n) /skɑːf/
school rules (npl) /skuːl 'ruːlz/
school uniform (n) /skuːl 'juːnɪfɔːm/
school (n) /skuːl/
science fiction (n) /saɪəns 'fɪkʃən/
scooter (n) /'skuːtə/
screen (n) /skriːn/
seafood (n) /'siːfuːd/
seaside (n) /'siːsaɪd/
secretary (n) /'sekrətri/
send (v) /send/
selfish /'selfɪʃ/
sensitive (adj) /'sensɪtɪv/
serious (adj) /'sɪəriəs/
shirt (n) /ʃɜːt/
shoes (npl) /ʃuːz/
shop assistant (n) /'ʃɒp əsɪstənt/
short (adj) /ʃɔːt/
shoulder (n) /'ʃəʊldə/
shout (v) /ʃaʊt/
shy (adj) /ʃaɪ/
sincere (adj) /sɪn'sɪə/
singer (n) /'sɪŋə/
single (n) /'sɪŋgl/
ski suit (n) /'skiː suːt/
ski (v,n) /skiː/
skiing (n) /'skiːɪŋ/
skills (npl) /skɪlz/
skirt (n) /skɜːt/
skull (n) /skʌl/
skydiving (n) /'skaɪdaɪvɪŋ/
sledge (n) /sledʒ/
slim (adj) /slɪm/
smoothie (n) /'smuːði/
snails (npl) /sneɪlz/
snow / snowy (n/adj) /snəʊ/ /'snəʊi/
social networking site (n) /ˌsəʊʃl 'netwɜːkɪŋ saɪt/
sofa (n) /'səʊfə/
sore throat (n) /sɔː 'θrəʊt/
soup (n) /suːp/
spare room (n) /'speə ruːm/
speaker (n) /'spiːkə/
spinach (n) /'spɪnɪtʃ/
sporting personality / sports star (n) /'spɔːtɪŋ pɜːsənæliti/
    'spɔːts stɑː/
sports centre (n) /'spɔːts sentə/
square (adj) /skweə/
stadium (n) /'steɪdiəm/
stall (n) /stɔːl/
stand clear of the doors (v) /stænd ˌklɪər əv ðə 'dɔːz/
start up (v) /stɑːt 'ʌp/
station (n) /'steɪʃn/
stationer's (n) /'steɪʃənəz/
stay in bed (v) /ˌsteɪ ɪn 'bed/
steak (n) /steɪk/
stomach ache (n) /'stʌmək eɪk/
stomach (n) /'stʌmək/

storm / stormy (n,adj) /stɔːm/ /'stɔːmi/ temporale /
strawberry (n) /'strɔːberi/
strict (adj) /strɪkt/
stud (n) /stʌd/
study (n,v) /'stʌdi/
subzero (adj) /sʌb'zɪərəʊ/
suffer from (v) /'sʌfə frɒm/
suit (n) /suːt/
sun cream (n) /'sʌn kriːm/
sunbathe (v) /'sʌnbeɪð/
sun-dried tomato(n) /ˌsʌndraɪd tə'mɑːtəʊ/
sunglasses (npl) /'sʌnglɑːsəz/
sunshine / sunny (n/adj) /'sʌnʃaɪn/ /'sʌni/
surf the web (v) /sɜːf ðə 'web/
surfing (n) /'sɜːfɪŋ/
surveyor (n) /sə'veɪə/
survive (v) /sə'vaɪv/
swimming costume (n) /'swɪmɪŋ kɒstjuːm/
swimming (n) /'swɪmɪŋ/

table (n) /'teɪbl/

table tennis (n) /'teɪbl tenɪs/
take photos (v) /teɪk 'fəʊtəʊz/
tall (adj) /tɔːl/
tattoo (n) /tə'tuː/
teacher (n) /'tiːtʃə/
team (n) /tiːm/
teen movie (n) /'tiːn muːvi/
temperature (n) /'temprətʃə/
terraced town house (n) /ˌterəst 'taʊn haʊs/
theatre (n) /'θɪətə/
theft (n) /ðeft/
thin (adj) /θɪn/
thoughtful (adj) /'θɔːtfl/
thoughtless (adj) /'θɔːtləs/
thriller (n) /'θrɪlə/
throat (n) /θrəʊt/
through (prep) /θruː/
thunder and lightning (n) /ˌθʌndər ən 'laɪtnɪŋ/
ticket (n) /'tɪkɪt/
ticket hall (n) /'tɪkɪt hɔːl/
ticket machine (n) /'tɪkɪt məʃiːn/
ticket office (n) /'tɪkɪt ɒfɪs/
toasted (adj) /'təʊstəd/
toe (n) /təʊ/
toilet (n) /'tɔɪlət/
tomato (n) /tə'mɑːtəʊ/
tooth, teeth (n) /tuːθ/ /tiːθ/
toothache (n) /'tuːθeɪk/
towards (prep) /tə'wɔːdz/
town hall (n) /taʊn 'hɔːl/
tracksuit (n) /'træksuːt/
train (n) /treɪn/
train station (n) /'treɪn steɪʃn/
trainers (npl) /'treɪnəz/
travel by train / plane, etc. (v) /ˌtrævl baɪ 'treɪn/ /'pleɪn/
travel /'trævl/

travelcard (n) /'trævl kɑːd/
trek (n) /trek/
trip (n) /trɪp/
tripe (n) /traɪp/
trousers (npl) /'traʊzəz/
T-shirt (n) /'tiːʃɜːt/
tuna (n) /'tjuːnə/
turn off (v) /tɜːn 'ɒf/
turn on (v) /tɜːn 'ɒn/
TV (n) /tiː'viː/
tyre (n) /'taɪə/

Underground (n) /'ʌndəgraʊnd/

unfriendly (adj) /ʌn'frendli/
unimaginative (adj) /ʌnɪ'mædʒənɪtɪv /
unplug (v) /ʌn'plʌg/
unreliable (adj) /ʌnrɪ'laɪəbl/
unselfish (adj) /ʌn'selfɪʃ/
upset (adj) /ʌp'set/
upstairs (n) /ʌp'steəz/
USB port (n) /juːes'biː pɔːt/

vaccination documents (npl) /ˌvæksɪ'neɪʃn ˌdɒkjəmənts/

vegetable (n) /'vedʒtəbl/
venue (n) /'venjuː/
vet (n) /vet/
view (n) /vjuː/
village (n) /'vɪlɪdʒ/
violin (n) /vaɪə'lɪn/
visit (v) /'vɪzɪt/
voice (n) /vɔɪs/
volleyball (n) /'vɒlibɔːl/

waiter / waitress (n) /'weɪtə/ /'weɪtrəs/

wake up (v) /weɪk 'ʌp/
walk to school (v) /wɔːk tə 'skuːl/
wardrobe (n) /'wɔːdrəʊb/
warm (adj) /wɔːm/
washing machine (n) /'wɒʃɪŋ məʃiːn/
watch TV / a video / a DVD (v) /wɒtʃ tiː'viː/ /ə 'vɪdiəʊ/ /ə diːviː'diː/
waterskiing (n) /'wɔːtəskiːɪŋ/
wave (n) /weɪv/
wavy (adj) /'weɪvi/
webcam (n) /'webkæm/
well built (adj) /wel 'bɪlt/
well-suited (adj) /wel 'suːtɪd/
whistle (n) /'wɪsl/
wind / windy (n/adj) /wɪnd/ /'wɪndi/
windsurfing (n) /'wɪndsɜːfɪŋ/
wood (n) /wʊd/
wooden (adj) /'wʊdn/
woolly (adj) /'wʊli/
wrist (n) /rɪst/

write poetry / stories / blogs (v) /raɪt ˈpəʊətri/ /ˈstɔːriz/ /
  ˈblɒgz/

yoghurt (n) /ˈjɒgət/

zone (n) /zəʊn/
zoo (n) /zuː/

Irregular verb list

Base form	Past simple	Past participle	Base form	Past simple	Past participle
be	was/were	been	leave	left	left
beat	beat	beaten	lend	lent	lent
become	became	become	let	let	let
begin	began	begun	lose	lost	lost
blow	blew	blown	make	made	made
break	broke	broken	mean	meant	meant
bring	brought	brought	meet	met	met
build	built	built	must	had to	had to
burn	burnt	burnt	pay	paid	paid
buy	bought	bought	put	put	put
can	could	been able	read	read	read
catch	caught	caught	ring	rang	rung
choose	chose	chosen	rise	rose	risen
come	came	come	run	ran	run
cost	cost	cost	say	said	said
cut	cut	cut	see	saw	seen
do	did	done	sell	sold	sold
draw	drew	drawn	send	sent	sent
dream	dreamt	dreamt	show	showed	shown
drink	drank	drunk	shut	shut	shut
drive	drove	driven	sing	sang	sung
eat	ate	eaten	sink	sank	sunk
fall	fell	fallen	sit	sat	sat
feel	felt	felt	sleep	slept	slept
find	found	found	speak	spoke	spoken
fly	flew	flown	spend	spent	spent
forget	forgot	forgotten	stand	stood	stood
forgive	forgave	forgiven	steal	stole	stolen
get	got	got	sweep	swept	swept
give	gave	given	swim	swam	swum
go	went	gone	take	took	taken
grow	grew	grown	teach	taught	taught
have	had	had	tear	tore	torn
hear	heard	heard	tell	told	told
hide	hid	hidden	think	thought	thought
hit	hit	hit	throw	threw	thrown
hold	held	held	understand	understood	understood
hurt	hurt	hurt	wake	woke	woken
keep	kept	kept	wear	wore	worn
know	knew	known	win	won	won
lead	led	led	write	wrote	written
learn	learnt	learnt			

HELBLING LANGUAGES
www.helblinglanguages.com

FOR REAL elementary Student's Book & Workbook
by Martyn Hobbs and Julia Starr Keddle
with Tessa Hall and Rob Nicholas

First published 2010

10   9   8   7   6   5   4
2014   2013   2012   2011   2010

ISBN 978-3-85272-235-1

Acknowledgements
The authors would like to thank all the people who have helped in the making of *For Real*:
• The teachers who contributed to the making of this book with their invaluable advice and feedback.
• The project manager Rosamund Cantalamessa for her capable and practical management, her commitment and good-humoured ability to stay calm at all times; the editor Clare Nielsen-Marsh, for her editorial input and expertise and her suggestions for improvements, and the research editor Imelda Hogan for her reports, ideas and suggestions.
• The designer Barbara Prentiss for her inspired, creative design solutions, and intelligent interest in the material, her can-do-attitude, and, of course, her invaluable advice on American culture; and designers Greg Sweetnam, Richard Ponsford and Barbara Bonci for their hard work and dedication.
• Francesca Gironi and Elisa Pasqualini for researching the wonderful photos, and making sure that the illustrations reflect the material; the photographer Charlotte Macpherson for bringing the story to life in a modern and motivating style.
• Paola Tite for her invaluable experience, irreplaceable eagle eye, and enviable multi-tasking skills on the Teacher's Book.
• The DVD company, 1410, for their creative and interesting ideas, exciting filming and imaginative interpretation of our requirements.
• The developers of the digital components for their incredibly skilled work behind the scenes creating an integrated digital resource.
• Thanks also to all the staff at the Helbling office for their support and encouragement.
• And last, but not least, thanks to Lucia Astuti, Managing Director of Helbling Languages for her innovative publishing vision, her responsive attitude, her never-ending energy and enthusiasm, and her ability to make authors' dreams and ideas a reality.

The publisher would like to thank the following for their kind permission to reproduce the following photographs:
Alamy p62 (barbequing on stall during Notting Hill Carnival), p82, p83, p84 (Internet Café), p137 (cake), p167 (teenage girl looking at Facebook website), p200; **Bloomsbury, J.K. Rowling, *Harry Potter and the Half-Blood Prince** p14 (cover image); **Clipart.com** p45 (get well soon); **Corbis** p10 (Mo Farah), p64, p78, p103 (Edmund Hillary and Sherpa Tenzing Norgay), p115, p116, p217; **Dreamstime** p21, p40, p43 (Hyde Park), p52 (tube), p54 (banknotes), p62, p107, p121 (terraced house), p123 (Jorani), p185 (girl), p191, p216 (lake), p230; **Flickr.com/** Matthew Black p13, Frans Schmit p64 (Beatles Museum), FRCH Design Worldwide p94, Angelo Leung p117 (Mong Kok), sylaf p122 (Škocjan Caves), bea-y-fredi p125 (Galway), Stefan Muntwyler p137 (camping at Exit Festival); **Fotolia.com** p47 (eating ice cream); **Getty Images** p10, p114 (vaccination campaign in Kabul); **Helbling Languages** p54, p102 (biro), p103 (tea cup); **©iStockphoto. com** p7 (teenage group), p12, p14 (sunglasses), p20, p22, p23, p30, p34 (handbag), p37, p38 (girl listening to music), p47 (painting; dancing), p53 (on the bus), p54 (snakes), p56, p58, p65 (nativity scene), p70, p73, p84, p97 (polar bear), p98, p105, p113 (pharmacist), p117, p121 (detached house), p122 (Tikal; the Route of Santiago de Compostela), p123, p127 (couple dancing), p130, p135 (French Villa; lake), p140, p151, p158 (Clark), p164, p170, p176, p180, p185 (boy), p216 (island; river), p218, p221, p224 (Kari; Kelly), p225, p232, p234 (Paris), p235, p238; **Lucia Astuti** p65 (Jesi streets); **NASA** p67 (The Earth seen from Apollo 17), p103 (Astronaut Buzz Aldrin on the moon); **NI SYNDICATION** p97 (Camilla Hempleman-Adams); **©Peace One Day, Matt Wolf** p114 (Jeremy Gilley in Sudan documenting the preparation of a food drop by W.F.P. in 2006); **©Peace One Day, Jim Jolliffe** p114 (Jeremy Gilley and the Dalai Lama in India in 2000); **Reuters Pictures** p61(The Turner Prize); **Shutterstock** p7, p14, p18, p23 (Innsbruck), p27, p34 (bracelet; chain), p35, p38, p40 (Tate Modern), p42, p43, p44, p45, p47, p54 (skulls; kitten; boat), p60, p61 (Tate Modern postcard), p65 (Panettone), p67, p70 (Suzy), p77, p93, p94 (pillow fight), p97, p105, p107 (Egypt), p112, p117 (La Paz), p121, p122, p127, p130 (Sophie), p132, p133, p135, p136, p137, p141, p142 (boy eating spaghetti), p153, p156, p158, p165, p167, p168, p181, p182, p193, p203, p204, p205, p213, p216, p224, p233, p234, p236, p237; **The Different Travel Company** p212; **Ubaldi fotovideo** p65 (Jesi); **United States Library of Congress's Prints and Photographs Division** p102 (Albert Einstein; first successful flight of the Wright Flyer, by the Wright brothers); **Wikipedia Commons** p98 (woman holding a Red King Crab), p103 (Titanic); **Yakutiatravel.com** p116 (Yakutsk); **123rf** p70 (Aisha), p113.

Illustrated by Roberto Battestini, Alessandra Ceriani, Giovanni Da Re, Stefano Fabbri, Michele Farella, Piet Luthi, Lucilla Stellato.

Commissioned Photography & Production by Charlotte Macpherson pp 9, 17, 29, 30 (Jack), 41, 49, 50, 53, 57, 68, 69, 89, 90, 109, 110, 118, 129, 138; Giuseppe Aquili pp 14 (bag), 33, 34, 52, 61, 81, 121 (block of flats), 142.

Designed by BG Prentiss, Studio Six
Cover photography by Charlotte Macpherson
Cover design by Capolinea
Printed by Athesia